A Skeptic Among Scholars

A Skeptic Among Scholars

August Frugé
on University Publishing

AUGUST FRUGÉ

University of California Press

BERKELEY · LOS ANGELES · LONDON

As Edwards Brothers, Inc., and The University of California Press celebrate their 100th anniversaries, Edwards Brothers is pleased to provide the paper, printing, and binding for the presentation copies of this commemorative edition to The University of California Press.

The Press also acknowledges the kind provision of the dust jackets for these copies by New England Book Components, Inc.

University of California Press
Berkeley and Los Angeles, California

University of California Press, Ltd.
London, England

© 1993 by
The Regents of the University of California

Library of Congress Cataloging-in-Publication Data

Frugé, August, 1909–
    A skeptic among scholars : August Frugé on university publishing / August Frugé.
      p. cm.
    "A Centennial book."
    Includes bibliographical references and index.
    ISBN 0-520-07733-4 (alk. paper). — ISBN 0-520-08426-8 (alk. paper)
    1. University of California Press—History. 2. University presses—California—Berkeley—History—20th century. 3. Frugé, August, 1909– . 4. Publishers and publishing—California—Berkeley—Biography. I. Title.
Z473.U623F78 1993
070.5′94—dc20   93-13477
                                                       CIP

Printed in the United States of America
9 8 7 6 5 4 3 2 1

The paper used in this publication meets the minimum requirements of American National Standard for Information Sciences—Permanence of Paper for Printed Library Materials, ANSI Z39.48-1984. ⊚

Title page photo: spiral staircase to the second floor of the Press building on Oxford Street. Photo by David Renick.

For Susan
Who Knows About These Things

Contents

Illustrations

I Fin de Siècle
End and Beginning

About one hundred years ago, when the old century was running to a close, as ours is now, when Sam Clemens was about to lose his shirt in a publishing venture and Sam Farquhar was three years old—both are part of what follows—the young and small University of California put up the sum of $1,000 to start a publishing program. A third Sam of this story, the diarist Samuel Pepys, had been in his grave for 190 years.

In 1868, shortly after the Civil War, or War Between the States, the new University had opened its doors to students. The first elected president, who declined to serve, was George B. McClellan, the Union general; the first faculty member hired was John LeConte, once an officer in the Confederate Army. In 1873 the University moved from Oakland to the open hillsides of Berkeley. Before the seventies were out there was a printing plant and, beginning in 1885, an editorial committee to oversee catalogues and announcements. The first scholarly publications were issued in 1893, a few months after the initial appropriation was made. Editing and production, it seems, were done more quickly then than they are now.

The first two scholarly authors were Andrew C. Lawson, a young professor of geology, and Milicent W. Shinn, a graduate student who wrote on child development. They turned out monographs, not books, although Shinn's work could have made a book had anyone been book-minded at the time. The Press of those days—meaning a faculty committee chaired by the University president—was firmly monograph-minded and so remained for more than a generation. The complete catalogue of the first fifty years of Press publications contained 13 pages listing books and 120 pages of serial monographs, 25 or 30 to a page. Such was President Wheeler's press, modified only a little since his time, when I came upon it at the end of that first half-century, in 1944. I exaggerate only a little and in the direction of truth.

If Lawson was a kind of father to the Press and Shinn a kind of mother—although there is no record of their even speaking to each other—then the godfather, in the Sicilian sense, was President Benjamin Ide Wheeler, who reigned over the University from 1899 to 1919, a despot, benevolent of course. He controlled the Press as he controlled everything else. It was he who obtained the second publishing grant, and from then on he created the Press in—if not in his own image then in the German image that he knew from his student days in Leipzig, Jena, Berlin, and Heidelberg.

I have not always known this. Although, as a publisher, I grew up with the University Series, lived with them for thirty-some years, and although I knew of the great Wheeler, it never occurred to me in all those years that it was he who invented the Press, determined its character. Reading in Albert Muto's book[1] that more than twenty new subject series were established in Wheeler's time, I got down the old fiftieth-anniversary *Catalogue* and checked the dates of first publication. There I found with growing wonder that all but a few of the great series, the prolific ones, those that made the reputation of the early Press, were begun under Wheeler. These included Alfred Kroeber's noted American Archaeology and Ethnology, which eventually ran to several hundred papers in more than fifty volumes. And there was the most numerous group of all, the several series in the life sciences: Botany, Entomology, Zoology. Although monograph series were less useful in the humanities, the Wheeler regime established Philosophy, Modern Philology (meaning modern European literatures), Classical Philology, and others.

1. *The University of California Press: The Early Years, 1893–1953* (Berkeley and Los Angeles, 1993). Many of these early facts are taken from Muto's book.

Wheeler permitted no publications but monographs in series, all written by Berkeley professors and graduate students. No books, no royalties, no advertising except bare lists, virtually no sales, no practices remotely commercial in nature. Distribution was primarily by exchange with other libraries. And this ancien régime survived the monarch. After 1919 there was no revolution and not much evolution. In spite of several early attempts at change, it was only much later, in its second half-century, that the University of California Press became a book-publishing house of the Oxbridge kind.

An early move for change came from Albert Allen, who in 1905 was made manager of the Press, meaning copyeditor, printing arranger, stock clerk, jack of all duties. He had ideas about what ought to be done and in 1914 took a leave of absence without pay—Wheeler would not let him go with pay—to visit the presses at Chicago, Harvard, and Yale. On his return, wishing to report his findings, he sought an audience with the president. This he never got. Three years later, about to join the wartime army, he turned in a written report, criticizing the Press as narrow and provincial.

To me it is not at all surprising that Allen never got his hearing, for I had some acquaintance with a later president whose style was not so different from Wheeler's. There was, I remember, an occasion in the 1950s when the Editorial Committee, composed of senior faculty members, requested an appointment with President Robert Gordon Sproul to discuss the future of the Press. They got the appointment—one year later. Sproul was also renowned in those days for refusing to take telephone calls. Since he would accept long-distance calls, I sometimes traveled to our Los Angeles office and called from there.

After Allen there was a succession of faculty managers or assistant managers of the Press, most of them scholars of Greek and Latin. The most notable of these, and also the last, was George Miller Calhoun, who was assisted and spelled by Ivan Linforth. It was the two of them, as recounted later in this volume, who transformed the Sather Professorship of Classical Literature into a lecture series with book publication. This was in 1920, one year after Wheeler. If the president had served—but that is not the *mot juste*—if he had continued in power for another few years, the finest classical lecture series anywhere might never have been born.

Calhoun, like Allen, had an interest in publishing as such. In 1930 he recommended to the new president, Sproul, that the Press be reorganized along broader lines. Now one could never be sure that Sproul read the memos that came to him, but perhaps he did read this one because a few years later he brought in the first outside professional manager, Samuel T. Farquhar, who was my predecessor and mentor. Farquhar's own recommendations, similar to those of Calhoun, were accepted, and a new era was at hand. Or so it seemed.

But the old system was essential to the research programs of a number of powerful academic departments; it continued to dominate. And Farquhar, although an educated man, was most interested in books as physical objects; he was more printer than publisher, having as background the fine printing movement in San Francisco. He came to Berkeley in 1932 as University printer, succeeding Joseph W. Flinn, who had been in charge of the plant for forty-five years. The following year Sproul gave Farquhar a second appointment as manager of the Press, approving his proposal that the two organizations be combined and be called the University of California Press. Out of that union (I say with hindsight) came more trouble and dissension than anyone cares to remember—anyone who took part.

Farquhar's printing exploits are worth some attention and will get that in a later chapter. In his clear mind he knew that his success had been gained in printing and book design, and by the middle 1940s he had observed other university presses, with their more lively publishing programs; he could see that the postwar years would require something comparable in Berkeley. So he made a number of new appointments, and it happened that I was one of these; a few years later he put me in charge of the publishing side of the Press. But the problems were great, the old way was resistant, and we were amateurs. Not very much had been accomplished when Farquhar died suddenly in 1949. He did not live to see the transformation of the Press as publisher.

Soon after I came, he took me to a university press meeting in wintry Chicago and introduced me to the presses of the east and midwest. Looking around to see what I could learn, I saw that a few presses—at private universities and at two state universities—were doing a professional job of book publishing, and I sat around tables in bars listening and asking questions. In those first days I remember especially the practical wisdom that dropped from the lips of Datus Smith of Princeton, Norman Donaldson of Yale, and Savoie Lottinville of Oklahoma. There were others, of course, not all of them directors. Among famous directors of the time was Bill Couch, first of North Carolina and then of Chicago, who was later to be fired for publishing a book when his university told him not to; although there was a California connection, we had nothing to do with either decision.[2] Two great directors I did not meet until later. Joe Brandt had moved on from Oklahoma and Princeton to commercial publishing; he will come into the California story in the 1950s. Tom Wilson of North Carolina and Harvard was just coming out of the navy.

From this handful of presses, competently run in the manner of a good trade publishing house, I formed the idea of what California ought to be, of what it might become. Although two of them— Princeton and Oklahoma—operated printing shops that were approximately as capable as ours, their directors and their other people talked like publishers rather than printers. What they and others said was enormously exciting to me. I went home with a head full of ideas.

Here I take up the California story as the second half-century of the Press begins, in 1944, describing first the old Press as I knew it, and then attempting a personal story of its transformation, including the many changes that have led up to the Press of today. As a partici-

2. In California Dorothy S. Thomas, head of a research project entitled Japanese American Evacuation and Resettlement, hired a number of people, including Morton Grodzins, to collect material for use in her books, *The Spoilage* (1946) and *The Salvage* (1952), both of which we published. She thought the material belonged to her, but Grodzins carried his off and wrote his own book. She (not the Press) complained to the Chicago administration, which told Couch not to publish the book. He, invoking freedom of speech, did so anyway. In an amusing twist, Grodzins later became director of the Chicago press for a short time.

pant, I offer not history but a memoir, an informal account of what happened. The great character change took place within my time. I coincided with it, paralleled it, survived it, arriving when the old style was still dominant and leaving after it had given way to the new.

The story as I remember it cannot be strung on a single chronological thread; topics will override chronology; and much will not be clear without glances before and after. For those before I depend on the research done by Albert Muto as set forth in his book, and especially on his examination of the papers of the University presidents, where he turned up many matters new to me, including some from my own time. I have also leaned on—have sometimes cannibalized—my earlier writings, some published and some not, especially on the booklet entitled *The Metamorphoses of the University of California Press* (Berkeley, 1986). For the years and events after the Press was made separate and allowed to seek a publishing future—for the greater part of this account—I must depend on a partial collection of my old papers and, for better or worse, on memory.

The memory has its own will. We cannot control what it brings to light and what it buries, although we can sometimes tease it—if not with madeleines dipped in tea then more prosaically with old letters. We can also do our best not to falsify, not to exaggerate beyond reason or in the wrong direction, especially in dealing with other participants. Most of those I deal with are no longer living. *De Mortuis . . . ,* it is said, but the dead deserve honest treatment. My small portraits, wherever possible, are double-sided, shown recto and verso, in the book terms used as subtitle to one chapter.

My portraits of the old Berkeley and the old Press will show clearly enough that I regret the passing of the one, which I observed, and have mixed feelings about changes to the other, changes that were in part my doing. We shall not see either again.

2　Berkeley in the 1940s
The Place and How
I Came to Be There

When I came back to Berkeley in the fall of 1944 the country was still at war, but the city had not yet taken up arms against the rest of the nation nor had it seen fit to adopt its own foreign policy. These adventures lay a couple of decades in the future. Berkeley was then, as when I lived there in the late thirties, a college and commuter town, where passionate commitments were more intellectual and personal than political. It was sometimes called a city of eccentric professors and of little old ladies in tennis shoes, up-ended in the garden.

Gardens large and small, public and private, were omnipresent, and surely they defined the character of the place as well as anything did. Still in existence, they no longer define. Then almost every house in the Berkeley hills had its private garden of shrubs and annuals, growing lushly in the mixed climate of sun and fog. Public ones included two splendid botanical gardens, the University Garden in Strawberry Canyon, behind the stadium, and the Regional Parks Botanic Garden in Tilden Park, just over the hills in Wildcat Canyon. One grew plants from all parts of the world, the other from every part of California. There was the fine, terraced Municipal Rose Garden in Codornices Park and the Salbach commercial garden high in the hills. Next door to Salbach my old library school teacher, Sidney B. Mitchell, tended his flower beds and wrote popular books about them, such as *In a Sunset Garden*. Ira Cross, professor of economics, hybridized chrysanthemums behind his tall house on Le Roy Avenue—a house built by

Rose Garden, Berkeley.

the architect Walter Steilberg on the ashes of the great Berkeley fire of 1923. My wife and I lived there many years later, as second owners.

A few words of nostalgia will not conceal—to those who know—the acute problems of university and town life or the toughness and combativeness of the inhabitants, including gardeners. Deer sometimes walked the streets of the hill districts and at night nipped the buds off rose bushes and devoured much else. On those streets to the east, bordering Tilden Regional Park, a sort of guerrilla war went on. Deer lived in the park by day and raided the town by night—as political activists were later accused of using the University as a staging area for attacks on the community. In one area a gang of three deer showed up every nightfall. Nothing could be done to stop the devastation, it seemed, until word got to James B. Roof, supervisor of the botanic garden in the Park, a man no less eccentric than any professor and no respecter of city or park regulations. Recruiting two friends and three shotguns, he lay in ambush one evening. The three deer appeared. The guns went off. Years later Roof told me that the first thing he heard, as blue smoke rose in the dusk, was a child crying: "Oh, they're shooting Bambi." The second sound was the voice of a housewife: "Did you get the sons-o-bitches?"

That was only an early skirmish; greater battles could be waged by the alliance of private and public gardeners. Some years later the director of all the regional parks was William Penn Mott, Jr., an ambitious man who was to become Ronald Reagan's director of the National Park Service. Mott decided to move that same Regional Parks Botanic Garden to a new site in East Oakland, and install in its place a pony-riding playground. One wonders, did he really think that botanic gardens were mobile, like some homes, and that he could pick one up and put it down elsewhere without mortal harm? The impulsive Jim Roof, who had spent twenty-five years creating the garden out of nothing on a couple of empty hillsides, might have taken the same shotgun to Mott. With uncharacteristic restraint he appealed to the private gardeners of Berkeley.

And it was they—a group that included a few professors of botany and physics, but mostly the embattled housewives of Berkeley—who fought a war with Mott, beat him down, and forced him to give up his plan. That little victory under their belt, this group of mostly amateurs organized itself into the California Native Plant Society and set out to save the native flora of California from bulldozers, developers, and the over-use of imported plants. From that small Berkeley beginning, the society has grown into a statewide group with active local chapters from Arcata to San Diego. And in imitation similar societies have sprung up in all the other western states. Some call this a nobler, a less self-serving, cause than other more strident ones.

Berkeley, of course, was not all gardens. Nor all hillsides. Social historians make much of differences between the hills and the flat lands to the west—perhaps too much. I lived years in both sections. In the thirties and forties we flatlanders felt no social distinction; the hills were handsomer and costlier, that was all, and we moved there when we could. Later a number of changes, including a new racial mixture brought on by war industry, had political repercussions. Even so, not everyone is a *zōon politikon*. In troubled times there were thousands who lived in Berkeley and paid little attention to the squabbling city council, who never walked past People's Park, or witnessed a riot. Such has always been the case, I suspect. But agitators make a better story.

But this is not an account of what happened to Berkeley. Here I wish only to sketch a setting for the Press when I first knew it, to give some idea—if only a personal and impressionistic one—of the environment in which it lived and grew. Berkeley was then more of a commuter town than it is now, one of the bedrooms of San Francisco. Trains to The City, as it was called, ran every few minutes along Shattuck Avenue, a block from the Press building, loaded with blue- and white-collar workers and with those who took the day off for shopping or pleasure. Editor Harold Small said that the riders, from early to late morning, were in turn the works, the clerks, and the shirks. The trains were more visible than they are now and a more vital part of the community.

I don't know how it came about that Berkeley was also a town of churches and theological schools; many of the latter were clustered around a hill just north of the campus, sometimes known as Divinity Hill. In early days the city had its own local form of prohibition. By the forties this was gone, but a state law made it illegal to sell alcohol within a mile of the University; for a drink one had to travel south on Telegraph Avenue or west on University. As a result, perhaps, there were then no truly good restaurants in Berkeley, no Gourmet Ghetto. For reasons more social than alcoholic the streets were safe. One could walk across the campus at night without fear. And housewives, including the little old ladies in tennis shoes, were not afraid to shop on Telegraph Avenue in stores that no longer exist.

The chief fact about Berkeley was, of course, the University, then generally respected in town although sometimes resented for taking property off the tax rolls. And lest nostalgia imply too mild a picture, we may remember that all is not harmony and good will inside a university. There may be partial protection from the commercial and political world—or at least there used to be—but strife is common within. Faculty and business officers do not see eye to eye. Power struggles convulse departments. Young teachers fight for tenure, older ones wage intellectual battles, sometimes against each other. There was the noted professor of history who had gathered, as some do, his coterie of loyal followers. Every noon master and acolytes sat around a large table at the Faculty Club, set apart from the ordinary run of academics. This little gathering was described by another professor as a sham giant surrounded by real pygmies. Intolerance there was, but no one invaded a professor's office or shouted him down at meetings.

The great expansion of the University came after the war, but slower change was going on in the early and middle forties. At that time Berkeley was still the center, the heart, the focus of greatness. The Southern Branch had become UCLA and moved to Westwood in 1929 and was on its way to claiming equality. Davis was an agricultural college, Riverside merely the Citrus Experiment Station, La Jolla the Scripps Institution of Oceanography, and Santa Barbara, not yet moved to Goleta, was trying to live down its normal-school beginnings. The only medical school was in San Francisco. Even so it was a great and widespread university if not yet the multiversity of Clark Kerr.

And the University Press? For the first forty years it had been little more than an academic committee with a secretary, sometimes called a manager, and with offices passed around from one University building to another. In 1933 it was grafted on to the University printing office, and in 1940 the combined organization moved into Sam Farquhar's handsome new building on Oxford Street, precisely between the campus to the east and the main Shattuck Avenue business district to the west. There it was when I visited in about 1940 and when I came to work in 1944.

The location now seems important. Although we never participated in municipal or local business affairs, we were slightly and subtly away from the academic center. Suppliers could come to us without bumping into classroom traffic. When we ate at the Faculty Club or called on a professor, we were almost visitors; we belonged and

did not belong. Later, with the new importance of the other campuses, that location, or a later one on the same street, was an essential
part of our stance as an all-University and not a Berkeley operation.
Later still, as part of the statewide president's office, we had little to
do with Berkeley as a campus or with the Berkeley administration,
even though faculty members, and the faculty as faculty, were central
to our existence. A vital distinction but a hard one to explain.

And the location made clear to us—when we thought about
it—that the Press had virtually nothing to do with students or with
the University as a teaching institution. We printed no student publications, published no standard textbooks. Our dealings were with
faculty members as scholarly authors. This lack of contact with the
student world and our location in the town business district, blocks
away from Telegraph Avenue, meant, two decades later, that the student wars scarcely impinged on our work or our daily lives. I remember one demonstration visible from our high windows. And once our
low windows were broken.

After Clark Kerr's reorganization, when our statewide status was
settled, we sometimes felt that we had the best of two worlds: the
Press was an administrative department and at the same time its function was academic, subject to faculty wishes. Although it would never
have done to play one against the other, the double character was
sometimes useful.

But I get ahead of myself. Such matters come later.

Since I am an unavoidable part of this story—the cord on which it is
strung, the glass through which it is seen—it may be useful to say
something about how I came to be on hand, about the accidents that
brought me to the Press. And to show how my peculiar traits were
formed, insofar as they can be formed by experience. I was raised in
two small towns on the Oregon side of the Columbia River. The first
of these, Hood River, sits beside a small stream of the same name,
whose lush, green valley, stretching to the south, was filled with apple
and pear orchards, some of them—like that of my mother's uncle—
planted on high rounded buttes. From some streets of the town one

Celilo Falls, with Indians fishing. The falls no longer exist, having been drowned by The Dalles dam. (Oregon Historical Society, #OrHi 86615)

could look south to the snowy volcanic summit of Mount Hood and north to an even higher peak, Mount Adams in Washington. Today the downtown district has changed almost not at all. And on a hillside above it still sits the first house—first home—that I can remember. With my grandparents we used to cross the Columbia on a miniature ferry to the village of Underwood, and from there go by horse and wagon up a dirt road to a part-time and unprofitable farm on the far side of Underwood Mountain.

The Dalles, not many miles to the east, was an old market and railroad town serving the farm country roundabout. On Saturdays stores stayed open until nine o'clock in the evening to gain trade from distant wheat farmers. Indians from Celilo—a few miles to the east and now lost under dam water—came to town that day and sat on curbs and in front of stores. No one bothered them.

The Dalles is set down in a splendid landscape just where the Cascade Mountains break off into dry eastern Oregon and on the banks of a magnificent river—more magnificent at that time, when dam waters had not yet drowned the great flat rocks and rapids that gave the place its French name. The town, unfortunately, could never match the setting. In the last century it had been a river port, the head of navigation, and a rowdy place that is said to have supported more than fifty saloons. Steamboats were long gone in my time and saloons had succumbed to prohibition, but vestiges of the old town survived, including a huge and abandoned old hotel, the Umatilla House, and a one-block-long Chinatown near the railroad tracks. But most of the place was ordinary enough, with wooden houses in mid-western style, as in other Oregon towns.

(Years later, during Editorial Committee meetings in the Press library, where I was dealing with some of the best scholarly minds in the world, there would sometimes come over me the feeling that I was out of place. Closing my eyes I wondered what sleight of hand, what wand of fortune had transported me from The Dalles, where I belonged, to the halls of Berkeley. It may be that others in the room also sometimes wondered at their presence there, but I always assumed that they belonged and knew they belonged, as I did not.)

Young people with literary or intellectual pretensions sometimes find it easy to look down on their bourgeois home towns. The Oregon writer, H. L. Davis—author of the prize novel *Honey in the Horn* (1935), who toward the end of his career lived near Berkeley, where I met him an only time—rechristened the town Gros Ventre in a bitter sketch published in H. L. Mencken's *American Mercury,* perhaps implying that the inhabitants were more than uncommonly greedy. For respectability, Davis thought. Before coming to The Dalles he lived in Antelope, a tiny sheep-country town in the southern part of the county. Antelope achieved fame of a sort a few years ago when the Bhagwan Shree Rajneesh settled there with a large flock of followers. He must have fleeced them well; the federal government eventually confiscated his fifty Rolls-Royces. Before that there was a fine series of controversies; the Bhagwan, it was feared, might be seeking to take over Wasco County; his disciples were said to have been responsible for a massive outbreak of salmonella food poisoning in The Dalles.

After high school I might have gone on to one of the Oregon universities, closer and more practical than others. Perhaps it was the snobbery of my surviving parent, my mother, as well as my own, of course—the poor looking down on those better off—that sent me instead to distant Stanford, where I managed by putting tuition charges on the cuff. Except for this and for travel back and forth, it was not then particularly expensive, although the coming of the Great Depression made everything desperate. But at Stanford, after a rather easy high school, I came up with a shock against the difficulty of competing with students from the better California schools, such as Lowell in San Francisco, and from eastern prep schools. They knew more than I did, had better work habits, and knew how to study, as I did not. It took most of a year to pull myself even. The son of my mother's employer failed to make it.

After spending most of a working life in Berkeley, so that Berkeley became a pervasive part of me, that Stanford interlude seems far away and unreal. But that is where and when were formed many of my intellectual tastes, including a fondness for French and Russian literature. And there I began to learn a few troublesome things about myself. Like others with humanistic interests, I had no use for a career in business—although later there was keen appreciation of the semi-business nature of scholarly publishing. I cared for literature and learning, for books, but was repelled by the notion of teaching—and what else could one do with such tastes, especially in the depression world? Even then I must have perceived dimly that I was not cut out to be a research scholar, although fond of intellectual matters. Long years of graduate study, and a hand-to-mouth existence, had no appeal.

With that impractical and impossible education, I got my degree, went back to Oregon, and was fortunate in the grim depression year of 1933 to get work in a furniture store, where I kept accounts, collected bills, delivered furniture, and sometimes tried to sell it, learning that I was not a salesman. Perhaps those two years provided some-

thing essential. After the passive and irresponsible life of a student—
and my own inability to see any acceptable line of work for the future—they did much to bring my feet down somewhere near the
ground. I rather enjoyed the active life, turning down a chance to go
back to Stanford as a teaching assistant, but had no thoughts about
how it might be combined with intellectual tastes.

An accident got me away. In the last desperate depression year at
Stanford, when all ways seemed closed ahead, I had taken the civil
service examination for accounting clerk in state institutions, work I
knew nothing about. More than two years later in Oregon came a
form postcard telling of an open job near San Jose. It was no better
than what I had in The Dalles, but it would get me out of a spot with
no future. I drove down and took it. And was soon intensely bored
with the routine, far deadlier than life in the furniture store. But
meanwhile a librarian friend at The Dalles, Mabel Kluge,[1] had moved
to Berkeley for further study, and it was she who suggested library
school. She recommended me to the dean of the school, Sidney B.
Mitchell, and helped me get a part-time job in the University library
at $50 a month. It was a desperate sort of move, like so many others
in the depression years. What else could one do with semi-intellectual
talents and no training?

There was an amusing incident before I left San Jose. Again I
took a civil service examination, the second of a series, this time for
chief accountant at state institutions. With ignorance tempered by my
old Stanford-learned knack for examinations, I somehow scored number one in the entire state on the written test. But when at the oral I
foolishly admitted having applied to library school, my score was
simply tossed out. By that time it was a kind of game, and I went
from first to last.

Once before I had been shown the futility of examination scores.
In my last year at Stanford I took a course from the celebrated Shakespeare teacher Margery Bailey but was frustrated when she let the

1. As Mabel Jackson, she later headed the Library of Hawaii, the statewide
system.

students lead the discussion; I had come to hear her. She must have seen the wrong kind of look on my face; one day she pointed a finger and told me to get out. At her office a day or two later she gave me a good chewing-out, probably deserved, for my supercilious attitude, allowed me a barely passing grade, and then advised me never to be a teacher: I was totally unfit for such work, she said. From her office it happened that I had to go to the Education Deparetment to get my score on a teaching aptitude test, taken in desperation, a test given to hundreds of students throughout the university. The man at the department checked the card file, gave me a strange look, and announced that I had come in number one. Even then, enjoying the ironical twist, I thought that Marge Bailey was probably right and the test wrong.

A student again at Berkeley and a few years older than most others, I found the competition in that special kind of school vastly easier than it had been at Stanford. The degree came and then a regular job in the accessions department of the University library itself, the beginning of a career that I could handle. At that time, when the library profession was dominated by women, it was sometimes helpful to be a man; we were scarce, and there were those who wanted to balance the sexes in the profession. But there could be problems, as when I applied for a temporary vacation job at the Berkeley Public Library. She would really like to give me work, said the distinguished librarian, but there was no men's rest room in the building. Amused but not indignant, I looked elsewhere. Imagine the outcry today if women were excluded on such grounds.

In the thirties and forties I worked for four different women administrators or managers, was comfortable with all of them, and admired them. One was Chinese American; no one saw anything unusual in her position of authority; prejudice was not so common then as some would have us believe. Later when I came to appoint department heads at the Press, it never occurred to me to consider the sex or race of candidates; one simply chose the person who seemed best for the job. Perhaps we will some day come back to the use of common sense in such matters, but I will not live to see it.

During my two years in the accessions department, one of my jobs was to work with a new and young professor of art history from Heidelberg, Walter Horn, who was eager to build up the library's then weak collection in his discipline. Years later Walter and I collaborated on the publication of many books; we even came into conflict, as I will describe.

In 1939 another state examination, a useful one this time, took me to Sacramento as head of the order department in the California State Library. It was not easy to choose the job over a similar offer at the University, but in Sacramento I could make my own selection of books to buy; my first wife was a librarian who had worked there; and the money was better. For the first time in my life, at $200 a month, I felt truly prosperous—a heady feeling that never came again. But the book budget was small and the library, in spite of its central position among public libraries, seemed a backwater. I stuck it out for five years, desperately bored toward the end—as so often before—and was once again saved by an accident.

Some of us belonged to the Sacramento Book Collectors' Club, a group of people interested mostly in California history and in the physical book, whose leading spirits were Mike and Maggie Harrison, she a bookbinder and he with an early start on his great collection of western books, now willed, books and building alike, to the University library in Davis. As for me, I lacked the soul of a true collector, then or later, but accumulated books when I could—not the same thing—and associated with those who collected.

Our little club, like larger ones of its kind, had taken to publishing a few limited editions, perhaps one a year, most of them from manuscripts in the State Library. And when the editor of one volume, also writer of an introductory biography, disappeared into the navy, his manuscript was left to be prepared for the printer. The task fell to Neal Harlow and me, and marked the beginning of a long friendship. Neal went on to UCLA, became chief librarian at the University of British Columbia, and then dean of the library school at Rutgers. He is celebrated among local historians for his elegant and scholarly books on the early maps of San Francisco, Los Angeles, and San Diego. And after both of us were retired I had the pleasure of sponsoring for the University Press his *California Conquered* (1982), a fine history of the Mexican War in California.

So we had a manuscript on our hands. Perhaps because the editor-author had been called away too soon, we judged that the writing needed revision, and spent long evenings doing what I have since learned to decry as over-editing—recasting the author's sentences and paragraphs. I am not certain whether he ever forgave us. Nor should he have, perhaps.

This happy editorial interlude ended with publication.[2] Thrown back on the old boredom, I thought of Sam Farquhar, who welcomed librarians on visits to the University Press. Calling on him in Berkeley I asked, with no good reason for hope, whether experience with books in a library was transferable to work with books at a university press. Perhaps so, said Farquhar, and he would think about it. I was at a good age for a move, he said, not too young. He must have been thinking about the kind of help he might need in the postwar years. And in those days, when the Press was less professional than it appeared from the outside, it made some kind of sense—as it did not later—to recruit people with more enthusiasm than experience. And the book we had just seen through the press was Sam's kind of book, a collectors' item.

A few months later, Farquhar called and asked me to take the place of his sales manager, whom he was about to fire—an invitation to jump over the fence from buying books to selling them. But a salesman I was not, as I had learned in Oregon, and there was an uncertainty in the job since rights to it were held by Dorothy Bevis, then on leave in the Coast Guard. Talking with Farquhar in Berkeley, I made what later seemed the only smart move of my life. I sought a real change of profession, said I, and would do the job if I could have the title of assistant manager of the Press,[3] with more general duties

2. John A. Sutter, Jr., *Statement Regarding Early California Experiences,* edited, with a biography, by Allan R. Ottley (Sacramento, 1943).
3. His was manager. The title of director, which then could be held only by members of the academic senate, did not come until 1957.

to come when Bevis returned. Farquhar agreed, subject to the approval of President Sproul. He wrote for that and I waited.

Meanwhile Dean Mitchell thought he might get me the open job of assistant librarian at a large midwestern university—Minnesota, says memory—and I spent anxious weeks fearing that the offer might come through. It was a bigger career opportunity than the Press job, and would be hard to refuse. That summer, while waiting, my wife and I spent the vacation weeks as guests of the Seattle Mountaineers at a camp in Paradise Valley in the heart of the Canadian Rockies. Although mountains had become a strong interest, my chief recollection of the stay is that one evening there came down from the hills and to our campfire the renowned Cambridge critic and philosopher I. A. Richards and his wife; she was a famous climber, and he must have been able to keep up with her. A few years later, as predatory publisher, I would have tried to get a book out of him, but that time was not yet. The talk was of peaks and glaciers.

With happy wisdom the midwestern library chose someone else. Sproul's approval came through, and I moved to Berkeley and the Press in October of 1944. There I would be for more than thirty years. And never again was I bored with my work. By accident and luck I had come to a place that was right for me. Not everyone thought, a few years later, that I was right for it.

3 The University Press in the 1940s
Recto and Verso

When you walked into the Press building—then home of the combined Press and printing department, now housing only the latter—to the left of the high lobby were the administrative offices, where Hazel Niehaus presided over several people in the large outer room. In 1944 she had worked for the printing plant and Press for twenty-four years, and she had another twenty-five to go, the last few for the Press alone. Past her desk and straight ahead was Farquhar's corner office and to the right that of V. J. McHenry, whose title was superintendent of the plant but whose work was more limited. With an assistant, Ross Cushing, he took in all printing jobs and did the estimating. Later, when I would bring in a book manuscript, he would weigh it solemnly in one hand, up and down, look out the window, look back at me, and say, "About x thousand dollars, don't you think?" And it really didn't matter much because we were expected to pay the actual cost as accumulated on the time sheets. And there was no real way to control that.

The front of the building along Oxford Street was three stories high, with the third floor given over to a library bindery and the second to editorial and sales offices. The much larger plant behind this front was all on one level. From the lobby leading up to the second floor was a handsome spiral staircase, whose exact curvature was often drawn and studied by students of architecture. Halfway up, the climber could pause and look through a wide window opening

U.C. Press Building on Oxford Street, 1940.

over the composing room, where men were busy at work. The more distant press room and pamphlet bindery could be seen through tall glass partitions. It was all quite impressive, and a closer look showed that the entire area was skillfully planned for flow of work from one function to another. Diffused light was provided by high saw-tooth skylights over the plant area and a south wall of glass bricks. The plant floor was made of upturned redwood blocks that cushioned the feet. Farquhar and his architects, Masten and Hurd of San Francisco, had known precisely what they were doing.

Farquhar himself must have taken an active part in the planning. That his older half-brother, Robert, was architect of the elegant Clark Library in Los Angeles suggests a family interest in such matters. The style of the Press building has been described as conservatively modern. A surviving unsigned memo of 1940 says "Simplicity in design and dignity without pretentiousness were sought by the use of lightly marked vertical accents" on the rather low main facade. Compared to other University buildings in Berkeley, it is small, harmonious, perfectly balanced—just the qualities that Farquhar sought in book design. I have sometimes thought that only one University building is more handsome—South Hall, the sole survivor of the 1873 campus.

The entire building was beautifully planned for the Press as it was then—for a good-sized printing plant and a small, attached, and sub-

Spiral staircase to the second floor of the Press building. Photo by David Renick.

sidiary editorial operation, with easy communication between editors and compositors. The second floor was all publishing. At one end was the oak-paneled library, with a complete collection of Press books and series volumes, a collection of works on printing, and a long table for meetings. At the other end was the sales department, more billing office than selling office, where I was about to install myself. And in between were half a dozen editorial rooms. That was it for publishing, and it was most of what we had for the next eighteen years. Publishing, unlike printing, can be done from almost any kind of office. When we finally moved in 1962 the chief gain, along with more space, was to distance ourselves from the printers—a gain that would have been incomprehensible to the editorial staff of 1944.

The chief editor, Harold Small, and his assistants were in almost daily touch with the print shop, and particularly with Amadeo Tommasini, foreman of the composing room. Given the conditions of the day and the conception of publishing then, it was an effective symbiosis. In a long job description written a few years later, Small described three essential skills of the "present editor." The first was the ability to revise manuscripts in many fields, the third an understanding of the "genus professor." Of the second skill, called equally important, he wrote, "The Editor must understand the mechanics of printing, and must have a discriminating knowledge of the design and manufacture of books, so that he can . . . collaborate fully with the supervisors of work in the mechanical plant at all stages of book production." Small was "the" editor, and one might describe his job in present terms as chief copyeditor and production editor; he did almost no procurement. In a letterpress plant all illustrations were printed from metal engravings, which Small, in close collaboration with Tommasini, scaled and ordered from an Oakland firm. Only later, when we came into conflict, did I realize how the two of them controlled between them almost the whole process of manufacture. It was Farquhar, of course, who had invented and still dominated the style of book design—as I will describe later—but with a looser control than in earlier years. Decisions were made one at a time, as the job moved along, and not all in advance as must be done when dealing with outside printers.

In our informal newsletter called *The Pierian Spring,* I once wrote a little piece that began, "Ever since we first wandered into the publishing business, we have been trying to determine precisely what an editor is. . . . The man eludes classification; the word evades definition. An editor doesn't fit a filing cabinet, can't be mounted on a slide, was never weighed in a scale or added up on an adding machine, moves too variously for an electric eye, and never stands still long enough to be measured by triangulation. Our friends the technicians, who think they can measure the goodness of an angel or weigh the thoughts of a lady while she pulls up her sox, have never been able to pin him down or fasten him up. Nor have we."

The overblown language was mine, of course, but the picture behind the prose was Small's own image of himself, as set down at length in the job description mentioned above. How serious was I at the time of writing? Perhaps as serious as was Small when he used to introduce me—in my first sales manager days—as the man who was going to "make us all rich." But there was truth in the self-appraisal. Largely self-educated after his degree from Colby College in Maine, he had picked up an enormous store of erudition and could hold his own in conversation with almost any humanistic scholar, as I saw when we went together for lunch at the Faculty Club. He himself wrote that "his qualifications and his successes" came from being brought up in a home where "good table talk was enjoyed and valued," from omnivorous reading, and from schooling in the old New England liberal arts tradition. True enough, I still think.

To this education was added miscellaneous information from some fifteen years of newspaper experience in Hartford and San Francisco. Among his stories was one about the New England lady proofreader who was too embarrassed to ask correction of a misspelled ad for fancy ducks, forty cents a pound, and the hilarity that broke out when the paper hit the street. Rival journalists at a Boston paper telegraphed to reserve several tons and claimed to be chartering a special train. This brand of masculine humor must have flourished in newsrooms of the 1920s. Similar goings-on made a highly successful Broadway play, *The Front Page* (1928) by Ben Hecht and Charles MacArthur.

Now as the erudite and unhurried editor of a scholarly press Small had found the right niche for himself. From there he could announce that all manuscripts must be written in *some* language. And that no book is ever finished but is only abandoned. And could classify the several kinds of academic prose. One, I remember, was the shingle style: each sentence overlaps the one before. In another the sentences follow each other in single file, like elephants in line, each trunk holding the tail of the beast ahead.

It was strange, I used to think, that an old newspaperman had no respect for deadlines; perhaps he had had a nose full of them and would no longer admit their existence. So the bad news, the verso of the good, was that authors could grow impatient; the Editorial Committee had, from time to time, risen up in anger over delays. The history of this I did not know at the time, but a new episode was soon to burst upon us. And I was to know the similar frustration of the would-be publisher with ideas about scheduling new books and planning their distribution. "The Editor," wrote Small, "must be able to give some assistance to the best manuscripts, to rewrite the worst, and to meet all degrees of demand between the extremes. . . . The editorial services given by the University of California Press are not duplicated by any other university press or by any commercial publishing house." That is the way it was, and I learned that no one could change Small's habits. Not even Farquhar, who in times of trouble might hire additional editors but could never get Small or his assistants to work in any other way. In my time he never tried.

When I first arrived Farquhar was still in vigorous good health and good spirits. His pronounced limp, from polio as a child, had little effect on his mobility. He was about to marry for the second time. At the Press, even if he could not control everything, as no one could, he was clearly in charge, ruling with vigor and good sense. Things had been going well. The Press had its own handsome type-

Sam Farquhar at his desk.

face, specially designed by Frederic W. Goudy, the foremost type designer of the day; in book design Farquhar had devised a splendid
house style and, with the help first of Fred Ross and then of Amadeo
Tommasini, had won many national prizes; the printing department
was soon to take on the design and printing of the United Nations
Charter.

Publishing income had almost doubled, largely from the sale of
Japanese-language textbooks and dictionaries, undertaken at the request of the U.S. Navy, which had licensed the reprinting of books
first published in Japan, a kind of authorized piracy. The books would
die quickly later on, but the wartime demand was great. Every morning, when the mail had been opened, Farquhar rang, and I would go
down to his office; together we turned over and discussed the day's
orders, not a very long task. The Japanese texts sold in quantity.
There were a few general books on the backlist but not many. Our
one "best-seller" among these, *Cézanne's Composition* by Erle Loran,

was out of stock. Paper was then rationed; we had no allotment for a reprint.

Like Small, Farquhar was a New Englander, coming from one of the Newtons, near Boston, and educated at Harvard. Although temperamentally quite different, the two men must have discovered something in common when they met in San Francisco. For more than a year, in 1927–28, while Small was book review editor of the *Chronicle* and Farquhar a member of the printing firm of Johnck & Seeger, the latter wrote a regular column on fine bookmaking, with emphasis on the notable printers of San Francisco. And in 1928 the two men were among the founding members of the Roxburghe Club of San Francisco. It is not surprising that one brought the other to Berkeley.

Also active in book circles was Sam's older brother, Francis—accountant, mountaineer, bibliographer, connoisseur of fine printing, historian of the Sierra Nevada,[1] and notable book collector. His great mountaineering collection is now at UCLA.[2] It seems likely, although I cannot document this, that Francis, with his many connections in San Francisco, may have had some influence on Sam's appointment as printer in 1932. For many years Francis edited the *Sierra Club Bulletin*, where David Brower got his first editorial experience before coming to the Press.

Sam Farquhar was less bookish, I think, than Small and much more of an organizer and manager, but he had a good humanistic education and was proud of his Harvard degree. Latin he remembered well, and he had recently audited a university class in ancient Greek—a step that I took after him a few years later. On one of our trips, eating in a Greek restaurant, he showed that he could make a stab at reading a modern newspaper in that language. And I should mention his irreverent sense of humor and quick wit. The Press had published a small collection of letters by Anthony Trollope, entitled

1. His *History of the Sierra Nevada* was published by the Press in 1966.
2. See James R. Cox, *Classics in the Literature of Mountaineering and Mountain Travel from the Francis P. Farquhar Collection* . . . (Los Angeles, 1980).

Sam Farquhar (second from right) presides over a staff meeting in 1942. The others are (left to right) Martha Willard, V. J. McHenry, Hazel Niehaus, Harold A. Small, Duane Muncy, Leura Dorothy Bevis, and Katherine Towle. McHenry was superintendent of the printing plant, Muncy assistant superintendent. Photo by John Brenneis.

The Tireless Traveler. Sam said it should have been called *The Tireless Trollope.* He had in his head a large collection of limericks, the erotic kind with a sting in the tail. I still remember how he recited these.

I could have no complaints about our new working relationship. Farquhar was a firm but generous mentor. He advised me on the University, saying that the faculty would accept me in about five years—an accurate appraisal of Berkeley reserve, at that time noticeably different from the more open style at UCLA. He told me also that in any dispute between the academic and the business sides of the University we must stand with the faculty, even though we were part of the administration. This recollection, I am aware, fits uneasily with Albert Muto's account of Farquhar's disputes with the Editorial Committee. Perhaps he had learned or had changed. I had good reason to remember the advice a few years later.

Farquhar saw the importance of the other campuses and branches of the University, especially those in the south, and he liked to travel by car, two interests that went well together. He no longer drove, but I did, and every few months we would head south in a University car, often on back roads, crossing the main highway now and then. Our first stop might be Riverside, where we had authors at the Citrus Experiment Station. *The Citrus Industry* (volume 1, 1943) and the *Color Handbook of Citrus Diseases* (1941), both with multiple authors, were important books in those days before the great southern groves were bulldozed into housing tracts. From there we went to La Jolla, like Riverside not yet a general campus, for a visit to the Scripps Institution of Oceanography, which then produced series papers if not books.

And then to Los Angeles, where the Press had a small office in the back of Royce Hall, and where the sole employee, the secretary, had little to do between managerial visits. Farquhar got along well with the southern members of the Editorial Committee (at that time three out of eleven), having worked with them to get Sproul's permission for the local office. Much of our business there had to do with journals: *Pacific Historical Review,* edited in the UCLA history department, at that time by Louis Knott Koontz and later by John Walton Caughey, and the new *Hollywood Quarterly,* an exciting but doomed venture that led, after political and other troubles, to the film publishing of today. In Los Angeles I was introduced to the two book clubs, Zamorano and Rounce & Coffin, and to the fine printers, librarians, and booksellers who made up the membership. Many became friends. One of them, the printer Ward Ritchie, became our first, and most prolific, free-lance book designer in the 1950s.

Sometime after my arrival Sam proposed that we revive the Book Arts Club, an informal student group that he had sponsored before the war. Members, changing annually, were the students in that year's library school class in Berkeley, especially those with an interest in the book arts. In 1937 I had been a rather inactive member. The students, in collaboration with Farquhar and the appropriate faculty member, chose each year a manuscript about fine printing or the history of bookmaking, and worked with Farquhar or Tommasini in putting together a design. The book was then printed in the plant in an edition of two or three hundred copies. The sales income was small, of course, and the printing bill had to be reduced, but Sam had been careful early on to obtain the approval of President Sproul for a project that was designed to benefit students. In spite of this care, he and I were later accused—he posthumously, I more vulnerably—of doing free printing for a club to which we belonged.

Six books had been produced before the war. The students, with our help, now brought out *Fifty Printers' Marks,* by Edwin Elliot Willoughby of the Folger Shakespeare Library, in 1947, and *Kamisuki Chohoki (Handy Guide to Papermaking)* in 1948. Farquhar's death, of course, put an end to the club and, indeed, to that kind of printing and publishing.

In her brief tenure in Berkeley, Dorothy Bevis had begun writing an informal newsletter about Press books entitled—by Sam, with his literary tastes—*The Pierian Spring.* It was similar in purpose, if not in style, to *The Pleasures of Publishing* put out by Columbia University Press about that time or later. Neither Dorothy at first nor I, when I took it up in 1945, pretended to drink deep at the spring of learning. The newsletter was intended, I once wrote, for those who "appreciate the sidelong rather than the headlong approach to book advertising." It was issued "at intervals." In it I wrote what I thought were light-hearted pieces about Press books, new and old, even some that were out of print, about the book trade as I was coming to know it, about editing, as quoted above, about anything that might interest librarians, booksellers, and even, possibly, book buyers. There was a spoofing piece about some of the titles of our monographs, such as *Is the Boulder "Batholith" a Lacolith?* (Geological Sciences, 1:16), *The Free-*

Living, Unarmored Dinoflagelata, one of the semicentennial publications, and a paper that I do not now identify on the three-toed
tree toad.

I have never been sure that this sort of thing sells many books,
although when we found a small cache of something old and desirable, such as Grinnell and Storer's *Animal Life in the Yosemite,* they
went fast enough. But it was a pleasure. Every publisher is a writer
manqué or a scholar manqué—except a happy few, the real McCoys.
But over the next few years we accumulated an appreciative audience;
there were letters from all sorts of people in the book and library
business and even from university presidents. If it had not been so
easy to make errors, we should have had to invent some; they pro-
voked correspondence.

For the first two or three years the intervals were short enough,
two or three months between issues, but in time the spring began to
run dry, and after the death of Farquhar—even before that, perhaps—
there were more serious things to think about. He who struggles to
keep his head above water is little concerned with drinking deep or
tasting lightly. Years later, when one of our editors suggested that I
revive *The Pierian Spring,* the idea was real enough to him, no doubt,
but to me it suggested a gone world—not just the great, changed,
outside world itself but also the smaller world in which we worked.
And I could not help thinking that it was I, more than anyone else,
who had done away with the old world of the Press.

There were three parts to that small ancien régime—three estates, we
might call them in pre-revolutionary terminology—the printing department, the Press as Editorial Committee, and the Press as book
publisher. And the third was least of the three. While the most visible
to librarians and booksellers, and destined to outstrip the others, it
was then smallest in size and perhaps in importance, overshadowed
by the others in two quite different ways.

Although the Committee's Press and Farquhar's Press used the
same imprint and financed some books jointly, they were really two
different endeavors. To the Committee the Scientific Publications (se-

ries and a few books of similar nature) were of first importance and were sometimes seen as competing for editorial and printing time with Farquhar's books (called General Publications). There had been hot arguments about delays, presumably caused by General Publications, and we were soon to see an attempt by the Committee to take them over.

The Editorial Committee spent nearly all its time on the monographs, which greatly outnumbered the books. In the 1893–1943 catalogue there are listed about fifty different subject series, of which perhaps forty were then alive and active. Of these, in the decade before the war, an average of more than sixty papers, large and small, were examined and approved each year. Even in the war years, when budgets were greatly reduced, the number of monographs was more than twice that of books, perhaps three times greater without the Japanese texts. It was not until the late fifties or early sixties that scholarly books began to exceed in number the great monograph series, and by then the two programs were no longer thought to be in competition. In 1944 it was possible to think of them as two programs with different purposes, almost as two presses.

When Sam Farquhar, with the blessing of President Sproul, put Press and printing office together in 1933 he had reason to believe he was forming a modern press, as well as one in a great and old tradition. For a long time after the invention of movable type in the fifteenth century the functions of printing, publishing, and bookselling were not clearly distinguished and were often combined. Even today the word *press* means a machine for printing and also means a publishing house. The invention of printing was, in a narrow sense, only a technological innovation, although writers on the history of the book sometimes seem to imply that the craft itself was a great cultural force. It was the combination of craft, choice of texts, and wide dissemination that brought on change. Each of the three was dependent on the others, incomplete without the others. Thus, the royal Letters Patent, the charter granted by Henry VIII to Cambridge University in 1534 not only gave the "power to print there all manner of books" but "also to exhibit for sale, as well in the same University as elsewhere in our realm, wherever they please, all such books and all other books wherever printed."

At the time of which I write the two great English exemplars, Oxford and Cambridge, had long operated combined printing and publishing organizations and were renowned for both. And on this continent, in the forties, more than a dozen university presses operated printing plants or had some kind of relation to their university plants. A few, such as Princeton and Oklahoma, were highly successful joint operations.

But printing and publishing, once so close together that the first term implied the second, have in today's world become incompatible. This is not the place to analyze the social and technological changes that have driven the two apart, but today I know of only two North American presses, Toronto and Princeton, that still do some of their own printing, and even the great Oxford University plant has been shut down—as a money loser and incompatible with publishing—and its remarkable collection of types put into a museum.

While printing can be thought of as an art or a craft, it can also be seen as a mechanism, a means to an end. While the publisher (or bookseller) may be a mere entrepreneur who buys cheap and sells dear (or tries to) he may also be judge and organizer of an intellectual endeavor. Printing as a craft and without sufficient concern for what is printed becomes precious. Publishing with too little thought for what is made public is mere commerce. The content of the work is of first importance. Or so reasons a publisher.

There is no mystique about publishing as there is about printing. Publishers are not craftsmen, as I learned and wrote many years ago, and they can seldom afford to have craftsmen on the staff, brutal as that may sound. Books should be eminently legible, as Farquhar proclaimed long ago, and it is a great gain if they are also handsome, as long as we don't let ourselves become more concerned with package than with contents. A publisher can be more than entrepreneur only by looking hard at the two chief functions, choosing and disseminating, especially the first of these. If he chooses well the fields of specialization, and in seeking books selects the excellent from among the good (instead of merely weeding out the bad), and distributes them well enough to attract the best authors, then the publishing house can develop a character of its own, and may come to have an intellectual value comparable, in its own way, to that of a first-rate academic department.[3]

But the Press did not publish in that way in 1944, and probably could not have, given its relation to the printing plant. One strategy for joint operation is for the plant to take outside work (as in Toronto now, I think). Another is to avoid the problem of balance by keeping one side of the union much larger than the other. Thus some small plants have been managed, not without difficulty, for the benefit of large publishing houses. In Berkeley in the forties it was the other way around, although I cannot be sure that anyone, except perhaps Farquhar himself, thought of it that way. The Press was grafted on to the printing office and provided only a fraction of the plant's business. As long as that ratio was kept, with not too much publishing activity, things went well enough, although there had been complaints since the last century whenever monographs were put aside for the more urgent announcements and catalogues. When a book program was added, books and monographs could compete for second and third places in line.

It was certainly not clear to me then—and probably not to others—that a successful symbiosis depended on keeping the number of books few. Few they were; neither Farquhar nor Small had strong publishing ambitions. From the beginning Farquhar's chief goal was to produce a few finely printed books that would win design awards, a goal triumphantly reached. The tastes of both men ran to the kind of book collected by bibliophiles. Of course they appreciated and worked competently on the scholarly books that came along, but they made no great effort to go after more of them.

In the nine years of 1933–41 the Press brought out a little more than one hundred books or about a dozen a year. Of these a number

3. I wrote something like this in "The Service Agency and the Publishing House," *Scholarly Publishing* (Toronto), January 1976.

were chiefly of book-collecting interest, and some were obligation books such as festschriften and the several series of lectures sponsored by the Committee on International Relations and pushed on the Press by President Sproul. There were also several unsalable foreign-language works, such as *Les sonnets de Shakespeare traduits en vers français,* and some volumes rescued from the monograph series. Substantial scholarly works and books of general intellectual interest—basic university press fare—were no more than two or three a year.

Nevertheless, during the war years these few included a number of important works, such as *Cézanne's Composition* and the two citrus books mentioned above. There were also the early titles in the United Nations Series, edited by Robert J. Kerner, large multi-author volumes about the Allied countries, beginning with Czechoslovakia and going on, after the war, to China, Brazil, Australia, Canada, and others. But the chief publishing venture, in a practical sense, was the large group of Japanese-language dictionaries and textbooks, all printed by offset outside the University plant, which could do only letterpress—hence no internal scheduling problems. It may be that the considerable success with these, the increased sales and income, together with the promise of the United Nations books, led Farquhar to anticipate an expansion of publishing in the postwar years. But he could not have foreseen—no one foresaw—what the growth of publishing, together with more active selling and the steep rise in printing costs, would do to his two-part organization.

4　An Unavoidable Conflict

When Dorothy Bevis came back from the Coast Guard, she decided not to return to the Press but to seek a career in librarianship, thus reversing the move I had made. Eventually she taught for many years at the University of Washington. And at my urging Sam Farquhar sought another sales manager, finding a young man in southern California, Thompson Webb, Jr., a Princeton graduate just back from service in the navy. Tom had been slated to succeed his father as headmaster of the Webb School in Claremont, but he and his wife Diana thought they would rather try something else. So Farquhar hired him, and he went up fast. After a couple of years in Berkeley, in sales and then in editing, he moved on to Madison and spent a long career as director of the University of Wisconsin Press.

But that is jumping ahead. In early 1946 I installed Tom in my second-floor sales office just above that of Farquhar, and moved myself down the hall. I now had what I had asked for, the position of assistant manager and relief from the sales job, but—but I had nothing to do. For days I sat there in my large and pleasant room, looking out over the green western expanse of the campus, shuffling papers, checking up on Tom now and again, and wondering whether I had talked myself out of a job. The uncertainty and self-pity persisted for a week or so; then I shook myself—I seem to remember—and said aloud to the room: "If you can't find something to do here, you can get yourself back to the library."

And indeed there was much to be done if we were going to make the Press into a scholarly publishing house of some consequence. That winter, as noted earlier, I had gone with Farquhar to my first meeting of the Association of American University Presses in Chicago and there began to learn something about how books were published by others. Sam himself was interested primarily in manufacture, and at that moment in paper quality, one of his great specialties, and we went up into frozen Wisconsin to visit a paper mill and a research institute—the name does not come back—set up to test the strength, opacity, and other characteristics of printing papers. After all these years I remember only one testing machine; it seemed to move in all conceivable directions, and we thought it must have been invented by the young man from Racine, protagonist of a favorite limerick.

AAUP meetings were then small. And the bitter weather held us indoors. After the formal sessions, now lost to memory, nearly all the delegates gathered around tables in one large taproom and talked. That informal talk—the exchange of information, the case histories, if you will—that was my education. Commercial publishers are noted for holding their cards close to the chest, but the most knowledgeable university press people were open and generous with what they knew, patient with the young and ignorant, willing to answer questions, most of which must have seemed naive. Of these early mentors I remember especially Datus Smith of Princeton, whom I came to regard—when he went from Princeton to his third-world work at Franklin Publications—as possibly the wisest and surely the most public-spirited of scholarly publishers. In the following years it was with Tom Wilson of Harvard that I held a thousand conversations and debates, many of them at his house on—appropriately named for me—Berkeley Place in Cambridge.

That early postwar time saw the beginning of a great development in university publishing. There were then only a handful of presses that knew how to do a fully professional job of publishing, and all of these, with a couple of exceptions, were in the great private universities of the east and midwest. Even today these remain the largest presses on the continent, joined in size only by Toronto and California. But we were not then in their class, nor were most state presses. As I listened to their ways of conducting author relations and business affairs, I began to understand why state university presses, wih their unbusinesslike institutional rules, were coming to bat with two strikes against them. For the next twenty years and more I had to expend much of my energy trying to break, or at least to loosen, those restrictions in Berkeley, succeeding with some and failing with others. Without some success in that struggle, our task would have been hopeless.

Today the national scene has changed out of recognition. There are more presses than I can count, large and small, state and private, that can promise their authors a complete and imaginative job of publishing. But in 1946 there was still far to go for many of us. In the next year the AAUP, led by Datus Smith, obtained the sponsorship of the American Council of Learned Societies and a grant from the Rockefeller Foundation for a survey of university presses as they then were. The survey report, written by Chester Kerr—later hired by Yale and eventually successor to Norman Donaldson as director there— was published in 1949[1] and allowed the presses a hard look at themselves and at each other. If self-knowledge is an early stage of wisdom, many of us, especially those from the more backward presses, could begin to probe our own weaknesses and to remedy some of them as best we could. After that there were many other cooperative efforts at learning, or self-teaching. For one thing, our record keeping was about as bad as it could be. It took many years for our financial wise men, notably Jack Schulman of Cambridge, to convince some of us— to convince our universities—to install the kind of publishing accounting that is essential for good management. State universities, especially, held fast to institutional practices that fitted only institutional thinking. As early as 1933 Sam Farquhar had asked for a title accounting system—standard in commercial publishing—but did not get it.

---

1. Chester Kerr, *A Report on American University Presses* (New York, 1949).

Back in Berkeley there was no lack of things to do. There was too much to do. I could look for manuscripts, of course, and did, but what could I say to skeptical authors, who wanted their books published in the full sense and not just produced? We needed advance planning from receipt of manuscript to marketing of finished book. But as soon as we tried to think in those terms, it became clear that our publishing office was no more than a sub-section of a printing plant, an editorial tail attached to a printing dog. When the dog barked, we wagged. Editor Small and his assistants had a useful place in the scheme of things, and so, in a smaller way, did a sales manager. But there was really no room for a publisher. The printers controlled the format and makeup of the books. They controlled schedules and costs, and for a number of reasons California printing, in our plant and in commercial ones, had become enormously more expensive than in other parts of the country. Book manufacture, I learned, was more efficient in plants that produced only books, but these plants were all in the east and midwest. Edition binding was even more critical at that time, done by machine in the east and by hand in the west at twice the cost. Western wage scales were higher, unions stronger.

I had to set myself up as a sort of part-time production manager, a standard job in most publishing offices but one often dispensed with when the plant was under the same roof. Before we could price reasonably on a national market, before we could sell effectively and keep promises to authors, we had to gain some measure of control over our own manufacture, which meant subjecting our printers to competition and buying outside some of the time. But this was a threat to the printers, to their pride and perhaps their livelihood. They demanded that all work remain at home. We could not publish if it did.

Farquhar was caught in the middle, between our publishing ambitions, encouraged by him, and the needs of his beloved plant. Or the wants, perhaps, since expanded publishing would provide additional work, if the printers could have seen it that way. Farquhar did what a sensible man would do in his place: he tried to compromise, make peace, keep the twain together, make it possible for both sides to live. Estimates were no longer made in McHenry's hand-hefting style but were calculated in detail, a new and uncongenial requirement to the plant. Occasionally we were allowed to send work out; at other times no. Sometimes when the cost of a book got out of hand, the bill was reduced and the loss spread over other jobs. Of course word got around and other university customers complained.

This kind of conflict does not arise all at once, but comes little by little as problems pile on top of each other, and as the participants begin to see, or at least to believe, that there is no reasonable way out of the difficulty. So I cannot say when it was that we passed from irritation to strife. Relations must still have been fairly good in 1947 when I was offered, and declined, the directorship of the press at North Carolina, after Tom Wilson had moved from there to Harvard and recommended me. Looked at rationally and without hindsight, that decision was a mistake, but I was loath to leave California and said to myself that Chapel Hill and I were not right for each other. They then found someone who was surely more right than I could ever have been: Lambert Davis, former editor of the *Virginia Quarterly Review,* who became a distinguished director for many years.

Memory retains few details of the following months. Farquhar was pleased with the growth in book publishing; he made me head of the publishing side of the Press and got Sproul to change my title to associate manager, with the promise of first consideration as his successor—little did I know how soon that would become an issue or how iffy were presidential promises. So I worked long hours seeking better manuscripts, with some success, and trying to coordinate all the publishing activities. There were only a few of us in the publishing group. I had moved Tom Webb to the editorial department, a better place for his talents; there he not only worked on manuscripts but searched our backlist and those of other presses for good books that might be reprinted and add substance to the front list. One of these was a book edited by Sam Farquhar's brother Francis and first published by Yale in 1930: *Up and Down California in 1860–1864: The Journal of William H. Brewer;* it eventually went into paperback and is still in print. The double experience in sales and editorial must have counted for much when Tom was chosen by Wisconsin.

As sales manager we appointed a former glider pilot, Albert J. Biggins, who had library training but no publishing background. In those days we never hired anyone with experience. Unlike Tom and me, Joe proved to be a natural salesman. When he walked in the front door there was no open job, but he was willing to gamble that he could recoup his pay from direct mail advertising of the backlist. After winning that little wager, he went on to the rest of the job and was soon on good terms with booksellers and reviewers, serving us well until there came a day when we no longer saw eye to eye. In the late forties and early fifties he did much to push our sales income up rapidly. If it had not risen, those difficult years might have proved impossible.

In the editorial department we found strength in Lucie E. N. Dobbie and David R. Brower, the latter back from service in the mountain troops. Both helped us into a new relationship with the Editorial Committee, described in the next chapter, and Lucie became executive editor, in effect chief editor, and contributed greatly to the remaking of the book program. There will be more to say about both of them.

In 1944 Farquhar was in high spirits, as I have said, and seemed in excellent health. Shortly after I arrived he married his second wife, Florence Walne, a teacher of Japanese who had returned to Berkeley after heading the Navy School of Oriental Languages in Boulder. A number of the Japanese-language texts that sold so well were compiled under her direction. Whether Florence or the Japanese books came first to Farquhar, I know not, but they were a happy conjunction.

Unfortunately Florence herself was in poor health, and she died suddenly in October 1946, after not quite two years of marriage and while Sam and I were in Los Angeles. Whether the later deterioration of his health was in any way the result of Florence's death, is impossible to say for certain, but it seems likely. His asthma became worse;

much walking was difficult. While he was at Princeton for the university press meeting in May 1949 the asthma turned into pneumonia.

Recovery was expected. Sam's third wife, Hazel Frost, married a few months earlier, had come on from Berkeley and was with him. I spent some working days in New York and, after being reassured by a telephone call to the hospital, took a circuitous route home by way of New Orleans and Houston, where I had relatives. News of his death came to me on a train going through West Texas.

In Berkeley the smolder of resentment between printing and publishing now burst into a flame that nearly destroyed the Press. That was long ago. Until recently a selective, and protective, memory has shielded me from the years of conflict, the harshness and bitterness, from recollection of a hundred incidents, large and small, that perhaps were better forgotten. But Albert Muto, writing his history of the early Press, went into the president's papers and dredged up most of the story as recorded in old letters, reports, and memoranda. Some of these I had never seen before; others I wrote or read at the time. There is no need to repeat here the account in Muto's book or to dwell on what happened.[2] A summary will do, and in the next chapter something about the role of the Editorial Committee. But if anyone should doubt the animosity of the parties, I have not forgotten a telephone call from the business vice-president who led the opposition to us—an enemy but more decent than some. I should keep an eye out for one person, he warned, who might be lying in wait for me. All this sounds a bit ridiculous so many years later; it seemed serious enough at the time.

There was of course competition for the manager's job, but beneath that and more important was the basic fight between publishing and printing factions. No quarter was given. The University business office maintained that the Press was a service operation, not so different from others, and sought control over publishing as well as printing. Faculty members, stirred up by us, thought otherwise. The

2. Muto, *University of California Press,* chap. 10.

president temporized, as was his wont. Eventually, with business office pulling on one end and faculty on the other, the Press was wrenched apart.

But it was separation, not divorce. Sproul, for all his great strength in some ways, would not or could not take the final step. We were called two departments of one Press; we lived uneasily under one roof, with no love and small civility. For the next three or four years, incredible as that may now seem, the separation was deemed tentative and temporary—while the University temporized, seeking ways to put Humpty-Dumpty together again. Or at least a way to harmony.

All this time there were special committees or boards to advise the president, and the chairmen of these were sometimes called co-ordinators and expected to mediate differences and decide which printing jobs could be put up for competition. That, of course, was the basic issue. Without some freedom in buying manufacture, we thought we could not control our own operation and would never become genuine publishers. The printers believed they could not run an efficient plant with a full staff unless they had all our work. One coordinator was a professor of English. Another was the former head of three university presses and a New York publishing house. Neither was effective or had any real power. Both departments worked around them and went on with the struggle—as in the old bull-and-bear fights of Spanish California, tied together so we could not get away from each other.

Neither department head had any security. I was acting manager of the publishing department of the Press, while William J. Young, who had been in charge of official publications—catalogues and directories—was made acting manager of the printing department, with Amadeo Tommasini as his superintendent. I had not known Jack Young. At our very first meeting he tried to throw me out of my office—Farquhar's old office, which Young thought should be his. There were angry words. He did not succeed, and I doubt that we ever spoke a friendly sentence from then on. But that was incident, not cause. Shortly thereafter he wrote a long letter to President

Sproul, declaring that Farquhar had lost control of the Press a few years earlier; thereafter the printing plant had continued to perform reasonably well but the publishing side was incompetent and needed a "thorough and complete housecleaning." Of course I did not see that document at the time, nor did our faculty supporters.

In this little civil war—or war of independence from our point of view—we were few and small. They were large and many, or so it seemed then. Their volume of business was three or four times greater than ours. They were supported not only by the strong business side of the University but by the president's chief assistant, George Pettitt, and even by our own chief editor. They were strongly backed by the printing and binding unions and later by the employing printers of San Francisco. Bills were introduced in the legislature to forbid sending printing work out of the state; fortunately they did not pass.

In almost every way the odds were stacked against us. And yet—when the dust settled in the late 1950s, the relative strengths of the two departments had been reversed. The printing plant was out of the book business, reduced to an office for University general printing, while the publishing side had grown into something like the Press of today—smaller, of course, but similar in nature. Somehow during those years—and I cannot say just how it happened—the struggle for survival was slowly won, and without any throats being cut, except metaphorically. We published what books we could, sought better ones, worked on the foundations of a publishing program as envisioned, or half envisioned, by earlier managers—Allen, Calhoun, and Farquhar.

In 1958, when Clark Kerr became president, the last ties were severed between Press and printing department, dissolving a marriage arranged by Sproul and Farquhar twenty-five years before. That the marriage did not work is the fault of no one, but the failure might have been recognized sooner. Under the new regime the printing department remained part of the business office, while the Press was placed under the academic vice-president, statewide, precisely where we thought it belonged. To oversee management and financial matters for the Press there was created a board of control, chaired by the academic vice-president and including other administrative officers as well as members of the Editorial Committee, north and south.

From the beginning the new system worked well. All members of the board, including the new business vice-president, were supportive and helpful. The academic vice-president, Harry Wellman, was also Kerr's first assistant, the chief operating officer of the University. An ideal superior, Wellman was quick to make decisions and made them well. If you could prove your case, he acted; if you could not, he said no. Once, when I informed him that the Berkeley purchasing office was holding up a requisition approved by the board, Wellman simply picked up the phone and ordered them to move it. After years of equivocation and infighting, at last we worked for someone we could talk to and who knew how to take action.

Establishment of the board was the beginning of financial health for the Press, a story for later telling.

5   How We Joined the Editorial Committee

By the time Clark Kerr ordered full separation of printing and publishing, he was recognizing a *fait* almost *accompli*. But how could the transformation have come about? We were not giant killers or clever politicians. We had no special credit with the old president, who sat back and let the fight go on. We ourselves were more stubborn than strong.

In our days of weakness I came to see that we had one great weapon if we could bring it to bear—the power of faculty opinion in a university where the faculty was strong enough to challenge the administration. Our access to this power was through the Editorial Committee, appointed by the faculty itself. But in the 1940s Press and Editorial Committee were going in different directions and looked on each other with suspicion. It could be said, as I have said, that they amounted to two different presses, one concerned with the monograph series and the other with book publishing and with printing standards. In relation to the Press staff, the Committee acted as a sort of watchdog, protecting the interests of the faculty, interests thought to reside in the series, where detailed academic research was published. The Committee criticized the Press for being slow, which we were, and for over-editing, which we did—matters that had brought on several battles between Committee and manager, a sharp one in 1939 and the most serious in 1947–48.

Many faculty members thought the Press unworthy of a great

university, less good than others. One of my brightest moments came quite a few years later when a distinguished scholar, about to leave Berkeley to become provost at a great eastern university, told me he thought the Press better than the University. An exaggeration, of course, but a sign that we had come of age. And now as I write, perhaps no longer an exaggeration; the University appears to have suffered more than the Press has from political activism and early retirements.

As the forties merged into the fifties, with Farquhar no longer there to keep an uneasy peace, we found ourselves thinking not only about how to survive but about what the Press was and what it ought to be. There was no conflict in those two thoughts; need and philosophy pointed in the same direction. Press and Committee, divided, could not withstand the business office forces; together we might. And if publishing was not a service activity, like printing, then it must be—had better be—academic in a broad sense. Indeed, I could see no justification for university publishing unless it was an extension of the academic university, an arm of the faculty. True that it need not, perhaps should not, be tied closely to the academic departments. True also that it must be managed like a business, but its raison d'être was—is—intellectual.

It made no sense, then, for Committee and Press to defend different goals. Surely the University of California was great enough, the Press could be large enough, to encompass two publishing programs, series and books, and if managed right the two could support each other, or at least could run on parallel tracks without collision. So to the Committee, and to anyone else who would listen, we preached the doctrine that university book publishing is an academic activity, and we invited the Editorial Committee to join the Press. Or perhaps we joined them. I am not sure that we ever put it into so many words, and certainly it was not the act of one heady afternoon, but in some way the two bodies were so maneuvered that they became one body. And it was more than a temporary alliance born of a common danger. This second marriage, unlike the old printing-publishing union, was made in a kind of publishing heaven. The benefits were mutual, and we thought we could live happily ever after if we could break the old connections.

For the first forty years, from 1893 to 1933, a faculty committee *was* the Press,[1] even though dominated for half that time by President Benjamin Ide Wheeler. After Wheeler's retirement in 1919 all publishing activities were planned and performed by the Committee and its secretary, called manager. One is reminded that the heads of the Cambridge and Oxford university presses until recently were officially called, in splendid understatement, Secretary of the Syndics and Secretary of the Delegates. Those bodies, of course, had financial as well as editorial powers.

From time to time, after Wheeler, the Committee as Press wanted to publish books as well as series monographs, and indeed it brought out two or three books a year, but these were treated pretty much like monographs, for the Committee had no funds but the series manufacturing appropriation, known as the Scientific Account, and no organization but the secretary-manager. In 1930, when Robert Gordon Sproul became president, there seems to have been general agreement that the Press should be expanded and reorganized for a broader kind of scholarly publishing—but agreement ended there. The Committee and its faculty manager, George Calhoun, expected to remain in charge. Instead, Sproul appointed an outside, nonfaculty manager, not responsible to the Committee, the man who was already in charge of the printing office—Samuel T. Farquhar.

When Farquhar drew up plans for reorganizing the Press, he took them to the Committee for advice—advice only, he made clear, because such matters were "beyond the jurisdiction of the Committee." At this distance it is difficult to judge the temper of those meetings in April 1933, but it is clear that Farquhar was doing two things: maintaining his independence as manager, including power to select book manuscripts for the new program, and at the same time seeking the support of the Committee for that program. With Sproul behind him

1. The Editorial Committee and its predecessor the Committee on Publications.

and the regents behind Sproul, Farquhar was in a strong position. When the Committee voted support, probably with some reluctance, it was approving the limitation of its own powers. All publications would still need its approval for scholarly quality and appropriateness, but books to be published on the new investment account, known as General Publications, were to be selected by the manager. Since the Committee retained full power over series monographs and could choose the occasional book financed entirely on the series fund, there were thus two classes or categories of publications. The Committee controlled one and looked on the other with a dubious eye.

The quality of the Committee-Press relationship in those early years cannot be recaptured, and the minutes, written by Farquhar, contain little evidence for speculation. He was an educated man, an appreciator of literature and scholarship, and he must have done his best to build a good rapport. Several Committee members, particularly some in Los Angeles, appear to have been good friends of his. At the very first meeting under the new regime he offered his new fund to help finance one of the Committee's manuscripts, thus saving money for the Committee and its fund. Joint financing became common thereafter, with Farquhar's General Publications Account assuming as much of the cost of a book-length work as he thought could be recovered from sales.

But Committee and Press were two; their publications, in spite of the occasional joining, were not thought of as one endeavor, as can be seen whenever trouble arose. And arise it did. Delays had once been attributed to the printers, who put scholarly work aside in favor of course catalogues, but after 1933 it appears that the chief problem lay in the editorial department of the Press. During the depression years, when there were funds for only a few series manuscripts, complaints were mild enough, but in late 1939, with more money and more approvals, the editing was said to be eighteen months in arrears, and an angry Committee retaliated by holding up two of Farquhar's book manuscripts.

He fought back. At the meeting of 3 May 1940 he read a prepared statement affirming his rights as manager and his intention to continue the program of general publications, as instructed by the president. In attempting to control that program by refusing to act on manuscripts, he said, the Committee was ultra vires, usurping authority. If it was dissatisfied with the operation of the Press, it could recommend changes to the president. But again he struck with one hand and offered peace with the other. He wished to cooperate. Admitting that the editorial department was the bottleneck, he said he had asked the president for an additional position and he now proposed to assign three-quarters of the editorial time to the series monographs and one-quarter to his general publications.[2]

That seems to have done the trick—for the moment. His manuscripts were passed. The editors began to catch up, and with the coming of the war the problem faded away. The budget went down; there were fewer manuscripts; and the new books were mostly Japanese-language texts and dictionaries, requiring little or no editorial time and printed by offset outside the University plant. But Farquhar could not have endeared the Press, his part of the Press, to faculty members when in 1943 he recommended to the president that the Committee's budget be drastically cut and that scholarly work unrelated to the war effort be put aside. The president was too shrewd to endorse the latter proposal, but he cut the budget.

Knowing nothing of this history, I was shocked when the attack came out of the blue, it seemed, in November 1947. Acting in response to a resolution of the academic senate about the slowness of publication, the Committee proceeded in a way that must have been planned in advance by at least some members. Discussion soon focused on the amount of editorial revision that could be justified, and the Committee then voted that "it is not the duty of the University Press to rewrite manuscripts." Since the meeting was in Los Angeles, with Harold Small not present, one can wonder how the discussion might have gone had he been there to listen.

2. Neither at this time nor before or after is there any indication that he asked Harold Small to change his methods, but it seems likely that he had once tried and failed. Authority over employees is never more than partial.

That much accomplished, the Committee moved on to the general publications—not to hold them up as it had in the past but to take them over. A subcommittee was asked to consider the limits of the Committee's authority as set forth in its rules, in the by-laws of the regents and the by-laws of the academic senate. Two months later, after listening to a long report, the Committee voted to change its rules and proclaim that it exercised supervision over, and was empowered to select, all publications, including those called general.

This time Farquhar did not fight back, as always before. I can say this was so, but not why it was. The lack of response may have derived from his declining health, noticeable after the death of his second wife, Florence. But perhaps not. He had always countered complaints of delay by hiring more editors; and as for general publications (books), he had turned these over to me as head of his publishing department, and he may have come to take less personal interest in them. His silence left both problems—editorial delays and threat to the books—in my lap. I had to take action on one; the other fell of its own weight.

What the Committee wanted for its series papers was precisely what I had been working to obtain for our books—to shift from what might be called a laissez-faire mode of production to a planned system with controlled schedules. At that November meeting I proposed to make one member of the editorial staff an expediter who would schedule series papers and monitor them from arrival to publication. He would examine incoming manuscripts and ask the Committee to throw back any that were poorly prepared and would require too much editorial attention, and he would then set up schedules of six months for shorter papers and a year for longer ones— not very fast really but an improvement and the first time a commitment had ever been made.[3] We would use free-lance editors whenever the load was too much for the staff. The expediter, David Brower,

3. According to Muto, the very first monograph in 1893 was edited and printed in three months, with type presumably set by hand. It is generally true, I think, that technological advances do not result in faster book production.

worked closely with Lucie Dobbie, who was soon to be in charge of all editors. In May 1949, just after the death of Farquhar, the new chairman of the Committee, Ted McCown, an anthropologist, compiled figures and announced, with satisfaction, that the Press had worked closely to the schedules proposed. So I gained some credit with the Committee, but not with Harold Small.

To proclaim is not to attain. The Committee could rewrite its own rule to grant itself power, but what effect could the new rule have? Sole responsibility for the investment account lay with the manager, who could not be told where to invest.[4] The only truly satisfactory way of working together was a collaboration of the two parties in an accepted balance of power, but that came later. Meanwhile, one member proposed that the Committee ask the president for a new fund to make up losses on general publications rejected by the Press and then approved by the Committee. The motion lost on a vote of nine to one, perhaps because wiser heads could see its futility, or because they judged they had gone far enough.

But I was instructed to report on all rejected manuscripts, and at each meeting for a time thereafter I made an oral presentation of all the projects recently proposed and rejected, including full descriptions of the more ludicrous and impossible ones. None of us smiled. The Committee then went through the motion—passed a motion—to reject them all. At the beginning of the next academic year McCown told me to forget the matter, and it was never heard of again.

For that one embattled year of 1947–48 the Committee chairman was Bertrand H. Bronson, distinguished scholar of Chaucer and Samuel Johnson and something of a literary stylist, but not an easy man to get along with. (I suspected that some editor, perhaps Small, had once done violence to his prose.) Cool, handsome, impeccably got up, he looked on us, looked down on us, with a critical eye. Some of

4. Years later one of our editors proposed that we make decisions by vote, and I had to tell him that his vote was smaller than mine. I carried the financial responsibility; losses would come down on my neck, not his.

us may have sympathized with his thoughts about over-editing, but we never shared the adoration of his girl students, one of whom was said to have rushed home to inform her parents that "Professor Bronson lives on Panoramic Way." To which her gruff father replied, "One might think he lived on Mount Olympus."

Happily for us, Bud Bronson went off the Committee at the end of the academic year, as did Edouard Meylan, the man who pushed for over-riding our rejections and wanted to ask the president for money to finance such gestures. The third active attacker was William Matthews of Los Angeles, who later became a rather good friend of mine but never again mentioned this episode. Over the years we published a number of his books, notably the new and complete edition of *The Diary of Samuel Pepys,* in eleven volumes. There will be more to say about this great edition and its two editors, who would gladly have throttled each other.

I cannot say precisely how the relationship of Press and Committee was changed, or when this was done. Such things happen day by day, little by little. With good will on both sides they move forward without a blueprint, until one day we realize that the change has taken place. Then we can codify it, as we could not have planned it.

For success in group trouble-making there is needed what might be called a critical mass. Three members out of eleven—the size of the Committee at that time—could provide mutual reinforcement, multiplying indignation by bouncing it off each other, and, with a plausible cause, could be quite effective. But a single dissident is lonely and, lacking an irresistible issue, is apt to subside into the general consensus. In all the years after that I do not remember any difference between Committee and Press that could not be ironed out in discussion, nor after 1951 was there any serious split within the Committee. New members sometimes questioned methods or policies, but sitting with the group soon convinced them. It was understood that we would not countenance any intercampus rivalry. Members might be chosen from or by campuses, but soon learned that they were not there to represent the interests of those campuses, but instead the good of the University and the Press. Only once, and that was early in the game, did a member from Berkeley, the chairman, talk down to the members from Los Angeles and thus question the standing of that campus. The other Berkeley members saw to it that he was replaced.

Our wish was to make this the best committee in the University, and we may have succeeded. Several years after my retirement, listening to a member who had never worked with me but only with my successor, James H. Clark, I was delighted to hear him state in public that the Editorial Committee is the best in the University, the most enjoyable, the most satisfying. The satisfaction comes in part because this Committee, unlike most others, does not merely recommend. It empowers. The joint decisions of Committee and director are final; they set the publishing process in motion, and a few months later the results, the books themselves, may be handled and read. But perhaps that could be true even were there dissension. The feeling of solidarity, the esprit de corps, if we may call it that, comes from the sense of being one body, two interlocking parts of one body, with a single purpose, going in a single direction. And that came about when Press and Committee joined forces after 1949.

Over the years, gradually, there was constructed a friendly balance of power. Since the Committee had to vote the use of the imprint, the manager—later director—could not publish without its consent. Since the director was responsible for the investment fund, and for the organization that supported it, the Committee could not order publication.[5] Collaboration was essential and natural. I should add that the Committee, in my time, never interfered with management, although always kept informed and invited to observe, and the director never took the Committee for granted[6] and accepted, with some show of grace, its occasional rejection of his projects.

5. It could, of course, with the monographs. There was no difficulty over them, and they gradually became a smaller part of the publishing program.
6. I have heard of an occasion at another press when the stock of printed books was covered by canvas while the editorial board met to approve the manuscript.

One result was that the Press never stood alone. The chairmen, backed by the whole Committee, were always ready to participate in negotiations with University powers—necessary from time to time even after the printing dispute was settled. The two parties, standing together, made a force that commanded respect. In 1957 the Committee, working through the academic senate, pushed the old president into arranging, through the regents, academic senate membership for the manager of the Press, thus changing his title to director. This step was, of course, a way of recognizing the oneness of Committee and Press as well as the basic interest of the faculty in the publishing program. It followed, as we have seen, that the new Board of Control, set up in the early 1960s, was a joint body of administrative officers and members of the Committee.

Beginning in 1947, there was a series of one-year chairmen: Bronson, McCown, and then, after Farquhar's death, James F. King, professor of history in Berkeley, and George R. Stewart. The standing together against a common danger began under King, and with it acceptance of the Press, the whole Press, as an arm of the faculty. We took up so much of King's time that year, as I remember, that he neglected his research and writing, and when he came up for promotion, his record of publication was short. With more flexibility than is sometimes understood, the promotion committee came to me for a statement in order that King's unusual service to the University—that publishing might not perish—could stand in lieu of so many printed pages.

The statewide committee on committees, wishing to provide a strong chairman when King went on leave, chose George R. Stewart of the Berkeley English department, a man of large reputation but no experience with the Press. George was famous for his books in the related fields of western literature and history, including the topography of overland routes, and had written successful novels about great natural phenomena such as *Storm* (1941) and *Fire* (1948). Another specialty of this versatile scholar was the study of American place names; in addition to his own books on this subject, he was one of the original sponsors—along with, among others, the two Farquhars, Francis and Sam—of our own large *California Place Names,* by Erwin G. Gudde (first edition, 1949).

But George's great talent was for individual, even solitary, work. As I was told by some who had dealt with him in departmental meetings, he was not a "team player." His quibbles, if I may call them such, could make it difficult for a group to act. Perhaps George was a lone dissident by nature, but not one who subsided easily. It was he who made the remarks about Los Angeles members and turned the Committee against himself. When he wrote to the president for the Committee, this accomplished writer would state the group's attitude in language less than clear and then append his own doubts and half-doubts in a way that made the letter equivocal and weak. After he was replaced, the two new chairmen, north and south,[7] acted and spoke in clear and direct language, and the Committee became a strong force once more.

At about the same time, there were mixed reactions to another "strong man," a noted former publisher who served on the Committee for three or four years and was also chairman of the president's first advisory board on the Press and printing department—Joseph August Brandt. Brandt was an Oklahoma boy who went to Oxford on a Rhodes scholarship and returned to a career of swift successes, several of them, and a few experiences that turned out less well. After working as city editor on a newspaper in Tulsa, he established the university press at Oklahoma, quickly bringing out books that received national attention. Paul B. Sears' *Deserts on the March* (1935) stirred up controversy over soil conservation. *Wah'Kon-Tah,* by John Joseph Mathews—an Osage Indian who also went to Oxford—was the first university press book to be chosen as a main selection by the Book of the Month Club, in 1932. At about the same time there was begun the long series of books entitled the Civilization of the American Indian, still one of the glories of the Oklahoma list. Brandt was made honorary chief of the Comanche Indian Nation. From 1938 to

7. At some time in the 1950s the chairman, from the north, and vice-chairman, from the south, were redesignated equal co-chairmen.

1941 there were further successes at Princeton University Press. In the seven years after leaving there, Brandt was successively president of the University of Oklahoma, director of the press at Chicago, and president of Henry Holt & Company, the New York publishers, staying nowhere very long.

Joe was large in stature, large in ideas, some of them brilliant, and gifted with the energy and enthusiasm that convinced authors to write the books he envisioned, colleagues to carry out his big projects, and both to look on him with devotion. He was a master salesman who could sell his ideas and his organization to book clubs, to institutions, to almost anyone—at least for a time. I have heard it said that as an administrator he needed a first-rate number-two man to oversee the working out of his best ideas and to shelve some of the others. At Oklahoma and Princeton he had just that kind of backup from men who later succeeded him and became notable directors.

In 1949 Brandt came to UCLA to establish a graduate school of journalism, and there spent the rest of his career as an academic. When he was appointed to the Editorial Committee in 1950, at the same time George Stewart came on, I thought Joe would be a tower of strength, that he would help interest the Committee in the problems of book publishing. And to some extent, so he did, but for reasons I know not he never became really involved in the Committee's work. Perhaps he had had his fill of book publishing and wished to concentrate on his new school of journalism. Or his fill of dealing with troubles and with the kind of infighting that must have plagued him in some of his larger jobs.

Joe believed in wide-ranging books, was impatient with the monograph series, and thought we might discontinue it. So I, having no talent for suicide, tried to explain that a move in that direction and at that time would destroy the bond between Committee and Press. And one day Joe came up with the idea that we should change the form of the imprint to include both Los Angeles and Berkeley. I could only show him some books and say we had been doing just that since 1940.

The two of us got along well enough, having a given name in

common, his second and my first, and sharing many friends at university presses. But as chairman of Sproul's special committee on printing and publishing—a kind of coordinator without clear powers—Joe was too easily led into damaging compromise, it seemed to me, perhaps because he remembered the joint printing-publishing operations at Oklahoma and Princeton. Twice he went along with business office proposals that all printing jobs be put in the University plant for an experimental period, a move that would have come close to destroying our position and had to be resisted. But on another occasion he shot off a thunderous letter to President Sproul, saying that the surest way to destroy the Press would be to put it under the business office. That may have saved us.

After Brandt the next "coordinator" was Arthur Hutson, professor of English at Berkeley and a member of the Editorial Committee. But he too was a compromiser, and nothing got settled. Strength in support of the publishing cause came from other members of the Committee. Beginning in 1951 and for the next several years we were fortunate to have two truly strong and wise co-chairmen: Robert L. Usinger, an entomologist from Berkeley, and Foster H. Sherwood, professor of political science at UCLA. It was they, backed by the whole Committee, who finally put an end to the University's equivocation about the separation of printing and publishing. But that dispute is another story, which the curious reader will find set forth in Albert Muto's book. Here I am concerned with the Editorial Committee and how it became a happy part of the Press.

It was under the two new chairmen, with the hesitaters gone or outnumbered, that we began to see how effectively Committee and Press could work together. All manner of problems, all new plans of the Press were discussed with the chairmen or with the whole Committee. Bob Usinger was particularly interested in the monographs, being closely involved with the Entomology Series, very active at that time and perhaps the best managed series on a statewide basis. But it was also Usinger who first suggested a series of popular books that later became known as the California Natural History Guides and is still going strong, with more than fifty volumes published. There

Joe Brandt.

could be a useful relation between series and books, or at least the same people could think about both.

For half a dozen critical years Sherwood was our chief faculty adviser on the Los Angeles campus. As we built up the Press office there from a room and a secretary to a full editorial office, parallel to the one in Berkeley, every step was discussed with him. Wise in the ways of the University, he also had a natural understanding of editorial and administrative problems. When he left the Committee and later became vice-chancellor, we found it good to have in the administration building someone who understood the Press. After those crucial years we had many excellent chairmen, some of whom will be mentioned later, but as I look over the old records and try to summon up recollections, I am struck by the key importance of Sherwood and Usinger at a time when Committee and Press, separately and to-

Bob Usinger.

gether, were taking on their enduring character. Never after that was there any doubt that the two were meant to be one.

There were occasional differences, of course, and I may paint too rosy a picture. But years later, in the early 1970s, when a group of journal editors criticized the Press—justly, in part—and mounted an attack on the Editorial Committee through the academic senate, it is worthy of note that Committee and Press stood together once more, this time against a faction of the faculty. That is for later telling.

In joining the Editorial Committee the Press gave in order to receive. If we invited the Committee into the book program, to discuss new fields and chart new directions, it in turn gave the kind of intellectual advice and practical help that we could find nowhere else in such measure. "Publishers," once wrote William Jovanovich of Harcourt,

Brace, "are men of strong prejudices and small scholarship. Like the English as a race, they are incapable of philosophy. They deal in particulars." I like to think there is a flourish of exaggeration in those words, but the most knowledgeable of publishers, the most imaginative—such as Joe Brandt—need to know what is going on in dozens of academic disciplines, more than a house full of search editors can cover adequately. Of course academic advisers can be hired and are, but there is no real substitute, we found, for a loyal committee that feels itself part of the press.

The Committee in 1944 consisted of eleven members, eight from Berkeley and three from Los Angeles. As UCLA rose in importance, the ratio was changed, and as other campuses grew up, their faculties were brought in until there were seventeen members from nine campuses.[8] Few outsiders will believe that our method of appointment is possible, let alone workable. At most presses, the editorial committee or board is chosen by the president or by another high university officer, often on nomination by the director of the press. At California members are appointed each year by ten committees on committees, nine from the nine campuses and a tenth statewide body to coordinate the choices. Most members are reappointed for several years if they wish. In my time the director had little to do with individual appointments, although I was often asked what our needs were, what subject areas would be most useful. (There was always the danger of getting too many professors of English, one from each campus.) And I was usually able to suggest new chairmen from continuing members who showed the greatest interest. This complex procedure, in spite of its lack of central control, has on the whole yielded excellent results, a whole succession of superior people. And everyone knows that it is better to work with first-rate minds, even strong-willed ones, than with those of lesser talent. I expect that this method of appointment is better suited to choosing a large group than a small one.

At some presses the faculty board or committee is regarded as a necessary nuisance, a hurdle—and so it can be. But should not be.

8. That was in my time. There are now twenty members.

There are many friendly relationships between presses and boards, but I wonder whether others have evolved—partly by intention, partly by the accident of a long common struggle—the kind of relationship that was formed here in the years after 1949. And that was carefully nurtured and protected thereafter by all of us—chairmen, members, director.

A recent survey[9] of thirty university presses revealed that California not only has the largest editorial board or committee, but is also the only press where every manuscript is read by a member of the committee. The two characteristics go together: only a large group could take on that much work. But to the best of my knowledge, no one ever thought of it in that way. The system grew out of the work of the old Press, when a subcommittee on manuscripts reported on all series papers up for approval, even though already read and recommended by subject boards. As the Press grew, the system was adapted but changed only a little.

The disadvantages of a large group are plain enough, as are the advantages of a small board that is more easily managed and less apt to cause delays. But there are compensations, especially within a great and sprawling university—more talent, a greater variety of talent and knowledge, more friends to speak for the Press among the several faculties, a stronger voice within the University.

At most of the thirty surveyed presses committee members read manuscripts only "occasionally" and at ten presses they read "almost never." Certain kinds of manuscripts do not require committee approval at all—multi-volume works issued one volume at a time, imports and other co-publications, paperbacks from the lists of other publishers, and the like. There are no such exceptions at California. All manuscripts must come to the Committee, most with at least two outside readings and a full dossier on author and background prepared by the sponsoring editor. Each manuscript is passed in advance to one member, who takes responsibility for reading all or part of it,

9. J. G. Goellner, "The Editorial Board: Friend or Frustration," *Scholarly Publishing* (Toronto) 21:3 (April 1990), 184–88.

describing it to the others, and leading the discussion, with participation by all present, including staff. With the usual large dockets, meetings take most of a day.

Good news and bad news, of course. It is a cumbersome procedure and, unless managed with considerable care, can cause harmful delays. Some scholarly publishers, who like to think of themselves as "professionals," would never be willing to put up with it. But there is another, brighter, side of the coin. The open discussion, the prolonged give and take in all-day meetings, the seeming waste of time—it is precisely these that bind Committee and Press together, with a sense of participation and belonging. We could never have had the one without the other. And since members come long distances, from all over the state, it is a short meeting that would waste their time. In my tenure I was convinced that the extra effort, all the time spent, was more than repaid by the sense of solidarity that has been the subject of this chapter.

In a recent book,[10] the former director at Toronto, the late Marsh Jeanneret, wrote that books considered "commercial," those that needed no university subsidy and were expected to make money for the press, were published there without reference to the editorial advisory committee. Although he had great success with these, and reaped no criticism, Jeanneret came to believe that any book purporting to be scholarly enough for the imprint should go before the committee, regardless of the budget.

I would never have given up our kind of meeting, but in my later years I came to favor some small change, believing that we had let the system become a little too rigid. The Committee appeared to agree, and on some kinds of books—multiple volume works, or those invited by the director with the Committee's assent, or books originally published elsewhere and reviewed—it was understood that the procedure might be short-circuited, with perhaps only one outside opinion or even just a Committee opinion. The director and associate

10. Marsh Jeanneret, *God and Mammon: Universities as Publishers* (Toronto, 1989), 223–26.

director described and presented some manuscripts. Of course these, like all others, could be voted down or held over if the evidence was not convincing. Thus we imparted a measure of flexibility to a system seen by all as basically good. But we continued to believe, all of us, that every new project, without exception, should pass through the Committee. I speak only of my own time.

Meetings came to be happy occasions and sometimes reconvened less formally in the evening, with drinks. Committee members and director looked forward to them as pleasant and often inspiriting encounters, a kind of intellectual dialogue not common even in a great university. One man used to fly back from study in Europe rather than miss a meeting. Another former member and former chairman, Hugh Kenner, has described the pleasure of these meetings in an article that I reproduce as an addendum.

6 A Kind of Metamorphosis

Our small war of independence, necessary as it was and desperate as it seemed at the time, was no more than a first step, or as Winston Churchill said of a larger matter, the end of the beginning. Its success, tentative in the early 1950s and definite by the end of the decade, left us with an opportunity, nothing more. What came next would be proof of the pudding, proof that had to be demonstrated quickly and would then need to be pursued for many years.

So how does one go about converting President Wheeler's old-style press into a modern scholarly publishing house? And the answer is . . . that I don't know. I remember some details, of course, but even in retrospect cannot come up with a formula or a large agenda. We never had occasion, or never had time, to sit down and draw up a five-year or ten-year or fifteen-year plan to get from here to there, although Heaven knows there were enough smaller plans. Perhaps smaller was better; we were not large enough for large plans. There were enough good models among the presses of the great private universities of this country, whose company we might join in a few years, we thought, while averting our eyes from those too old and too big, Cambridge and the polycephalous Oxford monster.

Things happen one at a time. If enough of them happen in the same direction, they may add up to something of consequence. What I can do here, perhaps, is to recall some of the small decisions, describe some of the not-so-great acts that, taken together over a number of years, produced a kind of transformation, one that I once called, in over-poetic language, a metamorphosis.

First, an example of no change. Or slow change. I spoke of converting the Press, but there could be no question of doing away with the University monograph series, the heart and soul of the old Press and the chief concern of the Editorial Committee. In the early fifties its value was still considerable, its use by a number of strong academic departments undiminished, and, as I had told Joe Brandt, I could see no future in suicide. We would simply operate two publishing programs, leaving the series monographs to flourish or not flourish as might be, while we concentrated on Farquhar's small book program and tried to make it into a first-rate scholarly press. He had already turned the books over to me; I had sought manuscripts and gathered ideas, but not much had been accomplished before he died. Almost everything remained to be done.

As for the monographs, we took them seriously—with the left hand perhaps, but seriously, helping the Editorial Committee manage them through a long series of adjustments to new conditions. Never, for a moment, would I allow any staff member to undermine them in any way. But gradually, as research patterns changed, as for example the number of taxonomic studies declined in the biological sciences, the monographs became fewer. With the development of a microfilm library in Ann Arbor, there was no longer need to consider most dissertations. Our changes came one by one, with no dissension between Committee and Press. So convinced were Committee members after a few years that they sometimes proposed to move faster than I thought wise.

Monograph, an awkward word sometimes used to mean any publication not in series, is more usefully employed to distinguish works of narrow interest from true books. Such were our old monographs, intensive studies of small but worthwhile topics, especially in fields that could make good use of publication in discrete segments—geology, the several life sciences, linguistics, some kinds of anthropology. We published—brought out—thousands of these, large and small, on the geology of this or that formation, on *Crepis* and other botanical genera, on the Tasmanian bandicoot and other animals, on surviving American Indian languages. Many of these were of lasting value to scholars, although perhaps we need not have given them elaborate editing and production in nearly perfect letterpress printing. But where should money be saved? One faculty member said he would accept offset printing when President Sproul rode the night bus to Los Angeles.

Later we did ask authors to provide cleanly typed copy for offset printing of the four or five or six hundred copies that went to libraries on exchange. In the end this became a rather efficient operation—although not real publishing—and still is for the few surviving series. Perhaps one of the electronic methods can make it even more efficient.

But the monograph formula proved a failure in the social sciences and most of the humanities. After years of foolish egalitarianism—opportunities open to some should be open to all—we came at last to see that a form of publication that was useful and accepted in a few fields was looked down on and thought second rate in others. We might have seen this sooner if we had been looking instead of thinking. There is nothing like thinking to confuse the issues. So eventually we *looked* and then discontinued many series. In history—for example—manuscripts would have to be good enough to make books, or they were not for us.

In the early fifties, if I remember aright, we sometimes brought out more than 80 series monographs per year and less than half that many books. By the seventies there were 150 or 200 books and only a handful of monographs.

To become a better press we needed better books. But before we could do much to build the book list we had to build some kind of organization separate from the printing department, and do it with one hand, quickly, while fighting to survive with the other. We had put together a reasonably good sales organization, headed at that time by Albert J. Biggins, but the editorial department was still in effect an arm of the printing plant, and we had no production department at all and no accounting office. Periodicals work was scattered. And in Los Angeles, a campus rushing to overtake Berkeley as a research center, there was only a secretary.

It is not easy to remember what was done when. Fortunately there has survived a report that I wrote in July 1952 and sent to administrators and selected faculty members, as well as to members of the president's board on the Press and printing department. At that late date, after three years of uneasy separation, there were still some who wished to put the two departments back together again. As we saw in the previous chapter, the board, now bolstered by Usinger and Sherwood of the Editorial Committee, finally knocked that idea in the head. My report may or may not have helped, but it now reminds me of what had been done by then.

The long-time chief editor, Harold Small, was not about to help streamline editorial processing. He was given special tasks, and the department was turned over to Lucie E. N. Dobbie, who managed it well until her untimely death in 1964. She also participated in the search for manuscripts.

Production work, the dealing with printers and binders, including the University plant, I had tried to do myself during the last months of Farquhar's tenure. I now turned it over to David Brower, the editor who had served as expediter of series papers. Like me, Dave had to learn the job as he went along, but he soon ran into trouble with Amadeo Tommasini, who had been made superintendent of the plant. Tommy could not attack me directly, but he could get at my assistant. Although it was clear then that he was undermining Brower, even setting traps for him, I might hesitate to write this if I had not recently seen confirmation in a report on the printing plant by J. K. Lasser & Co., a report not shown to me at the time. Before long I was told by Joe Brandt, chairman of the president's board, that he could no longer support me unless I replaced Brower. Dave could help me in other ways, I thought; for one thing, he chaired our small

Lucie Dobbie.

book-planning group until he went to the Sierra Club in 1953. There he won considerable renown for designing and producing the Club's large-format books.

Fortunately, a replacement was near at hand. John B. Goetz, a young southerner with experience in New York publishing, had come to San Francisco and was doing free-lance book design for us. As production manager he proved quite able to hold his own with Tommasini and others; working quickly and well, he never got flustered. In those early years it was he and Lucie Dobbie, more than anyone else, who kept the basic work going. John was also an excellent designer, as I will relate later. He and Ward Ritchie and Adrian Wilson gave us book design that matched, or more than matched, that of the Farquhar days.

At about the same time we pulled the periodicals work together and set up a new department under Virginia Bunting. A new accounting system—the first of several—was designed for us by Olaf Lundberg, university controller, and we set up an accounting and fulfillment department.

It is hard to believe, now, that we had got along without so many of these standard elements of publishing organization. Of six major subdivisions, including a Los Angeles editorial office, four had not existed when we began. The reason, surely, is that the Press had been a sort of branch of the printing office, which helped pay our bills but left us half dependent and half equipped.[1]

It was clear that we could not, should not, remain a Berkeley operation in a widespread university, especially given the rapid rise of UCLA. Somehow, as early as 1950, I got approval from President Sproul to put an editor in Los Angeles and, on recommendation of Joe Brandt, hired Glen Gosling, a former trade editor at Brandt's old firm of Henry Holt & Co. in New York. With Glen in Los Angeles we could seek manuscripts, deal with authors as we did in Berkeley, and get ahead of anyone who might want to establish a separate press in the south—a possibility that had to be kept in mind. Two years later we added a second editor, James Kubeck, and began copyediting southern manuscripts in Los Angeles. Other people were added as we developed the plan of two parallel editorial offices. Gosling later moved to Berkeley as assistant to Dobbie, and then for a time was director of the University of Michigan Press. Jim Kubeck stayed for his entire career, managing all processing for many years.

Even before the organization was in place, we had to think about where we were going and, in particular, about what kind of books we wanted and how many. The book list was small. In a great and rich university, spreading over nearly all academic areas, we had a list that was neither great nor rich. In a small university we might have chosen to keep the list tailored and homogeneous, limited to a few disciplines. But a neat little list would make small sense, we reasoned,

1. The reader who wants more detail on this matter may find it in Muto, *University of California Press,* chap. 11.

Jim Kubeck, mid-1950s.

in a huge university with several campuses and dozens of graduate departments. To do an adequate job and achieve wide acceptance in the parent institution, we had to build a varied list rather than a perfect one, as we had already chosen variety in book design instead of the old house style.[2]

So we had to publish in many fields and prepare ourselves for growth. But growth is not good in itself, is often the opposite. Uncontrolled growth can be cancerous, as some ambitious communities are beginning to find out. In book publishing it can bring on financial disaster if not properly funded, or can lead to a large and mediocre list, another route to the same disaster. It has to be carefully controlled. Better has to go along with bigger, not an easy thing to manage.

By great good fortune we had adequate capital, although no one

2. See Chapter 18.

seemed to know how much. Under the system set up by Controller Lundberg for Farquhar, new books were funded on general University accounts. Lundberg and his assistant Loren Furtado had also written down the old book inventory in order to give me a fair start. If we made good investments, then, and kept the inventory depreciated, there was for a time no limit on the number of new books. That had to change, of course, when the total investment became large enough to be noticed, but by then we had built up a salable backlist.[3]

Before thinking about fields to cultivate and how to do it, we made the conscious decision not to be a regional press. At that time the presses at North Carolina and Oklahoma had made wide reputations for books on the American south and the American west. A few years later Texas and Nebraska also gained fame for western books, Nebraska for a big paperback series and Texas for large books about that state, including art books. The director at Texas, Frank Wardlaw, became an eloquent exponent of regional publishing and could point to many fine books. We might have followed suit, especially since Farquhar's handsomest and best-known books were on western topics, and also since some of my friends chose to judge us in comparison to Oklahoma. But there were good reasons, intellectual and practical, to choose another main direction.

In spite of the great Bancroft Library and the renown of Herbert Eugene Bolton and other historians, western history was a minor field of study at the University of California. Far more academic attention was, and is, paid to the major regions of the world: Asia, Africa, Europe, and the rest of America. It would be more appropriate for us, we thought, to be a press of worldwide interests, like the University itself, than to build a provincial list, useful as that might be.

Then the practical reason. Books on California history, unlike some of those on other western regions, did not sell very well. The stores were full of them, it seemed, but these were either light and popular or collectors' volumes. The latter, often handsome and finely

3. The financial wars are discussed in Chapter 20.

printed, had a sure market but a small one, good for only a few hundred copies. In the years before 1949, excited by the coming centenary of the great gold rush, we and other publishers had anticipated a big market for California books. But our series, Chronicles of California, bombed. One book out of seven did well. A semipopular volume on the gold rush itself sat on the shelves. Other publishers' series, including one from Alfred Knopf, also failed.

A Texas book in Texas seemed to sell several times as many copies as a similar volume on California. I cannot say why this was, but have noticed on visits to Austin, for example, that there exists a fine attitude of loyalty to that state and its culture, something not apparent in California, except among the small tribe of book collectors. Perhaps immigration came too rapidly so that few people here have a genuine sense of belonging. So we had two good reasons to turn our main attention in other directions. We would do western history books when good ones came along but would not make a specialty of them. We were just then bringing out the first edition of Erwin Gudde's great *California Place Names* (1949), and in 1951 came the first volume of *The Larkin Papers for the History of California,* edited by George P. Hammond. And we began developing a specialty in the natural history of California and the west.

As every publisher knows, good books do not walk in the front door unless good books are already there. One author attracts another, as they were then doing at some presses, but our reputation was for monographs, a reputation that did no harm in the biological sciences but could be fatal in history, literature, and the social sciences, the most fertile areas in scholarly publishing. Slow, gradual change might take a generation, we thought. Faster change required drastic measures, some of which will be described in the following pages.

In building a larger list, it would not do, I thought, to let that list be shaped by a single mind. Or even by a good editor with an assistant or two. More heads were needed, more interests, more tastes, more experience, more idiosyncrasies. But the sponsoring editor system had not yet come to American university presses, and in any event we had no money to hire a second editorial staff. When we put an editor in Los Angeles in 1950, his assignment was territorial rather than topical. In Berkeley we had to press into service part-time every staff member who showed an interest in a subject or two, even copyeditors, although the copyediting mind, in my opinion, is not well suited to list building.

Here, perhaps, is the place to say something about the nature of editing, a matter not always well understood, it seems to me, and that is of first importance in regard to the quality of a publishing list. There are many kinds of editors, related but not the same: journal editors; series editors; those who work with newspapers, magazines, films, as well as with books. The two kinds that concern us in scholarly publishing are editors and copyeditors. Unfortunately, the first term is commonly used for both, the cause—or rather the result—of a confusion in thinking. Not only are the two different, they require different types of mind. Although a few exceptional minds can encompass both kinds of thinking, most do not, and the distinction is basic. To ignore it is to invite trouble.

To define and over-simplify—for the sake of what comes next— the editor's mind sees the entire manuscript, grasps the thinking behind it, clear or not clear, is trained to judge its intellectual quality and relation to other work, can spot a chapter or a section or even a paragraph that has gone awry, and can tell the author where to fix it and sometimes how. But this kind of mind is often impatient with lesser matters, does not relish the painstaking, and often painful, work of detailed correction.

The copyediting mind finds satisfaction in detecting mistakes that author and editor do not see or may not care about, in striving for consistency of sense and style, in making clear sense out of subheads, and many other such matters. This work, done with restraint and dispatch, is both good and necessary. The best copyeditors—and we had a number of them over the years—are jewels to be treasured. But unfortunately, this type of mind—not always but often enough— tends to grow authoritarian, putting too much stress on consistency, finding it difficult to overlook individual preferences in usage or de-

viations from house style. More serious—and this has often been encouraged by press policy—there is the urge to heavy revision, with
the manuscript sometimes looked on as the raw material from which
a book can be made. Impatience, that great quality of the other editorial mind, is not often found here.

An over-simple comparison, as promised, but basically true.
Things that appear alike are often not alike. Later, in connection with
the processing of manuscripts into books, and its cost in money and
time—a matter that became desperate in the early 1970s—I will have
something to say about copyediting in relation to production. Here
I am concerned with building a list of new books and the best way to
bring quality to that list.

We in university publishing are apt to think of heavy copyediting
as a guarantee of quality. This is not just wrong—it is the precise
opposite of the truth. For if we do a proper job of choosing manuscripts, turning back those that are ill written or ill prepared, then
light copyediting is sufficient. Heavy revision demonstrates a failure
in choosing; something has gone wrong with our quality control at
the place where it should be strong, the point of acceptance. The fault
here lies with management, and I have been as guilty as anyone. If
editors are allowed to take in poorly written or poorly assembled
manuscripts, then copyeditors must strive to make something out of
them, and the result will not be the best.

We may recognize that many academics do not write well and
that others will leave their work half done and expect the publisher to
put it in shape. So we must take what we can get or we won't get
much. I cannot say that I saw the flaw in this argument in the early
days, but it came clear later on. A publisher of small repute may not
have many choices, but if we became known for excellent books, we
thought, and if we built a strong staff of editors—later called sponsoring editors—then the opportunities would be many and we could
be choosy in our choices. Authors of promising but essentially unfinished manuscripts could be invited to revise. Or to seek help in revision, or in rewriting if their first language was not English. Quality

would come with tough-minded sponsoring editors and not by re-
working mediocre manuscripts.

What suits one kind of publisher may not be right for another.
Heavy copyediting, even rewriting, is proper enough in some types
of research institutes, where scientists unskilled in writing for the
public are asked to provide technical information to, for example,
farmers. Some authors in our old monograph series got this kind of
help until we—Editorial Committee and Press—refused to give it.
But a book publisher, we reasoned after some sorry experiences,
should not be doing the books of authors who cannot write. Any
author deserves a certain amount of help, but no more than that. If
we made a habit of giving more, we were taking in the wrong kind
of manuscripts, or unfinished ones.

There are, of course, those who disagree with the distinctions I
make or at least with the practice that derives from them, and who
fuse—I would say confuse—the two kinds of editing. Most notable
in my time, perhaps, were Leon Seltzer of Stanford and his chief
editor, Jess Bell, two of the most brilliant people in university publishing. Their minds were among those that can work in two ways,
but their emphasis on slow perfection in copyediting was, in my opinion, a mistaken policy. Nevertheless, their list was good, if small, and
may suggest that satisfactory results can come from opposing principles of action.

For a time we had to do our manuscript searching in the spare time
of staff members who had other duties, but it became clear that a
great list would require something more. So we became one of the
first university presses to set up a staff of specialized editors whose
job was to prowl the academic halls, at home and away from home,
personally and by letter, to seek out the best scholarly authors and
bid for their manuscripts. In our early innocence we proposed to call
them soliciting editors or procuring editors; after being warned that
we were stealing the terminology of another profession, we named
them sponsoring editors and encouraged each to think of his or her

Three directors: Lyman, Frugé, and Lilienthal in
the mid-1960s.

books as a small list within the larger list. Each could become a sort
of publisher, with limited powers of course but with a fair amount of
liberty, and each was expected to follow his books from acquisition
through the publishing process, conferring with production and sales
and looking after the interests of the author. Each worked in one or
more subject areas, but the lines were drawn loosely and could over-
lap. Jurisdictional disputes, harmful enough at any time, would have
been doubly so with two editorial offices four hundred miles apart.
The purpose was to get good manuscripts in any way we could.

The sponsors included director and associate director. It will be
assumed, I suppose, that the director would take his choice of fields;
in practice he found himself taking what was left over, filling in the
gaps. I had begun with an interest in literary translations; later most
of these were handled by Bob Zachary in Los Angeles. After I had
been around South America, surveying university publishing for the
Ford Foundation, and knowing a little Spanish and Portuguese, I
found myself acting as Latin American sponsor until there came an
editor willing to take over. Meanwhile the art editor resigned, and I

had to elect myself, Heaven help me, to nurse along her unfinished projects. My successor as director has published some of the correspondence of those trying days, reprinted here as an addendum. Later, through another combination of circumstances, I sponsored manuscripts in ancient history and literature, continuing to retirement and after.

As Harold Small said that manuscripts should be written in some language, a list of books, however varied, should have some shape and not be a mere miscellany. Manuscript searching is most effectively done by area or subject. Strength in a field attracts further strength. A group of related titles can be sold more efficiently than can a lone book. So it will be useful, perhaps, to say a little about the fields we chose to cultivate and how we chose them. In later chapters there will be space for more about some of these fields and about some large projects, either because they were important or because something about them sticks in my memory.

How does one choose fields of specialty? Sit down with a list of scholarly disciplines and another of the strongest departments in the home university, and then make a rational choice? That might have been best, perhaps, but I don't think we were ever so well organized. Even though the old list was small and uneven, we were not starting from a tabula rasa. So we found ourselves making opportunistic choices from small beginnings or from blank spots on the list if there was some perceived spark of opportunity. Literary translations had already started with a personal interest and the availability of the first translator. Latin American books were spurred by a grant from the Rockefeller Foundation. We might have done little in art history without the ambitions of Professor Walter Horn. Film books were attracted by the old *Hollywood Quarterly* and later by its grandchild, *Film Quarterly*. The Asian list is the only one I remember that was deliberately begun from nothing at all and because we deemed it bright with promise for us. Even here there was the personal interest of Philip Lilienthal, associate director and former editor of *Pacific Affairs,* and the anticipated help of the several Asian centers in the

University. As it happened, they did little; the list was fashioned by the single hand of Lilienthal, as a later chapter will show.

Other fields were chosen from areas where we had a start of one kind or another. One of the few early strengths was the series of Sather Classical Lectures, developed by the Berkeley classics department into one of the best lecture series of its kind in the world. With a start like that and some twenty titles published, we would have lacked all predatory instinct if we had not thought of this series as a springboard to greater things.

Even the monograph series were sometimes a help. In that heyday of taxonomic research the series in the biological sciences were perhaps the most prolific, and the same authors also wrote books and knew book authors elsewhere. With their help we put together a list of large books in natural history, particularly a shelfful of western floras, books that were expensive to set in type but continued to sell forever or thereabouts. Jepson, Munz, Mason, McMinn, Howell, and Kearney were some of the authors whose books still have a market. But after research patterns changed and taxonomy went out of fashion—for a time, at least—the old biological monographs and the related books stopped coming, and this part of the list ceased growing. But there has remained one large semipopular book series, the California Natural History Guides, brainchild of the late Professor R. L. Usinger of the Editorial Committee and edited by Arthur Smith of Hayward State University. There are now more than fifty volumes.

It is less clear whether another old and great monograph series, American Archaeology and Ethnology (later re-entitled Anthropology) had any parental influence on the later books in anthropology. It seems likely that many of the latter came out of the growing academic interest in Asian and African studies. Still another successful series, Ibero-Americana, had some influence in the Latin American area. Its best known authors, Carl Sauer, Lesley Simpson, Woodrow Borah, and S. F. Cook, termed the École de Berkeley by a distinguished French historian, turned to book writing in their later years.

But the existence of the series could be a handicap. One of our weaknesses paralleled a great strength in the university itself, European, British, and American history. When we confronted the distinguished academic writers in Berkeley and Los Angeles (before the other campuses had reached maturity) we found ourselves up against our own reputation. The old monograph series in History had taken in too many mediocre dissertations along with too few good things. It was not easy to convince our best scholars to lend their books to an undistinguished list.

Again, we could see that gradual improvement might take twenty years and looked for a faster way. It helped some to go hunting in other universities, where our reputation was not so well known, but we found bigger game in London, where many fine scholarly books were published by commercial firms, some of which were pleased to take on American partners for joint publication. In this way we acquired American rights to books by some of the best British historians and even to some by our own people who had British connections. After a few seasons, when these titles showed up in our catalogues we could stop apologizing to local people and approach them on even terms.

There were some presses that scorned joint publications, or imports as we called them, as an inferior kind of publishing, but such purity was not for us, who had to pull ourselves up by our bootstraps. It was good, we thought, to acquire needed books by using someone else's editorial staff and filling in weak spots in our own list. Half the market was still half the world and not to be sneezed at. And some of the authors first acquired in this way continued to work with us afterwards. Thus Peter Brown and Peter Green, who will come into the next chapter, and others.

The British firms were not always easy to deal with, and we soon learned to demand comparable retail prices, so as not to be undersold in the library market, and a reasonable cost to us. One of our earliest large imports, arranged by mail, was Michael Sadleir's *XIX Century Fiction: A Bibliographical Record* (two quarto volumes, 1951). At a gathering many years later, I ran into an editor from the British firm of Constable & Co.,who reminded me of the book and our importation of one thousand copies. "We thought you very brave," he said. "By brave you mean foolhardy," said I, "and you may have been right, but we did manage to sell all of them." It had helped that the UCLA library decided to purchase the entire huge Sadleir collection, basis of the bibliography. We were not always so fortunate, of course, but there were few real losers.

Joint publishing is a useful device and needs no defense. Many good scholarly books do not command enough market in one country but can be financed when the expenses are shared by two firms on two sides of the ocean. And authors like to be handled by a genuine American publisher, or a British one when the deal goes the other way, rather than by a branch office or an agency. Economy comes from printing the two editions together, with changes made on title page and book jacket. And the British cost of editing and subediting, as they called copyediting, was then far less than ours. Importing was not our invention, of course, but we were among the first university presses to make extensive use of it, with regular scouting trips to London and later to the fair at Frankfurt.

Like some other presses, we thought we should be publishing in the hard sciences, where so much of the University's academic strength lay, and we hired our first science editor in the early fifties. But success was never great in my time, although we managed to bring out a number of useful books. It seems to be generally true that scientists write either textbooks—not for us except in special areas—or journal articles. Few of them turn out the kind of scholarly books that are standard university press fare in other areas. Some do, of course, but our pursuit of them was never more than half successful. We also tried to develop a medical book program, again with partial success.

Although we never decided to make a specialty of English and American literature, there was no escaping it. Books of literary history and criticism will always be with us; the problem was then, perhaps is now, to get our share of the better books and to avoid the many that are merely adequate. I don't feel able to judge our results. In a related area we had to think about the publishing of new poetry and fiction, espoused by some university presses but resisted by us for reasons I thought compelling and that will be set forth later. We always welcomed editions of English and American classics, some of them modern.

Among the editions were a number of large projects, several from our own university and one, commercially published in England, that we went out after. In the early 1950s came *The Sermons of John Donne,* edited by George R. Potter of Berkeley and Mrs. Evelyn M. Simpson of Oxford, and completed handsomely, with a design by Ward Ritchie, in ten volumes. Beginning at about the same time and from the Los Angeles campus was the California edition of the *Works of John Dryden,* projected for twenty volumes and still in progress after more than thirty years. The founding general editors, Edward Niles Hooker and H. T. Swedenberg, Jr., have passed the torch to others, and the work goes on. One day in the 1950s I asked Swedenberg when they might expect to complete the edition. "You and I won't be around," said he. Now he is gone, and I am long retired. Both the Donne and the Dryden have received favorable reviews, even in the *Times Literary Supplement,* not always generous to American editions of English authors.

Similar remarks about the mortality of editors and publishers could have been made by more than one curator of the Mark Twain papers in the Bancroft Library, including the late Henry Nash Smith, not the first editor but the one who first dealt with the Press as publisher. We began with a separate book or two, then took on the Papers of Mark Twain, a selection in many volumes of the unpublished writings, including thousands of letters. Later came the Works of Mark Twain, a re-editing of all the published writings. And there is now a popular series, the Mark Twain Library. The work will go on. And on. And will be described later.

The largest and greatest of our imports, or joint publications, was surely *The Diary of Samuel Pepys,* the first complete edition, edited by Robert Latham of Cambridge and William Matthews of UCLA in eleven volumes from 1970 to 1983. Published jointly with G. Bell & Sons of London, the main text has spawned an *Anthology,* an *Illustrated Pepys,* and a *Shorter Pepys.* The nature of the text and of the new passages, together with the interactions of two publishers, who got along reasonably well, and two editors, who did not, is worth a longer and later account.

To remake our reputation and catch up with the larger and better presses, we had to seize on every stratagem that would help us with authors. Few people nowadays remember, or will believe, what a publishing desert the west coast was in the forties and fifties, how concentrated in New York was the book business, especially the distribution end of it. We needed a beachhead in New York, not so much for direct selling as for publicity, contact with reviewers, journal editors, paperback editors, book clubs, and others. We knew, of course, that we were too small to afford this but stretched ourselves, wishing to convince authors that we could do what others could do. After we had grown a bit, not so many people called us foolish. Later we joined with two other presses in a London office, this one primarily for selling, and because of our Latin American list we participated in a foundation-supported selling office in Mexico City, one that managed to reach the break-even point before Mexican inflation brought it down. It is true, if paradoxical, that some of these things were more important to a press that could not afford them than they were later to a large and powerful press.[4]

At about the same time we jumped into the paperback field before we were truly ready. A sensible director, sensible editors, would have waited until the backlist was large enough to support the venture, but again our determining thought was of how best to court new authors. In this country paperback publishing, long the norm in France and other continental countries, did not find a large market until after World War II. Whether it was the millions of armed services editions or the wartime Penguin Books in Britain that trained a new public, as some believe, I do not know, but suddenly there came a change, sometimes called the paperback revolution. First were the pocket-sized reprints of popular books, handled by magazine dis-

4. The several offices are described in Chapter 19.

tributors and sold in drugstores and railway stations at the now un-
believable prices of 25 and 35 cents. Success was considerable, and the
racks then carried better books than those now sold in this way at
$4.95 and more. Even we managed to sell at least one title to a paper-
back firm, Brewster Ghiselin's *The Creative Process,* to New American
Library in 1952.

Then in the mid 1950s came "quality" paperbacks at prices that
ranged above and below one dollar and brought out by regular trade
and textbook houses and sold in bookstores, especially college stores.
Many were literary classics or intellectual books of rather wide appeal,
or in other words, our kind of book in our market. The quick success
of Anchor Books and one or two other lines sent commercial editors
to the larger university presses—not to us—with checkbooks in
hand. Thus Anchor's early best-seller, *The Lonely Crowd,* came off the
Yale list.

So what were university presses to do, sell rights to their more
marketable titles or leap into a new kind of publishing? Selling rights
was the choice of some large presses with rich backlists, such as Yale
and Harvard. It was profitable, required almost no work, and avoided
the possible charge of commercialism. Yale continued the practice
until Chester Kerr became director in 1959 and Harvard even longer.
It was a couple of smaller presses that first ventured into the paperback business itself. First of all, as I remember, was Cornell, perhaps
because the director, Victor Reynolds, was an old Macmillan man.
Quickly thereafter came California, for reasons I have mentioned.

I can still see a group of us sitting in the old Press library on
Oxford Street, discussing whether to take the gamble and then choosing the first five titles from our meager list. One was a recent book on
scientific philosophy, one the collected papers of the anthropologist
Edward Sapir, one a Sather lecture, and two were translations, one of
these an original. It appears that we spread the subjects, wishing to
find out which areas might be suitable. Or, more likely, we chose
what we had. This first list came out in the fall of 1956, occupying
three pages in a seasonal catalogue of twelve pages plus cover.

The sale was uneven but generally good. Since all five titles were in print more than thirty years later, we must have chosen reasonably well, but there was nothing left for the following spring, so far as we could see. The second list came a year after the first, in the fall of 1957—six books of which three were originals, not because we were eager to experiment with original paperbacks—considered risky at the time—but because we had too few older titles. Five of the six were in print in 1990.

The long-term success of the two lists came not from superior wisdom in choosing, I think, but because we did not yet know the potential of the paperback market and made choices that might now seem obvious. After that, the backlist was growing, and we never missed another season. The spring list of 1958 included Mary Barnard's much admired new translation of Sappho. We had learned that the way, indeed the only way, to sell literary translations in quantity was in paperback at low prices.

The Press now brings out about one hundred new paperbacks each year, compared to five in that first year. New hardbound books are nearly twice the number of paperbacks. When I look at the twelve-page seasonal list of fall 1956 and put it beside that of fall 1991, seventy-two pages in larger format, describing better books, on the average, than we had thirty-five years ago, I find it hard to fit my mind around the extent of the change. It was in this direction that we pointed the Press in the early 1950s, but we could not have imagined what it would look like today.

7 Where to Look for Books
Athens in Berkeley

I n the early years of this century Jane K. Sather was left a considerable sum of money by her husband, a banker.[1] Living in Berkeley at a time when bankers were still honored there, she was generous to the local university, donating a granite bell tower, a bronze campus gate, and other things less monumental. Among these, and at President Wheeler's suggestion, were two academic chairs, one in history and the other a visiting professorship in classical literature, broadly conceived.

The first holders of that chair were invited to teach and not to write books. The very first of all—to digress for a moment—was John Linton Myers of New College, Oxford, who arrived in 1914, just ahead of the First World War. Leaving Berkeley, he went immediately into the Royal Navy and was given command of a small gunboat. The Sather professor of just fifty years later, Sterling Dow of Harvard, in a little book about those who came before him, tells this story about Myers. A huge and unexpected British battleship steamed into waters—near Greece, of course—where Myers had orders to let no ships pass. Interpreting orders to the letter, Myers ran up flags that spelled out "Stop or I'll open fire." The battleship, steaming on, replied, also in flags, "Does your mother know you're out?"[2] Myers was subse-

---

1. This chapter is based, in part, on an account of the Sather Lectures in the *California Monthly,* December 1979.
2. *Fifty Years of Sathers* (Berkeley, 1965).

quently knighted—for another action, I think—and came to Berkeley a second time in 1927, after the professorship had been transformed, and produced a celebrated book entitled *Who Were the Greeks?*, the sixth volume in the series of Sather Classical Lectures.

When we began in earnest to look for books, the best intellectual beginning we had, thanks to the Sather series, was in classical history and literature. By 1950 there were twenty-two volumes, and in the following year three more came into print, including two of considerable importance: *The Development of Attic Black-Figure*, by Sir John Beazley of Oxford, and *The Greeks and the Irrational*, by E. R. Dodds of the same university. Here we had something to build on if we knew how.

At first glance one might think the Sathers came about because the president of the University when the Press began was a professor of Greek, Martin Kellogg, and his successor, whom I call inventor of the old Press, was Benjamin Ide Wheeler, professor of classical philology. But neither had anything to do with them. Theirs was a press of serial monographs. Wheeler, as we have seen, thought books too commercial for a university; he established the Sather lectureship but there were no books until after he retired.

The transition began in 1920, one year after Wheeler, when the power of appointment passed from the president's office to the departments of Greek and Latin. Two professors of Greek, Ivan Linforth and George Calhoun, suggested that the professorship might be given formal distinction if each visitor were asked to deliver a number of public lectures that could be made into a book. Calhoun, it seems, must even then have had the scheming instincts of a publisher although he did not become manager of the Press until several years later. He asked that the lectures be prepared in form suitable for publication and expressed hope that the first volume might be devoted to Homer.

So began a great book series, by now perhaps the best in the classical field, a happy future that could be hoped for at the beginning but not predicted. Few book series rise out of mediocrity. A great series, like a great anything else, cannot be had quickly, nor can it be

THE DEVELOPMENT of
ATTIC BLACK-FIGURE

By J. D. BEAZLEY

UNIVERSITY OF CALIFORNIA PRESS
BERKELEY AND LOS ANGELES 1951
CAMBRIDGE UNIVERSITY PRESS LONDON

Ward Richie's title page for Beazley's *Development of Attic Black-Figure* (1951).

bought with high fees, if one has them, or with the promise of California sunshine, a promise not always fulfilled. The results can be controlled, in part at least, one hopes, by choosing the lecturers carefully, by appointing them a few years in advance, allowing adequate time to prepare a manuscript. More important, at a later time, is the quality of the already published books; if truly good, these can be a challenge to those who lecture and write after them. And another challenge, at least in later years, was the number of distinguished scholars in the audience, those in the classics department as well as classicists in other departments, such as history, comparative literature, philosophy, art history.

Perhaps even more important is the small matter of luck, particularly with the first few books. Without early distinction not much can be expected later on. Calhoun, if he was the prime chooser, must have been both shrewd and lucky. The very first book, *The Unity of Homer* (1921) by John Adams Scott, not only began at the beginning with the *Iliad* and the *Odyssey* but turned out to be enormously and widely influential. Epoch-making, Sterling Dow called it. It made the case for a single author of the two epics at a time when many considered them a patchwork by different authors writing at different times. Scott summoned up a vast array of evidence and won the day—at least for his own day. The series began not with a monograph but with a bang.

After this epic beginning there were volumes on other topics, Greek and Roman, history and literature, some of them highly regarded. But every few years the lecturers came back to the first fascination, the first arena, where the Homeric question continued to excite study and fan controversy. Fitting enough, we may agree, since the two epics were the centerpiece of education in the ancient Mediterranean world—a world that made us what we are, for better or worse, and in spite of attempts to claim otherwise.

One might think that 2,600 years or thereabouts—the time passed since the Homeric poems were written down—would suffice for scholars to reach some sort of agreement on their character and meaning. But no. Questions about them have continued to be hotly debated. Among new theories was that of Milman Parry—who happened to be a student in Berkeley at the time Scott lectured—that the two epics were composed orally and transmitted by memory and voice from one generation to another, with what changes we cannot be sure. A related development was the vast increase of knowledge of folklore and myth, ancient and modern. But the most striking change of all came about a hundred years ago when the old Sacramento banker Heinrich Schliemann dug up Troy, Tiryns, and Mycenae.[3]

Before Schliemann and his more scientific successors little was known about the actuality of Bronze Age Greece. After them there was the picture, incomplete but dazzling, of a brilliant Mycenaean civilization on the mainland and a more or less contemporary Minoan culture on Crete. Both were destroyed, the Mycenaean about 1200 or 1100 B.C., and Greece then slid down into what is called the Dark Age—whether the darkness properly describes the time itself or only our lack of knowledge about it. In any event the archaeological remains become fewer and lower in quality; the syllabic writing attested by the tablets from Pylos and elsewhere disappears; writing of any kind seems to be unknown for three or four hundred years until the appearance of a Greek alphabet, derived in part from the Phoenician. In the intervening years the Mediterranean world had changed out of recognition. (All this is over-simplified, of course.)

The Homeric poems purport to describe Mycenaean events but were not written down until much later, when the alphabet was available, and in a kind of Ionian Greek.[4] So where did they come from, and what are they? What society do they portray? How do they relate, or do they relate, to the Mycenaean world revealed by excavation? Who was (or were) Homer?

The Sather professor in 1930 was Martin Persson Nilssen of the University of Lund in Sweden. His book, *The Mycenaean Origins of Greek Mythology,* marshaled evidence to prove that the body of Greek myths that we know from historical times goes back in reality to the much earlier Bronze Age. Among other evidence, it is the cities and places of that age, authenticated as such by archaeological digs, that play a central role in the myths. So the memory of Mycenaean times,

3. Although Schliemann's stay in California was brief, it was during the great gold rush. He demonstrated his ability to make money and became an American citizen.
4. A mixture of Ionic and Aeolic, according to Bernard Knox in an attractive discussion of the Homeric question, part of his introduction to Robert Fagles' translation of the *Iliad* (New York, 1990).

transformed and re-imagined into the cyclic stories used by drama-
tists and others, carried over the Dark Age and into the later and
familiar classical Greece. Nilsson's book made possible a whole new
way of looking at Greek literature and religion. It has been reprinted
many times in paperback, most recently with an introduction by
Emily Vermeule, whose own book is described below.

In 1945 came Rhys Carpenter of Bryn Mawr, whose *Folk Tale,
Fiction, and Saga in the Homeric Epics* makes much of folk and mythic
material but finds little that is Mycenaean in the two poems. He pre-
fers northern and European elements; and he believes that the epics
were composed rather late, not long before they could have been
written down, and that there were two authors, one fifty years earlier
than the other. The *Iliad*, he says, was composed from traditional
material or saga; the *Odyssey* from folkloric elements.

Those who prefer history to myth were more attracted to Denys
Page's *History and the Homeric Iliad,* delivered as lectures in 1957 and
published in 1959. For Page, the Trojan War really happened, although not as described in the epic; it was a sort of war of succession
after the collapse of the Hittite empire in Asia Minor. Textual and
archaeological evidence, including the tablets from Pylos, are examined to make a compelling case for an *Iliad* that is much older than
Carpenter will allow. Although the form that comes to us is largely
Ionian, "after hundreds of years have elapsed, the *Iliad* still displays
the story of Troy in its Mycenaean setting." Page's book is two books
in one. The text moves along, swiftly, with a high degree of intellectual excitement. The notes are for the specialized reader, whose Greek
had better be good and who might profitably know a little Hittite.

An equally exciting and more visual Sather came out in 1979:
Aspects of Death in Early Greek Art and Poetry by Emily Vermeule, a
classicist and archaeologist at Harvard, whose chief specialty is again
the Bronze Age. Vermeule explores, in hundreds of incidents and
illustrations, the poetry and especially the iconography of death: re-
liefs, vase paintings, rings and gem designs, decorated cups and bowls;
sea monsters, sirens, Harpies, phallos-birds and ba-birds, winged and
other daimons. In a witty and lighthearted manner that belies or per-

Achilles and Penthesileia. From an archaic bronze shield strap from Olympia.

haps saves the subject matter, she considers burial practices; the nature of the soul (like a bird that flies from the body at death); ways of existence in the kingdom of Hades; the relation between mortality and immortality, and how to go from one to the other; the number of people killed in the *Iliad* (243); "the interpenetration of war and love, like the two sides of a drinking cup." Achilles, slaying the warrior-woman Penthesileia, "felt a shock of love for the Amazon queen just as he plunged his spear between her breast and throat." Or, quoting Quintus Smyrnaeus, he "could not control the grief in his heart, because he had killed her, and had not taken her as his glorious wife."

But I go on too long about one aspect of the series, and with Vermeule have brought the story up beyond the building period that is my subject. The books have never been all Homer. One of the 1951 volumes mentioned above, Beazley's book on black-figured vases, became a standard, if specialized, work for students. Years later I worked with Dietrich von Bothmer of the Metropolitan Museum to bring out a second edition with unchanged text but new notes and illustrations, published in 1986.

The other 1951 book, *The Greeks and the Irrational,* by the Irish scholar E. R. Dodds, may be the most celebrated of all the Sathers; it later became a mainstay of our paperback list and is still in print. If others opened a new vision on the Homeric world, Dodds suggested a fresh way of viewing the entire Greek experience. The common view, promoted by sentimental Hellenists, saw the Greeks as an eminently rational and well-ordered people, always in control of themselves. One wonders how this could be, given the violence of Greek history and the fury and madness that run through the literature (such as in the *Bacchae* of Euripides), but the thought persisted of a culture as serene and balanced as classical statuary. Employing the techniques of anthropology and psychology, Dodds assembled evidence for the other, the nonrational, element in Greek thought and behavior. Even the great Age of Enlightenment was also an Age of Persecution, and in any event did not last long. "An intelligent observer in or about the year 200 B.C. might well have predicted that within a few generations . . . the perfect Age of Reason would follow." It did not, of course, as it later failed to follow the hopes of the *philosophes* of the eighteenth century and the rationalists of the nineteenth. Reason, it seems, is a precursor of astrology, romanticism, revolution, and their ilk. In our own age of unreason, we can feel all too much at home with Dodds' view of the ancient world.

But fine as these books were, in the early 1950s there were only two or three that were both current and notable. Too few to make a list, they gave us a possible springboard. If we pleased a lecturer, we could ask about other books on the drawing board and could get introductions to friends and colleagues. If the lecturer were British, as so many were, we could get in touch with his London publisher and offer to take American editions of later books or of other books in the field. As the publisher of Dodds and Beazley, we were not just any hungry American press; we had some standing; new books would join a respectable company. Thus, after publishing K. J. Dover's Sather lectures on Lysius, we later obtained his books on Aristophanic comedy and on Greek popular morality.

There were pitfalls, of course. Most British firms were pleased to sell American editions; many of their more scholarly books could not easily be financed without a joint publisher. But there were others that demanded a return in kind, and we had little to offer. A couple of firms refused to deal with us unless we would sell them British rights to the entire Sather series, and that we preferred not to do, fearing that the series might become only half ours. One London firm— Methuen, I think it was—kept us on a sort of blacklist until the then managing director retired. Later we did considerable business.

One afternoon in Bloomsbury an editor handed me an untidy typescript, and the next day I read away hours over the Atlantic. The pages were amended and added to and written over, almost like a Proustian proof, but around and underneath the markings the reader could detect one subtle mind at work on another. This was the manuscript of Peter Brown's *Augustine of Hippo,* which we published in 1967 together with Faber & Faber. An intellectual and spiritual biography, it became a sort of classic and a long-time steady seller in paperback. It also gives a vivid picture of Roman Africa, which Brown has called the intellectual powerhouse of the later Western empire. Carthage was then the second city in the West. It is chastening to be reminded that North Africa at that time had been Romanized, civilized, for more centuries than our own country has yet survived, and that in Augustine's youth, in the mid fourth century, it was perhaps more prosperous, better ordered, than it has ever been in the 1,600 years since then. Good social history can help us see ourselves small.

Late antiquity, from about 200 to 700 A.D., has also been one of the dark ages, in the sense that we have known little about it. Scholars, concentrating on classical Greece and on the Roman republic and empire in the days of intrigue and glory, have paid these later centuries little attention. "It was a great civilization in itself," says Brown, who is one of those who have in recent years given special attention to this period. It was there all along, of course, but hidden behind the idea of Decline and Fall. The great Gibbon, dazzled by the Antonines, was not always sympathetic to what came after them. "I have described," he wrote, "the triumph of barbarism and Christianity." But Brown and others have pointed out that there was no decline and no fall; the political superstructure may have collapsed, but the texture of town and country life remained much as it was, with northern barbarians happy to be absorbed into Roman culture. The transformation was gradual as long as the Mediterranean world remained intact. "We live round a sea," said Socrates, "like frogs round a pond." Some think there was always a kind of unity until it was broken by the Muslim conquest.

Throughout these centuries there was both continuity and change. The living classical tradition, wrote Brown, "never stood still; it adapted to the rise of Christianity, the end of paganism, the formation of Rabbinic Judaism, the Arab invasions, and to many silent secular changes." The close study of this complex Mediterranean world has become in recent decades a major field of scholarly endeavor. Brown himself, a fellow of All Souls College, Oxford, when we first met him, later came to this country and joined the Berkeley faculty for a number of years. In 1979 he proposed to the Press the publication of a series of books to be called The Transformation of the Classical Heritage, with himself as general editor. There are nearly twenty books by now. So one thing leads to another in list building. A single book, imported almost by accident, may multiply itself years later and in ways not expected.

The line of causation is not always so clear. On another day in London, and without thinking of consequences, I took from a small English firm a book of essays entitled *The Shadow of the Parthenon*. The author, although English, was teaching at the University of Texas, and in Austin one day I invited him to the Driskill Hotel for a drink. Finding it easy to talk, we kept in touch. Years later, after retirement, I read the manuscript of Peter Green's *Alexander to Actium,* a large history of the Hellenistic age, and brought it to the Press. Meanwhile, during the long editorial gestation of this book, a number of Berkeley scholars had proposed another new book series to the

Press, this one to be entitled Hellenistic Culture and Society. In part, I think, the idea for the series grew out of a large book sponsored just before retirement, *The Hellenistic World and the Coming of Rome,* by the great scholar Erich Gruen. The Roman conquest of the Greek world, so often looked on as a phase of Roman imperialist ambition, is here viewed by Gruen from the other direction, seen in its Hellenistic context, with Greeks and Romans interacting and with the former sometimes manipulating the latter. The book is important, said F. W. Walbank of Cambridge, not only in relation to Roman expansion but for thinking about "any aspect of imperialism in other periods and contexts."

Peter Green's book became the first volume in the new series,[5] reminding me of my own dictum that a successful series should start with a bang—a big book and not a monograph. Again, we are talking about books in a field that is not new but has been neglected and is beginning to receive fresh attention. The Hellenistic age, the three hundred years or so between the death of Alexander and the Roman empire, has often been looked down on as an inferior time of quarrelsome monarchs and literature of little consequence. However that may be, it was a time of important change, when the eastern Mediterranean world became Greek in culture, at least on the upper social levels, and remained Greek through the Roman centuries and early Christian times. Having been neglected by all but a few, it is now a fertile area for study.

If I seem to dwell too long on trans-Atlantic maneuvers, this is perhaps because they appear more dramatic than home ventures. But the actuality was never so over-balanced; Erich Gruen was only one of many local authors. Jock Anderson of classics, erudite in more areas than I can mention, wrote on Xenophon, on military practices, on hunting in the ancient world. An editor tells that she once took some proofs to Anderson's office. His table was buried under a deep layer of books on many topics, journals, reprints, lecture notes, parts

---

5. The four general editors are Gruen of the history department, Anthony W. Bullock and A. A. Long of classics, and Andrew F. Stewart of art history.

of manuscripts; there was no place to spread out the proofs. For a moment Jock looked bewildered, as he sometimes could, but only for a moment, and then the problem was solved. A long arm swept the assorted wisdom onto the floor.

The wide-ranging Tom Rosenmeyer of comparative literature, subtle critic of many literatures, ancient and modern, at home in philosophy and drama, wrote about Theocritus and the European pastoral lyric,[6] then moved on to produce the elegant *Art of Aeschylus* and *Senecan Drama and Stoic Cosmology*. Meanwhile he found time to invent and act as general editor of a book series called Eidos: Studies in Classical Kinds. The first volume of this was a graceful account of the ancient lyric, by W. R. Johnson, who had meanwhile moved from Berkeley to Cornell to Chicago.

In 1964 W. K. Pritchett of Berkeley brought out the first part of his *Studies in Ancient Greek Topography* in the monographic series in Classical Studies. He continued—and continues—these studies, with six parts or volumes now in print. And there are five volumes of a parallel work, *The Greek State at War,* this one published in book form. Kendrick Pritchett's style is not the continuous narrative; he chooses topics or aspects of his large subject and treats each one discretely and exhaustively. Peter Green called him "the most formidable topographical bloodhound on a specific trail." And in a letter to me the late historian Sir Moses Finley of Cambridge, one of our Sather lecturers,[7] wrote that *The Greek State at War* had "moved to the status of a monument."

WKP is famous among scholars for dealing with the terrain itself as well as with artifacts and written records, scorning those who do topographical studies from a corner by the fire. At age eighty he was still climbing Greek mountains, walking ancient roads, and identifying forgotten sites, examining battlefields. He is also a great defender of the ancient historians against modern detractors. Woe to those

6. *The Green Cabinet* (1969; paperback 1973).
7. Author of *The Ancient Economy* (1973; second edition, 1985).

who impugn the veracity of Herodotos without completing their own homework; they will be demolished when the next volume comes out. Perhaps politely, perhaps not, but demolished. Quite recently a reviewer in the *TLS* called one of Pritchett's books "a disorganized, bad-tempered masterpiece . . . but a masterpiece for all that."

Pritchett, when he was chairman of classics, conceived the idea of an annual volume of shorter studies in Greek and Latin literature, history, philosophy, art, and other areas, nearly all by scholars from the several California campuses. I was able to get the Editorial Committee's approval, and the volumes, entitled *California Studies in Classical Antiquity,* appeared for about a dozen years. Bound in cloth and sold as books, they were a sort of cross between book and monograph series. Although there were enough classical writers on all our campuses and in several departments to provide articles, and although the rules of admission were not rigid, the publication could never quite avoid the look of a house organ, and the Editorial Committee eventually decreed that it be replaced by a true journal, open to all comers. In 1982 it became *Classical Antiquity,* with a board of five editors, and is still published under that name.

This may be a fitting place to say something about the role of the editor or publisher in building a book list. Most publishers, I think, are not true scholars, who like nothing better than burrowing in the depths of library or archives. Some like me, are not temperamentally suited to long, patient research but are fond of what can come out of it. Looked on charitably, the publisher may be an amateur of scholarship, amateur in the sense of lover. Less charitably, he or she may be called a sort of camp follower but not, we may hope, in the sense intended by the schoolboy who so translated *hors de combat.*

Publishers and authors are dependent on each other, forever thrown together. More compatible than printers and publishers, I think, but still not always happy with each other. The relation has been called one of *odi et amo,* with the *amo* not always apparent. A letter once came to the German publishing house Suhrkamp Verlag, proclaiming that one of the signs of Napoleon's greatness is that he once had a publisher shot. This from a sociologist.[8] A better-known detractor, about whom we have published a few books, Ezra Pound, once wrote of publishers and their readers: "These vermin crawl over and beslime our literature . . . and nothing but the day of judgement can, I suppose, exterminate them."[9] It is sometimes easy to smile at Pound's strong statements, but in this instance a reader for the publisher Duckworth, Edward Garnett, had recommended that James Joyce's *Portrait of the Artist* be "pulled into shape" and made less "sordid."

The publisher is usually a generalist, interested in many things, shoes and ships and sealing wax, Archilochos and the Zapotecs, excited not only by the results of the best study and research but often by the tools and methods used, the kind of thinking brought to bear. In a field chosen for cultivation the publisher may wish to learn something about what is known to scholars, what is obscure, what is controversial—learn enough to ask good questions, not always an easy matter, as demonstrated by television interviewers. Indeed, the publisher must know enough to pass judgment, after advice from knowledgeable people—who often disagree—on the importance and quality of manuscripts. But one must recognize one's limits, never challenge the scholars' expertise in their own fields—even on occasions when they may seem wrong-headed. The warning applies to both kinds of editing. The copyeditor who once majored in the field of the manuscript in hand will sometimes tend to do too much. On an occasion I know of a too-knowledgeable free-lancer who held up a manuscript for three years.

I came to the classical field accidentally and late, after working with literary translations, Latin American books, art books. Wishing to plug a hole in my education, I sat in on classes in ancient Greek taught by the same Kendrick Pritchett mentioned above and then by

8. Siegfried Unseld, *The Author and His Publisher* (Chicago, 1980), 1.
9. Quoted in Humphrey Carpenter, *A Serious Character: The Life of Ezra Pound* (Boston, 1988), 294–95.

Ronald Stroud, and so came to an interest in current classical studies. Or perhaps it was the other way around: the seeking of classical books impelled me to learn some Greek. Years have passed, and memory is not always precise. At about the same time my wife and I spent some weeks in Greece with our neighbor D. A. Amyx, professor of art history, and family. All this, together with sporadic reading, gave me some small knowledge of the field and a feeling for what was going on within it. By then I was old hand enough to avoid the error of some junior editor—claiming to know too much. But I knew what to look for and how to go after it, including the use of patience. It took fifteen or twenty years of pushing—not without irritation—to badger Dick Amyx into finishing his great *Corinthian Vase Painting of the Archaic Period* (3 volumes, 1988).

Prodding authors does not always work. At intervals over many years in London and Chicago and elsewhere, and by correspondence, I tried to get the noted historian Arnaldo Momigliano to turn loose of his Sather lectures, written but not, he said, in final form. He gave me early on and for safekeeping a copy of the first version. Years later over tea in Knightsbridge he pulled out of his briefcase the revised manuscript and let me look but not get firm hold on it. Back into the briefcase it went—for a little more checking, said he. More years passed; he died; the manuscript was found among his papers and was published in 1990, thirty years after the lectures were spoken in Berkeley.[10]

On another less than happy occasion the next Sather lecturer wrote to the classics department that he wished to speak on a topic used on another occasion—thus to make double use of lectures and writing. This would never do, of course, but no one in the department wished to tell him so and incur his wrath. So the publisher was elected fall guy, requested to bell the cat, to pass the black spot. Publishers, at such times, are expendable. And if Paris was worth a mass to Henri IV, good will at home in Berkeley was worth an enemy abroad. Like other bearers of bad news, I was executed—socially,

10. *The Classical Foundations of Modern Historiography.*

December 3, 1976

The director at his last Editorial Committee meeting. Drawing by Uli Knoepflmacher, a member of the Committee.

snubbed in Berkeley, ignored at one dinner party while the great man talked to my wife but not to me. He has never turned in a manuscript.

On a more happy note, the telephone rang early one morning in my London hotel, and I was dispatched by Bill Anderson, chairman of classics, to Cambridge to deal with another designated lecturer, who had threatened to walk out at the eleventh hour. The problem was settled—by our giving in, of course—and the lecturer, the same Moses Finley mentioned earlier, became friendly enough to read many manuscripts for me in the years that followed.

After I concentrated some attention on the field, and especially when trips to London became regular, the list grew rapidly. And it happened by the accident of appointment that for a time in the sixties and seventies there was no classicist on the Editorial Committee. So

I slipped into making the formal presentation of manuscripts in ancient history and literature. Like all other manuscripts, of course, these came with reports from outside referees, but still it was usual practice that each work be examined and presented by an academic member. That the Committee was content to have me do this is a tribute, I think, to the mutual confidence built up in two or three hundred all-day meetings since Press and Committee joined forces in 1949. Everyone seemed happy enough, but shortly after my retirement the Committee requested that a classicist be added to their number. I wondered: did they miss me, or did they fear that I might have misled them? Since then a number of classicists have served. One of them, Ronald Stroud, told his colleagues that we then had the best classical list in this country. I would never have said so much, but it was good to have someone else make the claim.

8 Looking to the South
Many Americas

I t is strange, some think, that peoples of the Americas tend to look east and west rather than north and south. About thirty years ago, when we first began to look for books from and about Latin America, this was plainly true; perhaps it still is. Often enough we have criticized ourselves for paying more attention to Europe and Asia than to the twenty or so countries to the south of us. But they too have looked to Europe for cultural ties, all the while complaining about the attitudes of their northern neighbor. Latin American intellectuals were, and still are, I believe, more at home in Paris than in any city north of them.

More at home in Paris, sometimes, than in each other's countries. And not always interested in each other. In Buenos Aires one day the lady manager of a large book store said to me, "We don't care about the Mexican revolution." That the memory of this remark remains with me so many years later shows that I must have been shocked— shocked perhaps into realizing that, in a very real sense, there is no such thing as Latin America. There are a number of countries, not all alike. They don't speak the same language. Nearly half the people speak Portuguese, and the Spanish of the others is similar but not the same. In Santiago de Chile my Mexican friend burst into huge laughter on seeing a newspaper headline that read, "Cohete norteamericano se chingó." What the North American rocket did to itself was splendidly vulgar in one country but not, apparently, in the other. Some countries (Argentina, Chile) are predominantly European in stock. Others (Peru, Bolivia) are largely Indian. Still others (Brazil, Mexico) are mestizo or mixed. But nearly five hundred years have passed since Cortés and the other conquistadores; the pervading culture is European, the sensibility Catholic, in spite of those intellectuals who would like to bring back Coatlicue and the Aztecs.

These are the impressionistic remarks of a nonexpert, a mere publisher, and are not to be taken as Truth, but perhaps they say something about our difficulties in understanding the other Americas, in distributing our books to them, in translating and publishing their literary and intellectual writings. When we ask God to bless America we mean the America north of the Rio Grande. When Mexicans write of *nuestra América,* that America is theirs, not ours, the one called New Spain for three hundred years. Included vaguely are the other Spanish American countries; along with the differences there is some sense of a common colonial origin, not like ours or Brazil's.

The several Latin American ventures, or adventures, of the Association of American University Presses came about almost accidentally; they had only grudging support from some member presses, notably those situated away from the Mexican border. At California the translation program—the larger part of our Latin American list in the sixties—was thrust upon us, willing as we were. In our university at that time there must have been more active scholars in this area—in the history, geography, anthropology, Spanish, and other departments—than in any other university. Without intention on our part, we at the Press found ourselves with the beginning of a Latin American list.

The old monograph series in History included a number of Latin American studies, and then in 1932 was founded the most distinguished of all the series outside the biological and geological sciences, Ibero-Americana. The first editors, led by Carl O. Sauer of geography, defined it as "a collection of studies in Latin American cultures, native and transplanted, pre-European, colonial, and modern . . . in the main, contributions to cultural history." By the end of the 1950s more than forty separate monographs had been issued, all but a few on Mexican topics. At first Sauer himself was the chief author, but the series came to be dominated later by the writings of Woodrow Borah, Sherburne F. Cook, and Lesley Byrd Simpson, of the history, physiology, and Spanish departments. In 1960 a noted French scholar, writing in the *Revue historique,* dubbed these scholars, along with some others, the École de Berkeley, in part, I think, because their methods bore some resemblance to those of the *Annales* school. Much later, in the 1970s, some of the series papers, along with new ones of similar kind, were issued as books, both in cloth and in paper.

Meanwhile, we were publishing the books on Latin American literature of Arturo Torres-Rioseco, a Chilean long resident in Berkeley, and a little later those on Peruvian literature by Luis Monguió, a native of Tarragona on the Berkeley faculty. Quite a number of these were in Spanish and thus not suitable for wide promotion, but when we started the paperback list in the mid 1950s, we included Torres' *Epic of Latin American Literature* as well as several of Lesley Simpson's literary translations. The *Poem of the Cid* and the *Celestina* were Spanish, of course, but there was also *Two Novels of Mexico* by Mariano Azuela, better known perhaps for *Los de Abajo,* translated as *The Underdogs* and published elsewhere.

A number of scholarly books, perhaps a dozen of them, happened along in the forties and fifties, notably Sanford Mosk's *Industrial Revolution in Mexico* (1950). Our first real success in this area was Simpson's *Many Mexicos,* whose title I have paralleled in the subtitle of this chapter. A lively and irreverent interpretation of Mexican history and culture, the book was first published by Putnam in 1941 and reissued by us in a third edition in 1952. Not often is it wise to take over books abandoned by commercial firms, but this time we were fortunate. Or, as Harlan Kessel would say, we did a better job of selling a good book. And it was Kessel, after he came to the Press, who did the most for it. In 1966 he planned and promoted a silver anniversary edition, with revisions, that had considerable success. Since the book still sells, the anniversary might now be golden.

So we had the beginnings of a list, but neither I nor anyone else thought of it as such. As for me, I had a tourist's interest in Mexico

How we went to San Javier, 1951. Photo by Neal Harlow.

and no thoughts about the continent to the south. In 1951, with Neal Harlow of the UCLA library, I drove an old military jeep the length of Baja California at a time when there was no paved road, only dirt tracks that branched off in various directions and, when we were lucky, came back together again. There were no service stations and only one ratty hotel between Ensenada and La Paz, nearly one thousand miles, but every farm on the way sold gasoline and beer. Gasoline was filtered through felt hats, the beer through us. One could stay in private houses if one knew where to ask. In Ensenada, by good fortune, we met a woman who had sisters in San Ignacio, Loreto, La Paz, and perhaps places I forget; we stayed with all of them, talking as best we could around the kitchen table, dictionary in hand. From Loreto we had to ride mules to reach Padre Ugarte's stone mission of San Javier, perhaps the finest in the two Californias. At Cabo San Lucas, at the end of the peninsula, where now there are at least six

Mission San Javier Viggé.

big hotels, a marina, and a tourist town, there existed then only a fish cannery and one beer joint. We slept on the sand under the very last rocks.

Two or three years after that, the painter Rico Lebrun (to be mentioned later as an author) and his wife Constance were spending the year in San Miguel de Allende, in the Bajío region north of Mexico City, and asked me to visit them. Leaving from New Orleans after a meeting, I was told I could go by way of Mérida or by way of Houston. Not that fond of Texas, I chose Yucatán and spent a couple of days at the great Mayan ruins of Chichén Itzá before going on to Mexico City. Only passenger on a small bus to San Miguel, I sat with the driver, dictionary on my knee.

In Mexico I made the first of our many calls at Fondo de Cultura Económica, perhaps the most intellectual publishing house south of the border, where we had a piece of business, now forgotten. Formed originally to bring out translations of books on economic matters,

Fondo had branched out into many fields and was selling its books all over Latin America. It was, I think, what is known as a *sociedad mixta*, a kind of mixed corporation peculiar to Spanish America, which could make use of both government and private money and could avoid the bureaucratic regulations that make state presses, here as well as there, so difficult to manage.

Such was my small experience of Latin America when things began to happen in the Association of American University Presses. In 1959 the annual meeting of the AAUP was held in Austin, and Frank Wardlaw, director of the press at Texas, talked us into holding a second session in Mexico City as guests of the National University there. A converted South Carolinian, Frank had become more Texan than a Texan, if that can be done, was building up a fine list of regional books, and always conscious of the border near by, was beating the drums for closer relations with Latin America. So about one hundred of us boarded a Mexican train in Laredo, survived a slow-down strike and a shortage of beer, and gathered with our Mexican colleagues the next morning.

Two things I remember about that meeting. One, through a large window looking south we could see the great volcanoes, Popo and Ixta, as their long names can be shortened. And two, since that was my second year as president of the AAUP, I had to respond to the speech of welcome. With some coaching I managed to read out a short talk in Spanish—with only one mistake, I was told by Jack Harrison of the Rockefeller Foundation. My mind retains little else of the meeting itself, but holds the memory of our driving with Harrison through the midnight streets of Mexico in search of band music, and over the hill to Taxco next day.

Berkeley graduate and friend of Ibero-Americana authors Borah, Simpson, and Jim Parsons, Jack Harrison, more than anyone else, brought about the events of this chapter. It was he who proposed me for the trip to South America; he was inventor of the Latin American translation program and sponsor of it through the foundation. With the third Latin American endeavor, the distribution office in Mexico (CILA), he had less to do. All three ventures are now things of

Jack and Barbara Harrison in Taxco, 1959.

the past, but the translation program resulted in many books of lasting value.

An organization optimistically called CHEAR (Council on Higher Education in the American Republics), with Ford Foundation money in hand, wanted to learn something about university and other scholarly publishing in the Latin American countries. So in the summer and fall of 1961 they sent two of us, one Mexican and one North American, on a survey trip around South America. We both traded our first-class tickets for coach tickets and took our wives along. Susan and I, before starting out, did what we could for our Spanish by attending Berlitz classes in San Francisco. With her superior ear she progressed faster than I with the spoken language. I could always read well enough.

My colleague was Carlos Bosch García, who taught history at UNAM (Universidad Nacional Autónoma de México) and was also distribution manager of the Editorial Universitaria, the press there. Like many intellectuals in Mexico, where university salaries were low, he needed two jobs, morning and afternoon, to support himself. Some of our friends took on evening jobs as well. Carlos' wife, Elisa Vargas Lugo, having written a monograph on the church of Santa Prisca at Taxco, was soon to become professor of art history. While she was Mexican-born, Carlos was a Catalonian from Barcelona, son of the rector of the university there, who at the end of the civil war had fled from Franco and eventually settled in Mexico. Carlos, by good fortune and good education, had some facility in five languages, four of which I heard him use in our interviews. The fifth, of course, was Catalán, which Carlos claimed as his first language. In Barcelona, said he, we learn Spanish at Berlitz.

Languages can be tricky, especially when they have many words in common. We all know about the *faux amis,* French words that look like English ones but differ in meaning. Carlos tells of a time when, as a very young man unsure of himself, he went to a dance across the French border. Dancing with a French woman, he stumbled and stepped on her feet, causing some pain. At this point one must remind the listener that the Spanish word meaning to tread on or step on is *pisar,* while the French word happens to be rather different, *piétiner.* Confused and contrite, Carlos could only accuse himself. "Ah, Madame," said he, "je vous ai pissé sur les pieds." Whether this truly happened to him or whether it is a standard Barcelona story, I do not know.

We began in Mexico with an automobile trip to the Universidad Veracruzana in Jalapa, five thousand feet up and foggy, the old colonial town that was once the first goal of incoming Spaniards, anxious to escape the malarial coast of Vera Cruz. To my surprise we found a young and enterprising university press, one of the most attractive in Latin America, publishers of original literature and of works about the archaeological findings of the region, including the *caras sonrientes,* the smiling faces, quite unlike anything Aztec or Toltec. After that little side trip, Susan and I went alone to Guatemala and Costa Rica, and then the four of us set off for Brazil and around the southern continent, traveling sometimes together and sometimes separately.

In Brazil we were accompanied by Helen Caldwell, who taught

Helen Caldwell in Brazil, 1961. With Susan Frugé.

Latin at UCLA but whose chief research interest was the novels of J. M. Machado de Assis, thought by many to be the finest fiction writer of all Latin America and the only one before Jorge Luis Borges to bear comparison with the best European writers. Along with Bill Grossman of New York University, Helen had been responsible for making Assis known in this country. *Epitaph of a Small Winner,* Grossman's version of *Memórias posthumas de Braz Cubas,* appeared in 1952 and Helen's translation of *Dom Casmurro* the following year, both published by Noonday Press. In 1960, shortly before this trip, California brought out Helen's book about *Dom Casmurro,* and in the years thereafter a biographical study of the writer and several more translated novels, as well as a volume of stories that she did together with Grossman.

Basilica of Bon Fim.

I get ahead of myself once more but would like to record that Helen Caldwell, who had never before been to Rio de Janeiro but knew the streets from her studies, led Susan and me through the old districts where Machado de Assis had lived and worked in the century before. And in Salvador da Bahia, the old northeastern capital city, the three of us got caught up in a popular religious procession, hundreds of people who had walked and sung from the basilica of Bon Fim in the outskirts, five miles away. They filled the narrow street from wall to wall and swept us along, with Helen singing "Ave María" at the top of her voice and muttering under her breath, "And I come from five generations of atheists."

In Brazil, I had thought, all educated people would speak Spanish as well as Portuguese. But none of them did, we found, not a one that we met. They would understand Spanish, more or less, reply in Portuguese, and as the conversation proceeded each speaker would adapt a few words, pronounce a little in the direction of the other until they were conversing in a tongue never known to man. Unknown to me, at least, but Carlos had a name for it, *españolete,* I think. It was a wonder to hear but too much for my fragile Spanish, which fell to the ground and shattered, never put together again until we reached the next country. Some in the offices where we went spoke

English, but at a university gathering in São Paulo one man insisted on German and another would speak only French. Carlos handled it all, and to me anything was better than the spontaneous hybrid. Brazil, we thought, was the most attractive of all the South American countries, but it was only later, when the Press was doing translations, that I came to appreciate the quality of written Portuguese.

Thereafter the language problem was less acute, or we became more adept at guessing or at making use of our Mexican friends. In Argentina we sometimes thought from a distance that people were speaking Italian, only to find closer up that it was Spanish with an unfamiliar intonation and some unexpected consonant sounds. Had there still been horses in the streets, we thought, one would have ridden a *cabazho en la cazhe,* with the double *l,* here transcribed as *zh,* pronounced like the *z* in azure or the *g* in my own surname. This, I was later told by my friend Luis Monguió, is an old Spanish pronunciation, abandoned in Spain and preserved in some parts of the new world. I have heard the name of the city of Medellín in Colombia pronounced in this way.

We visited universities at Rio, Bahia, Belo Horizonte, and São Paulo, in Brazil; at Buenos Aires and Córdoba in Argentina; and at Santiago de Chile, Lima, and Bogotá, and found them different from each other and quite different from our own. My information is out of date, perhaps, but in this memoir I must tell it as it was.

North American universities are descended through Oxford and Cambridge from the University of Paris, which in the interpretation of Luis Alberto Sánchez, then rector of the University of San Marcos in Lima, was a university of *maestros,* while those of Spanish America were formed in the image of Salamanca, deriving from Bologna, a university of *estudiantes.*[1] Hence the Spanish American tradition of student participation in university government, broken in the nineteenth century but renewed in the twentieth after a reform movement that began in Córdoba in 1918.

1. "The University in Latin America: Part 1, The Colonial Period," *Americas,* November 1961, pp. 21–23.

In Brazil no universities existed in the colonial period; advanced students went to Europe. The first universities were founded in the twentieth century by combining the several schools and institutes that existed in each city. In Spanish America, too, universities tended to be loose federations of faculties or schools; power was more decentralized than with us, and the chief officer, the rector, had relatively little control over the several parts of his institution. Schools of law and medicine were often quite powerful, and sometimes the *facultad de filosofía* (humanities) thought of itself as the true university. There were a few exceptions of course, but usually the rector was elected by students and faculty for a term of four, five, or six years, and some professors were also elected. The political climate, then, was quite different from ours, more chaotic and subject to frequent change. Later in the sixties, listening to the agitation for student power in Berkeley, I recalled the South American universities and thought that reforms could move backwards as well as forwards.

It was also true that research, both organized and individual, was far less central to Latin American universities than to ours. They never experienced the remodeling on European lines that took place in this country in the second half of the nineteenth century, and, for better or worse, missed the great flowering of scholarly writing and publishing that took place here. Historical and literary writing has flourished, and at that time there began to appear works in economics and other social sciences, but these were not many.

In all South America we found only one university press—in the University of Chile—that operated on lines familiar to us. Most worked in the old print-and-exchange system, printing occasional books from the several faculties, some of them collected articles or speeches. One press, EUDEBA at the University of Buenos Aires, had gone to the opposite extreme. Operating as a *sociedad mixta,* it brought out small popular books, selling them from kiosks on street corners. Whether they have survived the political upheavals since then, I do not know. In Mexico I have already mentioned the Universidad Veracruzana. The University of Mexico itself had a large press, with an organization partway between the old and the new styles; they had their own printing plant and were publishing about one hundred books a year and distributing them with some success, partly by barter with other universities, a practice strange to us but evidently workable for them.

A number of university officers, we found, anticipated that a foundation might help them buy new printing equipment, but we judged, rightly I think, that the greatest need in Latin American university publishing was for better distribution, particularly from one country to another but also within the countries of origin, and we recommended that, if CHEAR and the foundations wished to do something to improve matters, they might concentrate on that aspect and perhaps set up a number of distribution centers in major capitals. A committee of the AAUP, after spending some time in Mexico, made a similar recommendation.

I have sometimes wondered whether those who are asked to study problems do not feel a compulsion, internal or external, to recommend large cures. It might often be sensible to write in a final report: Yes, the problem is serious; something should be done about it, we suppose, but a move for change is apt to encounter difficulties one cannot foresee; large measures may bring small results, and perhaps it will be best not to attempt too much.

A notable example occurred in the 1970s, when there was a widespread belief that the whole system of scholarly communication in this country—writing, book publishing, journals, research libraries—was in trouble, trouble too various to be spelled out here. A group of scholars, publishers, and librarians spent three years on the problems and came up with a number of individual studies, the most useful being perhaps one by Datus Smith on the foreign distribution of university books. But no large solution was in sight, it seemed, and perhaps should not have been looked for. At the eleventh hour, with three years of work to justify, the board of governors voted to recommend a great new central library system, parallel to the Library of Congress; this, it was hoped, might make (expensive) sense of the entire system of scholarly communication. Fortunately, the plan was never implemented. It is mentioned here merely to illustrate the mental set that leads investigators to propose whole new structures when it might be more feasible to whittle away at the edge of the old ones.[2]

It is possible that in the 1960s we fell into a trap not so different from that one. Diagnosing the problem correctly, we felt that an interested foundation might do something useful. The difficulties were clear enough; how intransigent they might be was less clear. And for reasons that now escape me the two foundations, Ford and Rockefeller, decided to fund only one distribution center, in one capital, Mexico City, hoping it might do something to improve the movement of scholarly books throughout the hemisphere. Mexico was the obvious choice, close to us and of greater interest than others, but not a choice that was understandable, or useful, to book people in Buenos Aires, for example. The plan may have been too small rather than too large. Or both too small and too large. It succeeded in part, and for a time, and in one direction more than in the other.

This is not the place for an account of the Centro Interamericano de Libros Académicos (CILA), but it was one of our major Latin American endeavors and may be worth a comment or two. The Centro was opened in 1965 in modest quarters in a good location on the Avenida Sulliván, with a handsome display of North American and Mexican books along with a handful from South America. A board of directors was appointed: three from the United States, appointed by the AAUP; three from Mexico, appointed by the rector of the National University; and three from South America, chosen in a way I forget. To the best of my recollection, only one South American ever attended—José Honorio Rodriguez of Rio de Janeiro, author of a book that California translated and published, entitled *Brazil and Africa*.

The Mexicans gave us a distinguished group: Jaime García Terrés, who shortly thereafter became ambassador to Greece, where Susan and I later called on him; Manuel Alcalá, then head of the national library and later ambassador to UNESCO; and Rubén Bonifaz Nuño,

2. See my "Two Cheers for the National Enquiry: A Partial Dissent," *Scholarly Publishing* (Toronto), April 1979, pp. 211–18.

The original CILA group: Chester Kerr, Frank Wardlaw, Carlos Bosch
García, August Frugé, and Rubén Bonifaz Nuño; Mexico, 1963.

head of the press at Mexico and for a long time the second in command at the university. García Terrés and Bonifaz Nuño were also,
and still are, distinguished poets, and the latter has published translations into Spanish of Pindar, Ovid, and other classical authors. He
served as chairman of the CILA board for nearly the entire time.
Understanding English quite well, Rubén would never try to speak
it, and Carlos Bosch sat next to him and translated what he had to
say. And because his appearance seemed to fit the part—black hair,
dark three-piece suit, necktie with stick-pin, huge ring on his finger—we always called Rubén, to his great delight, the Riverboat
Gambler. Retired now, he continues to write books and is one of my
faithful correspondents.

We North Americans could not expect to match such distinction
but tried to balance it, as best we could, with knowledge of scholarly
publishing. Our first group was Frank Wardlaw of Texas, Chester
Kerr of Yale, and I from California. Serving thereafter were Jack

Schulman of Cambridge, Willard Lockwood of Wesleyan, Bill Becker of Princeton, and others. The executive secretaries of the AAUP, from Dana Pratt to Jack Putnam, served as secretary of the group. We met in Mexico two or three times a year and worked quite hard, going over the inventory, checking the accounts, visiting bookstores, calling on the American ambassador, for reasons I forget, and planning with the staff. Carlos Bosch García of Mexico was director, and Jonathan Rose of the United States, assistant director.

It was difficult, of course, to sell expensive hard-bound books, except for a few about Mexico, but some paperback editions, including our *Many Mexicos* by Lesley Simpson, were attractive to tourists and could be sold in quantity to bookstores. CILA did a good job of distributing in Mexico, but national boundaries proved even higher than expected and more encumbered with red tape; books crossed borders less easily than did people, legal or illegal. The staff made a trip or two to South America with results that hardly repaid the cost.

The greatest success came in selling Latin American books to university libraries in the United States. These latter, often unable even to learn what was available, were pleased to place standing orders for everything published in certain categories. South American organizations, not much on buying, were happy enough to sell. CILA bought, had the paper-covered volumes bound at Mexican prices, and resold north at a good profit.

After some retrenchment of the original plan, operating with one executive instead of two and putting the North American directors up at cheaper hotels, CILA managed to operate in the black for a number of years until Mexican inflation and rules of employment became too much to overcome. Whether the dozen or so years of effort had a lasting benefit, it is hard to say. Something was gained at the time.

And we, the North American directors, made many friends and came to feel at home in Mexico City. It was indeed a splendid place before being overwhelmed by too many people—a remark that might also be made about southern California. There was time to visit the university as well as the Colegio de México, an advanced school originally set up under the name of Casa de España to provide teaching posts for refugee scholars from Spain, and later Mexicanized. And there were peripheral activities, such as heckling Chester Kerr when he called a press conference to publicize a new Yale book entitled *The Vinland Map* purporting to prove that Norsemen reached America before Columbus. The map was a forgery, some of us claimed, and perhaps it was. And no one, we said, could interest Mexican journalists in a book written in English to discredit the discoveries of an Italian who had sailed for Spain. But Chester proved to be a press agent of genius, and was given polite attention, more than the book received, I think, from Italian groups in New York.

We also called on Fondo de Cultura Económica, where I had first gone nearly fifteen years before and could now sell translation rights into Spanish. The director at that time was a left-wing Argentine businessman named Arnaldo Orfila Reynal, who made a show of disliking things North American. At luncheons, when I went there alone, he liked to place me between two people who spoke no English and watch to see whether I could survive. On another occasion, when several of us arrived for a talk, Orfila dismissed his English-speaking secretary, while Chester Kerr grew red with anger. The incident is of no importance but shows the kind of attitude we sometimes encountered. Other Fondo officers were helpful, and several years later our friend Jaime García Terrés became director there, and always welcomed us.

We sought out authors when we could, and translators too, although most of the good ones translated *into* their native language and could more easily be found at home. One of the very best, however, was the American wife of a Mexican intellectual. Prompt, literate, knowledgeable, she also possessed a quick wit and a sharp tongue, and we may call her Melissa. She used to drive to the airport to meet two of my colleagues. More standoffish or less charming, I was not so privileged, but could say that she translated books for me and not for them.[3] The game was all quite innocent, of course, but at

---

3. Later she did a book for one of them.

a later time something happened to the marriage, and her husband, whose *nom de guerre* can be Pablo, found himself an *amie*. The latter came from Austria, and Melissa was soon referring to her as Pablo's Tail from the Vienna Woods.

Preceding and paralleling the CILA venture was the translation program, a genuine success. The idea came from Jack Harrison of the Rockefeller Foundation. With his help Frank Wardlaw and I wrote the proposal, and in 1960 the foundation granted $225,000—worth much more than that sum is worth now—to the AAUP to help finance translations of literary and scholarly books from and about Latin America. Individual grants were made to pay translation and other manuscript costs in order that translated books might start out even with those written in English. Without this help, it was reasoned, the expense of translation had to be laid on top of all the usual expenses, making publication impossible unless the book promised a big sale or came as a labor of love from the translator. And big sales were not likely. Latin American books were notoriously more difficult to sell than those from France, Germany, and other European countries. Alfred Knopf, for example, made an effort to publish Latin American novels in the 1940s and 1950s; they sold only a few hundred copies each.

When he proposed the program to the chief officers of the foundation, Harrison remembers, they brought in Knopf to evaluate it; he recounted his own sorry experience and said there would never be an adequate market in this country. Harrison countered with the report that Frank Wardlaw at Texas had sold 20,000 copies of *Platero and I,* a work of poetic prose by the Andalusian poet Juan Ramón Jiménez, then living in Puerto Rico. In disbelief, Knopf checked the story, found that the sale had been even higher, and advised that Latin American books deserved another try.

The association appointed a committee of university scholars to receive proposals and approve individual grants. Thus at some presses, such as California, each project had to get over two hurdles, the home editorial board and the national committee. But in the next five years more than eighty books were approved, mostly in the humanities at first, after that nearly half in the social sciences. About twenty presses participated, but the greatest number of projects came from Texas and California, the two presses most willing to do without manufacturing subventions. The translated books were a major part of the publishing program at Texas. At California, as part of a larger list, they were less central but quite important.

It is worth noting that nearly half the California books were from Brazilian Portuguese, and several were from French. The Brazilian books included Helen Caldwell's translations of Machado de Assis, but there were also economic studies by Celso Furtado and a number of historical and cultural works. It is difficult, I learned at this time, to be confident about originals in a language one does not read—read enough at least to get a feel for the nature of the work. The opinions of others are essential, of course, but one is still in the dark without some first-hand knowledge or impression. And so, to make myself feel better, I had to get hold of a Brazilian-Portuguese grammar and teach myself to read. The language, I found, was in some ways less like Spanish than it looked; the syntax, fortunately, was more like French. I began to share the enthusiasm of Helen Caldwell.

Friends told us about three exceptional books written in French and for some reason never put into English, perhaps simply because they were about Latin America. Most notable and first in period covered, was Robert Ricard's *La conquête spirituelle du Mexique* (1933), the story, says the translator, Lesley Simpson, of "the profound revolution in Mexican life brought about by the Mendicant friars." The author himself wrote, "In the religious domain, as in the others, the sixteenth century . . . was the period in which Mexico was created, and of which the rest of her history has been the almost inevitable development."

François Chevalier's *Land and Society in Colonial Mexico: The Great Hacienda,* published in 1963, concerns the Mexico of the great landed estates formed in the seventeenth century after the military and spiritual conquests had come to a halt. Like the Ricard, it is still in print in paper after all these years. So also is *Latin America: Social Structures and Political Institutions* by Jacques Lambert.

Out of the Homeric sixteenth century, as Lesley Simpson called it, came the *Historia de la conquista de México* by Francisco López de Gómara, published in Zaragoza in 1552 and translated as *Cortés: The Life of the Conqueror, by His Secretary* (1964). Suppressed by the Crown, perhaps on advice of Bartolomé de Las Casas, the great enemy of Cortés and Gómara, it survived outside Spain but has been neglected in modern times. Intellectual fashion in Mexico is to denigrate the Spanish conquerors, as Las Casas did, and to exalt the Indian component of the heritage. In English Gómara's book has been pushed into obscurity partly by the popularity of the contemporary chronicler Bernal Díaz del Castillo. Gómara, said Bernal Díaz, gave too much credit to the leader, Cortés, and not enough to the soldiers, or even to the horses, and he was not even there but wrote from a distance. But he was a great writer, as Simpson tells us, and seems to have had much of his information from Cortés himself. In English there was no modern or adequate edition of a chronicle parallel to, and equal to, the *True History* of Bernal Díaz, and we were pleased to publish it in Simpson's version.

Although most of our Spanish American books were Mexican, there was also Aldo Ferrer's *The Argentine Economy* (1966) and *A Cultural History of Spanish America* (1962) by Mariano Picón-Salas of Venezuela. *Country Judge* (1968), a novel by the Chilean writer Pedro Prado, was one of several literary works gathered in by the translation net. And because our paperback list was proving successful with poetry and other literary classics, as hard-cover editions were not, the translation impulse carried over to works not eligible for the AAUP grant, such as books by the Spanish poets Antonio Machado and Rafael Alberti, translated by the American poet, Ben Belitt.

Foundation interests change like any other fashion, sartorial or intellectual. When the Rockefeller money was exhausted after the allotted time of five or six years, the AAUP made strenuous efforts to obtain a second grant but was never successful. We no longer had Jack Harrison on the inside, he having gone first to Texas and then to Miami to head Latin American centers. And the enthusiasm of many presses was limited, they having less interest in Latin America

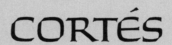

CORTÉS

THE LIFE OF THE CONQUEROR
BY HIS SECRETARY

Francisco López de Gómara

TRANSLATED AND EDITED BY LESLEY BYRD SIMPSON

Jacket by Adrian Wilson.

than had Texas and California. They wanted manufacturing subsidies while we were usually content with funds for translation and illustrations. So the game came to an end, but not before we had made a considerable splash. A couple of decades later, a former student of Helen Caldwell, Joan Palevsky, established at the Press a fund to support literary translations. Although this was not limited to works from Latin America, I like to think, because of Helen, that there was some kind of relation between the two grants.

The Rockefeller grant, I think, and the six years of working on it, had a salutary effect on Latin American studies in this country. We—all of us—managed to bring into English, along with many current studies, most of the classics and standard works that had long been unavailable; they may now be assigned to students in survey courses where the foreign language is not required. Scholarly editors around the country became used to thinking about what is written in the countries to the south of us. And as for current literature, it is noticeable that new Latin American novels are now regularly translated and published by commercial firms, the same firms that could not make a go of such works a generation back. Although it may be that current writings, including those in the "magic realism" genre, are more to North American and British tastes than were the older works of fiction, there is reason to believe that our efforts had something to do with the change.

The Press came out of the endeavor with one of the two best Latin American book lists among American scholarly presses, the other being that at Texas. Since then interest has declined somewhat, perhaps, but retains a part of its strength. If fortune should send along another Lesley Simpson—our most prolific author and translator—we might see another flowering.

9   Looking West to the East
Pel and the Asian Books

One day in the fifties, sometime after Phil Lilienthal became assistant director (later associate director) of the Press, he and I sat in my office discussing whether to make a concerted effort to build a publishing specialty in Asian books.[1] At that time we had almost nothing: a few odds and ends from the late forties and early fifties, things that had wandered in or imports offered by London publishers. Some were good books, but taken together they were odds and ends. Thus I don't remember how we got acquainted with Charles Boxer, the great and unconventional English historian, whose *Christian Century in Japan, 1549–1650* we published in 1951. Perhaps through our Latin American connections.[2]

Asian studies, the province of a few before the war, were expanded quickly thereafter in the major universities, including Berkeley and to some extent our other campuses. There were set up research centers for Chinese, Japanese, South Asian, and Southeast Asian studies, bringing loosely together scholars from several departments, especially history and political science. We looked at this

---

1. "Pel" to me will always mean Philip E. Lilienthal. That is how he signed his office memoranda.
2. Boxer's chief scholarly interest was Portuguese expansion around the world. We brought out his *Colonial Age of Brazil* in 1962 and *Four Centuries of Portuguese Expansion,* in cooperation with Witwatersrand University Press, Johannesburg, in 1973. Both Boxer and his wife, the writer Emily Hahn, were prisoners of the Japanese during World War II.

growth of research interest in one of the two large cultures of the world, and thought it a ripe field for picking manuscripts. And that if we did not bestir ourselves the flying editors from Harvard, Princeton, and elsewhere would gather all the fruit. But a halfhearted move with a junior editor would not do in such a huge field; we had better make a big effort or none.

We had Phil, with his wide experience in the Asian field, if we chose to divert the larger part of his energies, and we thought we might obtain the active help of the various centers. So Phil and I sat there that day, knowing that we had to make a decision. I asked whether he wanted to throw himself into the venture—for twenty years perhaps, although we always avoided distant visions. He asked whether I wanted him to. We were not batting the ball into each other's court, as it may seem. We had the same wish, I think; each was making sure of the other. So Phil said yes, and went off to his desk and began making phone calls and writing letters—those splendid letters that became known to so many in and out of the Asian field.[3]

Although he had many other interests and an education that was broadly European, Phil was involved with Asian peoples and Asian studies for almost his entire life. After leaving Harvard in 1936 he went on a *wanderjahr*, or maybe two. With no knowledge of his itinerary and remembering only the occasional remarks he let fall, I believe that the greater part of his time was spent in India and Southeast Asia. Returning home to New York, he went to work for the Institute of Pacific Relations, then perhaps the primary agent of study and publication in the field of contemporary Asia. Not long thereafter William L. Holland of the institute put Phil in charge of a printing and publishing program in China, editing and producing IPR books for markets in Asia and elsewhere. Holland remembers—in a recent letter to me—that Phil found time from his frustrating struggles with

---

3. When he retired a few of them were gathered up and printed in a booklet entitled *Letters from Phil* (1980).

Shanghai printers to join a volunteer fire-fighting brigade there. "You can imagine what an extraordinary time it was for him, especially knowing that the Japanese military were all around him waiting to pounce. By the time he came back he had acquired a remarkable knowledge of copy-editing, proof-reading, paper-purchasing, type-faces, shipping, sales promotion, currency exchange, and much more."

In Shanghai Phil became acquainted with John S. Service, an American consulate officer, who many years later, retired in Berkeley, helped us with some difficult editorial revision of Asian books. Of their Shanghai meeting more than fifty years ago, Service recalls, in another recent letter: "He was already—in his youth as well as later in life—a wonderful, kind, out-going, intelligent, imaginative, quietly impressive person."

During the war Phil worked for the Office of War Information in San Francisco as chief of the Chinese Division, supervising, among other things, shortwave radio broadcasts to Asia. Among those who worked for him then was Max Knight, né Kühnel, an Austrian refugee by way of Shanghai, who later came to the Press and served for many years as one of our senior copyeditors. In 1946 Phil returned to New York and spent several years as chief editor of *Pacific Affairs,* the journal of the International Secretariat of the IPR.

During the cold war hysteria the IPR was heavily attacked by the McCarthy and McCarran committees of Congress; some of its left-leaning officers were forced to leave, and financial support dwindled drastically. Of the senior officers only Holland remained, and it was he who held the organization together until it was dissolved in 1960.[4] Meanwhile, Phil, who had not been attacked, resigned and moved to California. In 1954, with an introduction from Jim Hart, then professor of English and later director of the Bancroft Library, he came to the Press, looking for work.

The only open job we had—several months later—was one that

4. Taking *Pacific Affairs* with him, Holland then moved to the University of British Columbia as head of Asian studies. There I knew him in the early 1960s, when I visited Vancouver on editorial scouting trips.

he was vastly over-qualified for, writing advertising copy in the sales department. He took it willingly, with no false pride of position, and went to work with the incredible efficiency that we all came to know. But at that time the Press was expanding, and I had felt the need for someone of high ability to help me plan where to take it and how to get there. A few months of observation were enough; I asked Phil to become assistant director and wrote to President Sproul for approval. Phil himself was willing but hesitant, suggesting that Sproul might not allow me to make the appointment. Although not himself attacked during the IPR troubles, he had signed a protest against persecution of intellectuals and had got his name on a list of people acquainted with communists and possibly sympathetic to them. Phil seemed sensitive about the matter and never discussed it. I was not concerned and thought the president would pay no attention.

In this I was wrong but never knew it until recently. Papers found in the University archives show that someone called that list of names or another to the president's attention. Sproul held me up for a few days but must have found nothing of consequence because he allowed the appointment to go through.

Phil always had a strong sense of social justice and throughout his life worked in his quiet way for the American Civil Liberties Union and for other organizations whose purposes he thought worthwhile. To me he seemed one of a rare breed, the hard-headed liberal. He once told me, speaking of his work with the NAACP, that he was not about to bend over and invite kicks, as so many white liberals did in those days. And after retirement, when he did volunteer work with prisoners in the San Francisco city and county jail, he offered help but not sympathy.

When Phil accepted my offer, neither of us could have known what we were letting ourselves in for. Possibly he did and decided to gamble on me. For better or worse, and without knowing much about each other, we began a sort of working *mariage de convenance* that lasted for more than twenty years. It was not easy or straightforward, especially at the beginning. When a director wishes to take on a second in command, the easy way to avoid trouble is to choose someone inferior to himself. Some executives, including a friend or two at other presses, have worked in this way, and not without success. But little venture, little gain. When one chooses an equal, or perhaps in some ways a more-than-equal, then it is a chancy business that may blow up in both their faces. But if they can synchronize their aberrations (as a friend of mine said about marriage itself), ride out the storms, and find a way of working together, then the rewards will be there.

There were difficulties, not all of them our own. The Press had just come out of—or rather, was not yet quite out of—the fight I have mentioned with the printing department and the University business office. These were the dying years of the long Sproul regime, and neither he nor anyone else would or could cut the ties that bound us, however loosely, to the printing office. We lived uneasily under the same roof, outwardly polite, inwardly thinking: "Smile when you call me that." The tension did not go away completely until we moved out of the building in 1962.

Within this tense environment we worked out our own problems. Both Phil and I were strong-minded—bull-headed, if you like. Some people have taken his modest speech at face value, but behind that almost oriental self-disparagement lay a fierce sense of pride. He knew his value and very occasionally stated it. He is one of three people I have worked with, all quite superior and all now gone, whom I used to characterize as mixtures of arrogance and humility. The words are strong, but no others will quite do. But I should add that the two qualities were so intertwined, so blended into each other, that neither ever appeared quite alone—to those who knew them well enough. It was an attractive mixture, one that I always admired.[5]

If Phil was not an easy person, neither was I. The great intra-University fight had taught me diplomacy for use where essential but

5. The other two were Thomas J. Wilson, late director of the Harvard University Press, and Michel Loève, mathematician and member of the Editorial Committee. Other superior people did not show quite the same blend of qualities.

had also stirred up for part-time use what may be called the combative side of my nature. Both sides had been needed for survival. So neither of us was relaxed, but fortunately, we both had the good sense, or the instinct, not to throw out challenges, and the patience to ignore opportunities for trouble. There were times when Phil blew his temper at me, which may surprise those who never knew he had one, and other times when I could see him exerting control. The learning process went on tacitly, without discussion, never laid out on the table or put into words, each making his own adjustments, until we evolved or discovered a kind of harmony. We came to know what each other was thinking or was about to think, and eventually learned that we thought alike most of the time. How this happened I cannot say. Perhaps, out of some kind of instinct, we played down the ways in which we were different and made daily use of the ways in which we were much alike. Two measures of the relationship: I trusted him completely, and he turned down offers of higher-ranking jobs elsewhere.

In the later years, when this unexplained kind of understanding had worked itself into place, Phil was a great joy to me in our weekly meetings with the Berkeley sponsoring editors. By that time there were quite a number of them, all capable, some brilliant, with various backgrounds and interests. Phil was in daily charge of the editors, especially after we moved that department to a separate building, but I had begun my work at the Press with a deep concern for the kinds of books we published, a concern that might be shared but could never be given up. So the two of us, by now thinking much alike, acted jointly to exert general control over the book program and to keep it going in directions we thought best. The weekly meetings became, in part, times for the exchange of ideas, for the younger editors to try out their plans, even to challenge their elders. But in part these were also training sessions, although never called such. In our parallel Los Angeles editorial office, relations were rather different. Occasionally we all met together.

None of the Berkeley sponsors, capable as they were, had a gen-

Phil Lilienthal. An informal moment.

eral education equal to Phil's or a wit as quick as his. When in the course of our discussions I might make a sidelong literary or historical reference, never explaining it, I found myself glancing around at a room of blank faces—except Phil's. Always there was a small sign, movement of an eyebrow or slight change of expression, nothing obvious, that showed he had picked up the point and understood its relevance. It was satisfying. Points missed are breath wasted; points explained go flat. What I observed had more to do, perhaps, with a generation gap or a difference in education than with anything else, but the occasions were not few and they enhanced our (or at least my) sense of being joint mentors.

Oral wit seldom reads well on paper, but one small exchange sticks in my head. A sponsor, momentarily prey to the solemnity that bites us all at times, remarked, "You may not know that I am descended from kings."

"By the back stairs, no doubt," said Phil.

There was another mixture of qualities that I do not remember seeing in anyone else: Phil was both brilliant and methodical. Ordinarily one becomes methodical to make up for lack of brilliance. Brilliance, whatever it is and however defined, leads one to work in occasional bursts, starting late and catching up. How Phil came about his great and sometimes somewhat rigid sense of discipline, I cannot say, but he could always begin at the beginning of a project and work straight through, or at the beginning of a day and never let up until evening came. In a letter to an author, he once wrote, "Placing the one foot in front of the other, and then repeating the process though not with the same foot, seems to have a certain effect, doesn't it?"

With this habit of work along with the ability to move fast without seeming to—hare and tortoise combined—Phil could handle about twice as many books as could any other sponsor. One who knew him said, and of course I have no figures, that he sponsored about a thousand books in twenty-five years at the Press, along with many other duties performed. It is the Asian books that first come to mind, but he also handled the many volumes that came from the great

Mark Twain projects, some of them involving complex relationships with another university. He also managed the huge symposia on mathematical statistics and probability—six of them, the last in six volumes—brain children of that great scholar and entrepreneur Jerzy Neyman of the Statistical Laboratory in Berkeley. And with his left hand, just as a change of pace, Phil could always put through a few literary translations, personal accounts, and the like.

In the years before retirement, when he and I and others had got the Press into pretty good shape, I began to feel—perhaps like the solemn editor mentioned above—the need to pontificate and so began writing articles on university publishing and on the relation between a press and a university.[6] Thus I came to learn something about how Phil related to his authors. I used to work my way through two or three drafts of a piece, and then, thinking it about ready to go, would write "Pel" at the top and toss it into the circulation basket. Back it would come in less time than expected and with a little note that said something like this: It is fine, it will do nicely, but—but you might want to take another look at this part or think again about that part or change an emphasis or two. Just details, one might think at first glance, but by that time I knew Phil well enough to know when to read small suggestions large. Putting paper into the typewriter, I began to see—his suggestions touching off my own propensity for revision—that the whole thing needed to be torn apart and recombined before it could make the kind of sense that he knew I had in mind. On one occasion I rewrote the entire article except for one page. And threw that page away.

Many academic authors received more drastic advice than that. To one young author he wrote, "If your academic situation permits such a course, you would almost certainly be well advised to put your manuscript on a back burner and allow it to marinate for a year or

6. Most of them appeared in the 1970s in the journal *Scholarly Publishing* (Toronto).

more. . . . Time, it is said, is a great healer; the conventional wisdom fails to remark that it is also a helpful editor."

Regardless of how much he may have contributed, Phil never allowed authors to give him printed credit or thanks in their books. To Irv Scheiner, author of a book on Meiji Japan, he wrote, "For many years now I have deleted my name from the acknowledgement sections of books in which I have been interested—this for no particular reason that I can identify but simply in response to some axiom that I may have heard at one time or another." Many years later, composing an obituary, Scheiner mentioned this and added: "But none of us who worked with him will ever forget." The urge to self-effacement or the strict editorial conscience may seem excessive to some but defined one part of Phil's nature, a part that does not quite fit either of the contrasting qualities that I ascribed to him early in this chapter.

Along with critical suggestions, he could write the most graceful of compliments, as he could also say them to his friends on the right occasions. To one distant author and his wife: "This spring instead of ingesting the usual patent medicines to counteract the effects of the season, we are contenting ourselves with simply thinking of you both: the effect is immediately tonic and long-lasting."

Looking back at our old seasonal catalogues, spring and fall, I note that in the mid fifties there was only the occasional Asian book, accidentally acquired. After a few seasons of effort this part of the list can be seen gathering force, gaining numbers. By the mid or late sixties, each year saw publication of fifteen or twenty books on China, Japan, India, and Southeast Asia, and in a number of disciplines: anthropology, economics, political science, history, art. It would be foolish for me to pass judgment on our Asian list in comparison to others, but I remember how we felt about it at the time—we being the rest of us rather than Phil. By the end of the sixties we believed that our Asian books were quite equal to those of our two chief competitors, Harvard and Princeton. And I used to say that the Asian field was the greatest of our specialties, not in sales perhaps but in richness and variety of scholarship.

Among so many good books I cannot make choices. But it may be worth noting that a number of our early titles, before we had solidified our own lines of communication, were imports from British publishers. In this way we obtained books from some of our own faculty members, such as Joseph Levenson and Wolfram Eberhard, as well as books from outsiders, including Ron Dore, of Vancouver and London, and Michael Sullivan, who was at the University of Malaya when we brought out his *Chinese Art in the Twentieth Century* (1959). Sullivan provides an example of what can follow the experimental importation of a distant and unknown author. There followed *An Introduction to Chinese Art* (1961), which later changed its title to *The Arts of China* and became a standard work for classes. Sullivan moved to London and then to Stanford and went on writing books. The initial volume of *The Birth of Landscape Painting in China* (1962) became the first title in our art history series, described in another chapter. And it was to Sullivan and his wife that Phil wrote the springtime compliment quoted above.

Among the hundreds of other titles, many by distinguished scholars from within and without our own university, most were our originals and were edited and produced by us. Although the books paralleled the work of the several centers and institutes in the University and although these gave occasional help, it was Phil Lilienthal himself who made the list into what it became. We had thought, when we began, that the centers would turn to and make common cause with us, that some of them might even bring in books for us, as John K. Fairbank was doing for the Harvard press, but it never worked out that way. If I remember correctly, Henry Rosovsky, head of the Center for Japanese and Korean Studies while he remained in Berkeley, was the only one in the 1960s to work systematically with Phil. Many other faculty members, of course, gave informal help and advice. But this great publishing list was really constructed by a single hand, and it was the finest editorial effort I have ever witnessed.

IO Ishi, Don Juan, and the Anthropologists
A Tale of Two Best-Sellers

At the beginning of this century, when the Press was only a few years old and the academic science of man— man as *anthropos*—was nearly as young, there were still Indian villages in California where daily life was carried on in the traditional way, where men and women spoke the Indian languages and remembered the history and myths of their people. What better could the first California anthropologists do than seek to understand and record this civilization before it was lost, as soon it would be? In the year 1900 a young man named Alfred Louis Kroeber, soon to get his degree under Franz Boas at Columbia, arrived in San Francisco as curator at the California Academy of Sciences. A few weeks later, having put the collections in order and with $100 of expense money in his pocket, he set off by train and stage coach to the Klamath River in the redwood country of far northern California. There he began the study of one of his favorite Indian peoples, the Yurok.

Although much of Kroeber's early work with this and other tribes was in recording languages, he also collected myths. For a time he intended, once those of the Yurok had been published, to write a history of that people. But he never did, and years later told his wife Theodora that perhaps he could never write of them in this way, saying: "I feel myself too much a Yurok." This she tells us in the foreword to *Yurok Myths,* published by the Press in 1976, sixteen years

Alfred Kroeber, 1911.

after Kroeber's death. His remark may foreshadow later controversies about inside and outside observers.

In the years after that first northern visit Kroeber published many books and hundreds of papers and articles. But his greatest publication, perhaps, was one not entirely his own, one shared with other university scholars—the famous monograph series, American Archaeology and Ethnology. Known everywhere in the world of anthropology as AAE, this series began in 1903 and added up to fifty volumes and about 300 papers before it was superseded in 1964 by a new series, called simply Publications in Anthropology, with no geographical limitation. And alongside AAE after 1937 was another series, Anthropological Records, designed for less expensive publication of field notes and raw data. Of all the numbers in AAE the best known was number 38, Kroeber's *Cultural and Natural Areas of Native North America* (1939), a large cloth-bound book.

I am not sure whether the Press ever had what might be called a list in anthropology; certainly we never thought of it as such; but over the years we must have published more pages on the California Indians than did all other publishers put together, and also much on Mexican native peoples, which led in the sixties and seventies to two of the most widely read books that we ever turned out. The first of these was distilled in large part from several AAE monographs.

But first a glance backward. The very first book of the Press, an accidental one in the old monograph days and one that had no successors for many years, was *The Book of the Life of the Ancient Mexicans, Containing an Account of Their Rites and Superstitions* . . . by Zelia Nuttall. In 1890 Nuttall, an amateur scholar and resident of Mexico with Harvard and California connections, came across in the national library in Florence a sixteenth-century Mexican manuscript that came to be known as the Codex Magliabechiano. With permission of the Italian authorities she had two hundred facsimile copies printed by what was then termed chromolithography. Intending to have the Codex published by the Peabody Museum at Harvard, where she was an honorary assistant in American archaeology, she set to work on an introduction and translation. But she worked slowly, or perhaps she dawdled, and in 1903 was told by another scholar that if she did not publish at once, he would bring out his own edition. Putting aside her partially done commentary, Nuttall hastily wrote a preface and introduction, which she had set up and printed in Cambridge. But the Peabody was not ready to cooperate, and she turned to her friends in California, where she was a member of the advisory committee for the new department of anthropology. With money from a donated research fund, the Florence and Cambridge parts were put together, bound in flexible leather, and issued in 1903, with the imprint "University of California."

It is a handsome volume, with colored reproductions of drawings by an unknown Indian artist and of handwritten text by a Spanish friar. It was called Part 1 and the high price of $25 entitled purchasers to a second part to come, translation and commentary. But Nuttall, although she lived another thirty years, never completed the work. In 1927 Kroeber told an inquiring Press editor that Nuttall would never, in his opinion, finish this book or any other.

All her papers appear to have been lost. Eighty years passed, and in 1983, the Press brought out a reproduction of the book, a facsimile of the facsimile, together with a second volume containing a translation and commentary by Elizabeth Hill Boone of Dumbarton Oaks. To the best of my knowledge none of the original purchasers showed up to demand their copies of Part 2.[1]

Early one morning in the summer of 1911 an exhausted and starving man wandered down out of the mountains to a slaughterhouse near Oroville in the northern Sacramento Valley. Cornered by dogs, he was rescued by the sheriff and, for protection from by-standers, locked in the local jail. No one, white or Indian, could understand him, and the newspapers reported that a "wild man" had been found.

---

1. This wonderfully tangled tale is told in detail by Muto in chapter 4 of *University of California Press.*

Reading these accounts in San Francisco, Kroeber and his colleague, T. T. Waterman, guessed that the man might be a Yana Indian of a tribe virtually extinct. With a written vocabulary in his pocket, Waterman took the train to Oroville and established partial communication with the man, who turned out to be a Yana of the Yahi subtribe. He was put into white man's clothes and taken into a world he had never known, transported by train and ferry to the University museum in San Francisco. There he lived for five years, the rest of his life. He was known as Ishi, the Yana word for man. It was Yana custom to keep the personal name private.

In the decades after the great gold rush white settlers had rapidly filled the Sacramento Valley, pushing the native peoples out of the way. There was trouble, and in the 1860s, about the time Ishi was born, settler bands massacred Indians in the farm country and pursued them into the hills, seeking to exterminate them. The campaign against the Yahi, the southernmost group of Yana, succeeded almost completely; only a small group, remnant of a remnant, escaped into the canyon country of Deer Creek and Mill Creek, where they hid themselves and managed to survive for more than forty years, subsisting in the old ways, hunting by bow and arrow. Eventually there were only four people left, and then there was only one, Ishi, then about fifty years old. Alone, depressed, and delirious, he wandered down to the valley, the last wild Indian in North America.

What does it tell us that a middle-aged man, transported directly from his stone-age culture into the complex world of the twentieth century, could make a quick adjustment and live with some comfort in the new environment? For one thing: that our technology has changed far more than we have. Ishi, befriended and given quarters in the museum, adopted the white man's ways, taught the anthropologists the crafts, language, and religion of his people, demonstrated fire making and other crafts to the public, and moved easily about the city. In the spring of 1914 he journeyed with Kroeber and others to the area in the foothills of Mount Lassen where he had

Ishi in two worlds.

spent his early life. There he led them to all the old spots where he and his vanished companions had managed to eke out a living. He was indeed a man who had lived in two worlds, as Theodora Kroeber put it in the title of her book.

I first heard of Ishi sometime in the 1950s, when Bob Heizer, professor of anthropology, told me that the department was looking for someone to write this story for the general public. There had long ago been monographs in the AAE series, among them Waterman's *Yana Indians* and Saxton Pope's *Yahi Archery,* both papers containing much learned from Ishi himself.[2] For the wanted general book an author was at last found in Kroeber's own household, his wife Theodora, who had demonstrated her capacity in *The Inland Whale,* a retelling of nine stories from California Indian legends—the title

2. American Archaeology and Ethnology 13:2–3. This volume of nine papers, published 1917–23, is almost entirely concerned with the Yana.

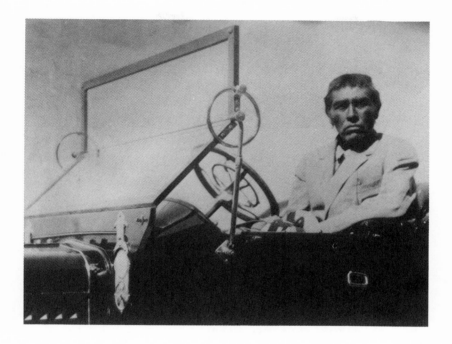

story from Kroeber's favorite Yurok tribe of the far northern region.[3] The retold stories were called by Oliver La Farge "literature, in the best sense of the word." When she came to the larger task, the story of Ishi, she had as source material Kroeber's personal recollections as told to her, along with fifty pounds of old documents made available by Heizer. From these she distilled the book *Ishi in Two Worlds: A Biography of the Last Wild Indian in North America,* published in 1961, the year after Kroeber's death. At once it became a classic and a best-seller.

I had known Kroeber in connection with his publishing activities, books and monograph series, but had only the slightest acquaintance with Theodora until we came to publish *Ishi* after his death. There followed other books and other occasions until I knew her well as friend and neighbor, knew also the fine old house on Arch

3. Indiana University Press, 1959. Paperback edition issued by California in 1963.

Street, built by Berkeley's most famous architect, Bernard Maybeck. So my knowledge of Theodora had virtually nothing to do with Kroeber himself, except as she wrote of him. It says something for the vividness of that writing and also of her talk that I came to feel the illusion of having known her and her daily life from long before we first met.

Many of us live more than one life, I suppose, even if not so drastically as did Ishi. The several lives of Theodora Kroeber were more distinct than most: girlhood in a Colorado mining camp and first widowhood; then the long central period as wife and partner of a man much older than she; and after his death, a final twenty years as author and noted public figure, with a third marriage to a younger man. She came to writing late. When her youngest child was fifteen, the older ones away, husband recovering from a heart attack, she made, she tells us in her book about Kroeber, the "first tentative beginning toward writing." She was always tentative, I think, even later when she had won some fame and must have been well aware of her talent. Her first book, *The Inland Whale,* was published when she was past sixty.

When the manuscript of *Ishi* first came to the Press, half of it was written in her own words while the other half was a set of strung-together quotations from the sources, including the monographs of Pope and Waterman. I suggested that she take the manuscript home and redo the quoted parts in her own language. As first submitted the book fell apart into two sections, unlike in style and in effect on the reader. As redone, source material rewritten, the book was triumphantly one thing, perhaps the finest account that we have of American Indian life.

Ten years later, when she brought in her biography of Kroeber,[4] there was a minor repetition of the incident. In one section she tried once more to string quotations on a thin line of commentary, something she could not do effectively, that no one should do. Why she

4. *Alfred Kroeber: A Personal Configuration* (Berkeley, 1970).

tried is a mystery, related perhaps to the tentativeness mentioned above. When she rewrote in her own style, without leaning on borrowed syntax, the improvement was beyond compare. She told me then, I remember, that I was wasting myself as an administrator and should spend my time editing.

Theodora was no scholar, nor ever pretended to be one. She listened and absorbed. Her strengths as a writer were understanding, intuition, simple words well placed, strong feeling understated, an unexplained ability to project herself and her reader back into another time and place. This is the ability of the historical novelist, one of them at least, and it helps us to see how she could breathe life into the unliving transcripts of Indian tales, unliving because set down literally in an alien idiom. It is this gift of re-imagining that distills reality out of old papers and re-creates Ishi as an individual person, not fully comprehended of course but quite as alive and eccentric as my grandfather. It is a very great gift, that of making us part of a life we never took part in, of allowing our presence where we never were, of raising up a gone world. In another kind of life, no husband's career to assist, no family to raise, she might have made herself into a considerable novelist. But we are fortunate to have what she wrote in the latter part of her life.[5]

The great success of *Ishi*—half a million copies in print, said our ads in 1976—was bound to attract other publishers. Of course we would never sell the paperback rights, as we did later those to another anthropological best-seller, deemed less suitable to our list. But one day Lucie Dobbie came to my office and said that a local publisher, specializing in juvenile books, wanted Mrs. Kroeber to write a children's book about Ishi, and did I have any objection? A children's book would not affect our market, I thought in one of my naïve moments, knowing too little about that business and perhaps about that publisher. Permission was given for a children's book.

---

5. A few of these paragraphs, somewhat changed, are taken from the introduction that I wrote to her oral history for the Bancroft Library.

A year or two later we woke up to advertisements for a general book, implied to be *the* book about Ishi for all readers. The new version was being pushed in the adult market, our market.[6] Although it was said to be written for young adults—a book trade term for twelve-to-fifteen-year-olds—there was no indication of age group on book or jacket or in the ads; on the jacket our book was passed off briefly as an "anthropological story" of Ishi and not a biography, as it was. One might have excused some of this but not the marketing.

The book itself, though perhaps allowing the kind of sales treatment that confused book buyers, was entirely different from the original book. A fictional account with imagined incidents, conversations, and some invented characters, it tells Ishi's story from his own viewpoint, concentrating on the years of concealment in the hills and the deaths or disappearances of family and friends. The story is one of almost unrelenting decline and sadness until the years in San Francisco. It seems to me, and I no judge of "children's" books, that the parts set in Ishi's mind, his thoughts and memories, are not entirely successful, perhaps because too explicit. In calling up a past world and making it live, the author is more successful, I think, when she sticks closer to real events, when the writing is more objective and restrained. Here perhaps I contradict my earlier words, and perhaps am prejudiced by knowledge of what really happened, but that is how a re-reading strikes me. And I find it disconcerting that she leaves Kroeber entirely out of the latter part of the story. But some parts, such as that on the first train journey to San Francisco, are fascinating.

When the other publisher—Parnassus Press of Berkeley—would not see the matter as we saw it, we had recourse to the University attorney. After some wrangling, during which we had to explain to Bob Heizer that we were not attacking Theodora, the publisher agreed to stop advertising to the adult market. He then made an attempt to sell movie rights; Harlan Kessel, our marketing manager, had to call him off. Harlan himself was dickering with a studio; a

6. *Ishi: Last of His Tribe* (Berkeley, 1964).

script was written, I think, but no picture was produced at that time. It could be argued, I suppose, that the story itself is in the public domain, but nothing truly good could be done without Theodora's interpretation. As this is written I am told by Dan Dixon, rights manager of the Press, that there are now to be two films. A documentary, done on an NEH grant, was first shown in October 1992 at the Marin Film Festival. A feature film is being done commercially.

Approaching retirement, the Press in good shape, financially and intellectually, I found time to think about books we had published, including *Ishi,* and it occurred to me that perhaps there should be a fully illustrated edition, somewhat like the handsome volumes produced in color and black-and-white by George Rainbird Ltd. for a number of London publishers. So we got Dave Comstock, formerly of our production department, to design and produce one, first going through all the Ishi documents and photographic files in the Lowie Museum (once the University museum, where Ishi lived, but now in Berkeley) as well as through many contemporary publications. Living in Grass Valley, Dave was pleased to visit the Ishi country, not far away, and photograph the terrain. In rather larger format than the original edition, the book came out in 1976.

The next step followed from that one. With readers wanting more information about Ishi, I thought we ought to publish a volume of the documents themselves. This appeared in 1979. Edited by Bob Heizer and Theodora Kroeber, the thirty-seven documents, including early newspaper clippings, personal accounts of Indian fighters, and detailed studies by the museum staff, are divided into four sections: Before Ishi, Ishi Enters Civilization, Ishi Among the Anthropologists, and Death of Ishi. It is called *Ishi, the Last Yahi: A Documentary History.* With this, I thought, perhaps we had done full justice to the story of Ishi, a great story in several ways: scientific, historical, and merely human. Ishi, born to a fleeing remnant of a persecuted people, having spent more than forty years in hiding, became a celebrity twice: once after 1911 as a stone-age man come to the city, living with the anthropologists, and then again fifty

Theodora.   Ishi.

years later in the writings of Theodora Kroeber, widow of his early benefactor.

Quite different is the story of don Juan, a Yaqui Indian famous in the 1970s and who may or may not have existed. In 1967 there came to the Press office in Los Angeles a manuscript by a graduate student in the anthropology department there. Based on a term paper or intended as a thesis—I am not sure which—it recounted the experiences of the student, Carlos Castaneda, as apprentice to an Indian shaman in northern Mexico. "In a series of remarkable dialogues," says our advertising copy, "Castaneda sets forth his partial initiation into don Juan's perception and mastery of 'non-ordinary reality.' He describes how peyote and other plants sacred to the Mexican Indians were used as gateways to the mysteries of 'dread,' 'clarity,' and 'power.'"

A university press, faced with such a "non-ordinary" manuscript, will be interested but skeptical. Such was the reaction of Robert Y. Zachary, head of the southern editorial office, and he decided that the critical readings should be more extensive than usual—four of them instead of two. To begin with there was a statement from Clement Meighan, an archaeologist at UCLA and leader of at least one field trip in which Castaneda took part. Another was obtained from Edmund Carpenter, former collaborator of Marshall McLuhan in Toronto, a man expected to be sympathetic. I reveal these names because their participation was public; some of Carpenter's remarks were later quoted on the book jacket. Two other readers were promised anonymity, the standard practice. The crucial reading, says Zachary, was from a noted ethno-botanist, a level-headed person familiar with the medicinal plants mentioned. Rather to the editor's surprise, it was quite favorable, as were all the others.

The manuscript was also read by a fifth authority, Walter Goldschmidt, then a member of our Editorial Committee and chairman of the department of anthropology at UCLA, although not at that time acquainted with Castaneda. He recommended approval to the Committee and also offered to write a foreword, placing the author as a graduate student in anthropology. In later years he must have regretted doing this—not for what he wrote, which was cautious enough, but for putting himself in the line of fire. His most persistent critic jumped and jumped again on Goldschmidt's very first sentence, calling the book "both ethnography and allegory." Logically impossible, said the critic, as it surely was to his type of mind. In his acknowledgments the author mentioned help from six other members of the anthropology department. One senior member, as we shall see, was adamantly opposed.

So in the spring of 1968 we published *The Teachings of Don Juan: A Yaqui Way of Knowledge*. On the jacket Edmund Carpenter wrote, "I cannot adequately convey the excitement I experienced on reading this account. I kept putting down the manuscript and walking around. . . . Suddenly so much of what had hitherto been ambiguous made sense. . . . *The Teachings of Don Juan* reports a human reality, not an equivalent of that reality."

In the summer of 1960, wrote Castaneda, when he was on a field trip to collect information about medicinal plants used by the Indians, he met in a Greyhound bus station near the Arizona-Mexican border an old Indian named Juan Matus, said to be a sorcerer. Later he sought out Juan and visited him many times. A year after the first meeting Castaneda abandoned his objective role and began serving as apprentice to don Juan—thus going from outsider to insider, from observer to participant. In the book he recounts a number of extraordinary experiences, not fully understood by him and not full explained. All this is set forth in simple and unemotional language that contrasts with the things told and enhances a believable story. (After ten years of apprenticeship, we learn in a later book, Castaneda becomes a "member" of the sorcery and is able to "stop the world," and to perceive another reality without the aid of psychotropic plants.)

It was clear from the beginning that interest in *The Teachings of Don Juan* was not limited to the usual academic market. Harlan Kessel advertised in the alternative press as well as in the standard media, and he arranged an extensive speaking tour for Castaneda in university communities. Success was quick. The book became famous. Castaneda and don Juan became cult figures to the young, not just in the counter-culture but to many others who were feeling the general dissatisfaction of the times. If there is such a thing as a zeitgeist, it was there to greet Castaneda and don Juan.

And so we sold a million copies. Or did we? Friends, impressed by the successful publicity, called Kessel to ask how many copies so far, and he put them off, not wishing to reveal the true figures. In the first several months we went through a couple of substantial printings, a good result but not sensational, nothing like the early sale of *Ishi*. What Kessel had suspected was now clear: the true market was not in cloth; the natural readers were not buyers of hard-bound books but of paperbacks; the great potential sale could be reached only in paper. We knew how to sell a paperback, of course, but had no time to cope with the off-beat inquiries, the special events, the countless telephone calls, the general commotion; we had a hundred other books to sell in the scholarly market. So Kessel licensed paperback rights to Ballantine Books for a substantial advance on royalties, shared with the author of course. At the end of the first licensing period, after some disagreement about accounting records, he transferred the license to Simon and Schuster. Meanwhile our Los Angeles office had found Castaneda an agent, Ned Brown, who sold his future writings to the same publisher. From then on we watched with interest, collecting royalties on the volume we had published. Castaneda wrote more books and became wealthy.

In March 1973, shortly after publication of the third book, *Journey to Ixtlán,* the magazine *Time* printed a long cover story entitled "Carlos Castaneda: Magic and Reality." Because Castaneda would not allow a straight photograph, the cover picture was a shadowy montage of his head in outline, and inside it a thin Mexican in a sombrero. Below were flowering plants and a single cactus. In a gossipy, semi-literate way, the article must have been intended as a demystification of Castaneda. The magazine tracked him back to childhood in Cajamarca in Peru, interviewed his sister in Lima, and uncovered small facts about his life in this country. He was quoted on the difficulty of judging one culture in terms of another, and on how a Navajo anthropologist might ask about white European culture.

Carlos, a friendly and intelligent fellow, continued to come into the Press office to ask about royalties and for conversation. I talked with him a number of times in Los Angeles but never knew him so well as did others. He considered Zachary a snob, says the latter, and with him conversed about philosophy, while with some junior editors he discussed girls. To Jim Kubeck, managing editor, he told long stories of childhood in Brazil, abandonment by a father who ran off to Paris, schooling in Argentina, near death from a bayonet wound in Korea, and work as a border spy in Texas. He must have known that the sober and rational Kubeck, onetime student of anthropology, would not believe so many things, at least not after the first episodes, but perhaps that was no matter. In the Peruvian Andes the teller of tall tales, says Kubeck, is expected to mix fact and fantasy and is admired for the richness of his invention. But some skills, I think, can be learned only by those with a natural gift.

The young people who came to hear Carlos at Cody's Bookstore in Berkeley and in other places were always shocked, says Harlan Kessel, when their cult hero appeared in a three-piece suit and necktie. That is how he always dressed, looking oddly out of place on the UCLA campus where no one but an economist, says Walter Gold-schmidt, ever wears a suit. Goldschmidt says also that Carlos looked like your gardener on his way to church. A popular magazine wrote that he resembled a Cuban waiter. But snide remarks give a wrong impression. Shrewd and intelligent, Carlos surely knew exactly what he was doing. The Brooks Brothers suit, he once told Zachary, per-haps in jest, was a kind of armor, covering the confusion within. More likely, it seems to me, he knew that to meet an audience in sandals and open shirt would be to bring himself down to the level of his hearers and eventually to lose respect, as some well known gurus did.

It was surely part of Carlos' persona, built up over his entire life-time, perhaps, that he should always be something of a mystery—as also was don Juan. Not too much should ever be certain. A factual biography would have diminished him. One wonders to what extent this pattern was thought out, calculated, or whether it had all become so natural, so much a part of him, instinctive rather than learned, that the quotidian man was no longer there, the persona more real than the person.[7]

The true con man, I think, is born, not made, although he may sharpen his skills over time. One thinks of another successful con man—so called by himself—of about the same time, Werner Erhard of EST. Werner was not always entirely convincing but never quite unconvincing, and could perform remarkable mental feats. His mind was quick and supple; one could never pin him down or even catch up with him, and to dispute him was to risk humiliation. As with Carlos, some hearers became true believers; some, the practical minds, pro-nounced him a fraud; others admired without fully understanding.

In any event, and in more banal terms, Carlos created in himself a character more complex than his don Juan, if indeed don Juan was

7. In the second chapter of *Journey to Ixtlán* (1972) don Juan tells Carlos that he must "erase" his personal history, wrap a fog of uncertainty around himself.

Carlos' creation. We don't know that he was or that he was not, and given the nature of the story—or the thesis—we cannot know. But there were those who thought they did know, one way or the other. At UCLA, where Castaneda submitted the manuscript of *Journey to Ixtlán* as his doctoral dissertation, there were a few detractors but more supporters. One senior professor, Ralph Beals, considered the work a fraud and would not have granted the degree, but he retired, and a committee of several others examined the manuscript and approved the doctorate in 1973. In its dissertation form the work was entitled "Sorcery: A Description of the World."

A couple of years later there came along a man named Richard de Mille, with a degree in psychology, who embarked on a five-year endeavor to prove that the Castaneda books were not just a mixture of fact and fiction but amounted to a great hoax, like Piltdown man. In one of his lighter moments de Mille invented the term *Uclanthropus piltdunides Castanedae*. And he quoted the bon mot of a friend: that Castaneda's one successful piece of sorcery was in turning the University of California into an ass. But surely no one with a genuine sense of humor—sense of the ridiculous—would devote five years of his life to such a quixotic project, and write two books about it.[8]

De Mille hectored the UCLA faculty, especially Goldschmidt, demanding that the department admit error and rescind the degree. It is hard to know how serious he was when he wrote in the second book that he could not have finished writing it if the department had made public confession of its sins. In 1978 de Mille, Goldschmidt, Beals, and others took part in a raucous session at the annual meeting of the American Anthropological Association. Castaneda declined to appear.

De Mille's second book—I have not seen the first—contains 519 pages of gossip, innuendo, burlesque, and some genuine evidence, which I make no attempt to weigh. There are also a number of pieces

8. *Castaneda's Journey* (Santa Barbara, 1976) and *The Don Juan Papers* (Santa Barbara, 1980).

by others, including an article favorable to Castaneda by the noted anthropologist Mary Douglas. Of special interest is an interview with Barbara Myerhof, fellow student of Castaneda and once a close friend. Goldschmidt considers this piece damning, but another reader might think it a partial validation. De Mille, on the attack, has Myerhof backed into a corner; as he presses her to declare the books a fraud, she keeps answering, "yes, but . . . yes, but." Yes, Castaneda seems to have adapted material from her work and from others, but there is more to him than that.

I find it striking that attitudes to Castaneda's work relate so closely to the type of mind of the critic. In over-simple terms: those of a mystical or quasi-mystical turn of mind tend to be sympathetic; the practical or engineering mind cites the lack of evidence and the obvious fact that Castaneda does not always tell the truth. At UCLA his supporters, with some exceptions, were of the first type. The distinguished and beleaguered Goldschmidt, who fully fits neither type, gave loyal support for a long time without accepting everything, but now seems close to judging that Castaneda mined "the literature of psychic phenomena, largely material from India, for his insights." And that "Don Juan is himself a literary creation."[9]

In our own Los Angeles office I have already mentioned the contrast between two experienced senior editors, both now retired. The sensible Kubeck, detached, amused, remembers Carlos as charming friend and liar. The subtle Zachary, no mystic but with mind honed on philosophic studies, says that the demystifications of *Time* and others are not the whole story. And continues thus:

> The importance of Castaneda's work does not rest upon the veracity of the don Juan story. Even if much of it is fictitious—and I doubt that it is entirely so—the point of the work for anthropology revolves about the so-called emic/etic (insider/outsider) distinction set forth in 1954 by the linguist Kenneth L. Pike.
>
> Oversimply: the inhabitant of a culture speaks emically. A scientist observing and describing speaks etically. Emic speech conveys an inside

9. Goldschmidt to Frugé, 1 April 1991.

truth, not available to the etic (outside) speaker. But the intellectual convention is that scientific truth is expressible only etically. A radical dilemma arises: if "inside" truth is the "real" truth, then the scientist-observer will always wander in outer darkness. But if the truth is real only when it is scientific, then the insider must be a prey to endless delusion . . . is in the purest sense one of Plato's cave-dwellers, seeing only shadows on the wall. Question: Can there be such a thing as a participatory observer, at once an outsider and an insider? Clearly there is danger: the scientist who wants to speak emically may simply "go native" and lose his scientific perspective. But if he is inflexibly etic, he sits above and outside the culture and winds up talking vacuous abstractions.[10]

We may remember—from the early part of this chapter—that the great Alfred Kroeber once said he could not write a history of the Yurok tribe because he felt himself too much a Yurok.

Zachary says that Carlos, in many conversations, almost never discussed magic, drugs, and the like, but showed himself much concerned with the insider/outsider dilemma and interested in the writings of Merleau-Ponty and Gadamer. And indeed we find the following in Castaneda's dissertation abstract:

> This is an emic account of an apprenticeship of sorcery as it is practiced by the American Indians of modern Mexico. . . . The sorcerer's contention is that the world at large, and our physical surroundings . . .
> are the product of the perceivers' agreement on the nature of what they perceive. . . .
>
> This basic premise of sorcery does not deny the objectivity of the world. For the sorcerer the world is not an illusion, quite the contrary, it is real, but its reality is not a fixed condition. In fact, it can be altered in part, or it can be changed altogether; thus the alleged magical properties of sorcery practice. This process of change is called "stopping the world" and can be explained as the volitional interruption of ordinary consensus. The "techniques of stopping the world" entail that at the same time the ordinary consensus is interrupted another one is ensued [sic] and in this way a new "description of the world" is brought into being.

10. Zachary to Frugé, 21 February 1991.

And there I shall leave these matters—hanging in the air. Perhaps there is no plain answer to questions about the nature of Castaneda's writings—perhaps not even in his own head. Was it the Lady or the Tiger waiting behind the door in Frank R. Stockton's old story? Each reader, I seem to remember, was told to supply his own conclusion. Such uncertainty once troubled me. I am older now.

II Hollywood and Berkeley
Getting into the Film Business

In the mid 1940s Sam Farquhar experienced a brief encounter with Hollywood. Out of this came a book, *Writers' Congress: Proceedings* (1944), and a magazine, *Hollywood Quarterly* (1945–). The book lived its short life and expired, as symposia
are apt to do. The *Quarterly* endured political troubles, survived,
evolved, and then underwent a curious metamorphosis into something the progenitors had never intended. And in this new form it
has spawned a long shelf of rather unHollywoodian books.

The Writers' Congress, out of which came the book, was held on
the UCLA campus in October 1943 and was sponsored jointly by the
University and the Hollywood Writers' Mobilization, an "independent war propaganda and information" agency[1] that was launched
the day after Pearl Harbor and worked with several government agen-
cies in promoting the war effort. It can be speculated that Farquhar
and the Press became involved through two Los Angeles members of
the Editorial Committee, Gustave Arlt and Franklin Fearing. The
book was published in October 1944, the very month when I came to
the Press as Farquhar's assistant.

Meanwhile, and probably out of discussions at the congress,
there came the plan for a new journal that would draw on the combined talents of the University and the more intellectual side of Hol-

---

1. So called in *The Inquisition in Hollywood,* by Larry Ceplair and Steven Englund
(1980).

lywood, as found in the Mobilization and in the Screen Writers' Guild. An uneasy alliance, one may think now, but all things seemed possible in those days of the second Popular Front, when communists, liberals, and even nonpolitical types thought they could work together toward a common goal.

In presenting the plan to the Editorial Committee and asking for use of the imprint, Farquhar stated in August 1944 that the journal would carry "articles by professional writers, for the most part those who write for the screen and radio, addressed to other professional writers." Unmentioned but surely intended—and borne out by the contents of the journal—were research articles on mass communication, the specialty of Franklin Fearing, one of the University supporters. Once more the Hollywood Writers' Mobilization was to be cosponsor. The name *Hollywood Quarterly* was chosen to indicate the double character of the enterprise—*Hollywood* for the profession, *Quarterly* for academia. The format was to be academic: text only, no pix.

In asking President Sproul's approval, as well as that of the Editorial Committee, Farquhar stressed that intellectual control would rest with the University. Two members of the editorial board would be appointed by the Mobilization, two by the UCLA provost while he, Farquhar, would be the fifth member, with the swing vote. He had already insisted that there be no propaganda, no ideological slant to left or right—so he put it, meaning left. The Tenney committee of the California legislature had been at work spotting communists, real and alleged, in Hollywood and trying to find others in the University, but it is doubtful whether anyone concerned guessed at the greater threats to come.

On advice of the administrative council of deans, Sproul at first disapproved the proposal but later, after persuasion from UCLA faculty members, he and the council reconsidered. The first issue came out in the fall of 1945. Enthusiasm ran high. Subscriptions rolled in, solicited by the Mobilization. Copies were placed in stores and on newsstands. I can remember selling quantities to a large sidewalk stand on Cherokee, just off Hollywood Boulevard.

In this first issue, just after the end of the war, the editors asked: "What part will the motion picture and the radio play in the consolidation of the victory, in the creation of new patterns in world culture and understanding?" The *Quarterly* would seek an answer, they said, "by presenting the record of research and exploration in motion pictures and radio in order to provide a basis for evaluation of economic, social, aesthetic, educational, and technological trends." A large ambition, one may think. Four years later the *Quarterly* called itself, more narrowly, "a journal of the media of mass communication" and mentioned television.

The first editors from the Mobilization were Kenneth Macgowan, a producer at Paramount, not much involved in politics as far as I know, and John Howard Lawson, a screenwriter who later became one of the Hollywood Ten and went to jail for contempt of Congress. The two from the University faculty were Franklin Fearing and Franklin Rolfe, from the UCLA departments of psychology and English. That was a long time ago, and I remember nothing substantive about the board meetings I attended; I do remember that they were lively and that the two Hollywood members struck me as sharp and quick-witted.

Every year thereafter brought changes. Farquhar was subpoenaed, along with UCLA Provost Dykstra, as a witness before the Tenney committee, which investigated the *Quarterly* in 1946. Jack Lawson (and one other, I think, from an expanded board) resigned when they came under fire from the House Un-American Activities Committee. Kenneth Macgowan left Hollywood and joined the UCLA faculty—despite Senator Tenney's protests—as professor of theater arts; there he served as chairman of that department during its great period of growth and eventually had a rather grand building named after him. The Mobilization declined in the chill of the cold war and was disbanded in 1947. An independent group calling itself the Hollywood Quarterly Associates was formed to act as joint sponsor, but with the Winter 1947–48 number the University took over sole sponsorship. In 1949, however, there were still four Hollywood members on an editorial board of eight—John Collier, James Hilton,

Irving Pichel, and Abe Polonsky—but the *Quarterly* had become practically a publication of the theater arts department. There was an assistant editor, who did most of the work for the board—at this time Sylvia Jarrico, who with her husband Paul became deeply involved in the fight with HUAC. She departed after the University imposed a loyalty oath later that year.

Eventually the Hollywood connection disappeared, and beginning with the issue for Fall 1951 (vol. 6, no. 1) the journal was renamed the *Quarterly of Film, Radio, and Television*. Under this name it continued for another six years, running gradually down—or so I seem to remember—as the emphasis became more sociological and less cinematic. After Sylvia Jarrico came a succession of assistant editors, or managing editors as they were sometimes called, who worked under the editorial board but who were paid as members of the Press staff and who did not always fit in well. The last of these, who need not be named, made a practice of threatening to resign in order to get her way. One day in 1957, when I was visiting the Los Angeles office, she tried this ploy once more. Accepting the resignation, I bid her good-bye. There was no visible distress in the office.

I then braced myself for trouble with the editorial board. But when Macgowan, the chairman, came in to discuss the matter, there was no blood in his eye. Appearing to understand our staff problem, he wondered whether they could find another qualified person. In the end, and after a quiet talk, he sighed and said that perhaps the time had come to bring the enterprise to a halt. He himself—here I speculate—was again involved with his early love, the theater, and perhaps retained only a diminishing interest in film, or in the sociological aspects of it. The other editors put up no fight, for what reasons I know not, although the subscription list was down to about three hundred, mostly libraries. It is a wise editor who knows when the time has come to stop. Journals are not immortal; like the flu they eventually run their course, although the running down is not always plain to those most concerned. And so the old *Quarterly* died with neither a bang nor a whimper but with a shrug of the shoulders.

That should have been the end of the affair, but I hesitated. The

Quarterly had a University subvention, as did our other journals, including funds to pay the part-time editor. We might have let the money revert to the state, as it would have if left long enough, but an idea had begun to form itself, fed from two sources. Now and then, between appointments in the Los Angeles office, I had whiled away the time by looking at other film journals received on exchange for the *Quarterly,* particularly *Sight and Sound* (London) and *Cahiers du cinéma* (Paris). The latter was especially attractive; I still remember a rambling but illuminating interview with Jean Renoir. There was no American review comparable to these two, intellectual but not academic and devoted to film as an art and not as communication. By accident we found ourselves with the means to publish one—if we chose and if we knew how.

I had also been talking to my one friend in the film business, an eloquent young Frisian named Andries Deinum, whom I had met through the painter Rico Lebrun. Deinum had been teaching film at the University of Southern California, but in 1955 he too came up against the House Un-American Activities Committee. After testifying that he had for a short time been a member of the Communist Party in Hollywood, he refused to name the names of others. For this refusal he was dismissed at USC.

Deinum and I had spent some time discussing film and related matters, I testing my amateur and rather literary interest against his knowledge and his great ability to talk and, talking, to enlighten. So when two things coincided—the thought of a new journal and his lack of a job—it was natural to put them together and ask whether, if we started a journal, he might be willing to take the job of editor. The answer was no. The University, he said, would never allow me to hire him. I thought it would. The loyalty oath, in its objectionable early form, was long gone; the air smelled reasonably free. I had never intended to consult President Sproul, as Farquhar would have done in the old days; in the expanded university Sproul was no longer second-guessing our decisions. To ask permission was to invite trouble. Better to decide what was best and go ahead. But Deinum was right on another score: his own incomparable ability was for the spoken word, for the give and take of teaching, the quick flash of discussion. Soon thereafter he began teaching at Portland State University, where he remained until retirement, much loved by his students.

Meanwhile he made a suggestion. Perhaps you don't know, said he, that you already have a film critic on your staff. He then mentioned Ernest Callenbach, who at that time was writing book jacket copy for our sales department and whose cinematic past was unknown to me, in spite of his contributions to the defunct *Quarterly*. My recollection is that Callenbach was reluctant to take on the new job, or perhaps only cautious, wondering whether it might forestall any other future he might have in mind for himself. Wondering also whether enough good critical material could be found. But we talked, and he considered.

Before making up his mind he suggested Pauline Kael, who was then living in Berkeley and had made a local reputation writing blurbs for the pictures shown in a repertory movie house near campus—more illuminating, some of us have thought, than her well-known later reviews. She came in for a discussion, and it was, in Callenbach's words, an oil-and-water situation. Almost immediately it became clear that she and I did not think alike and would never be able to work together. For one thing, she wanted a completely free hand, which we would not give. So off she went, but during the next few years she contributed a number of pieces to the new journal before going east, where she made her reputation in more popular magazines.

Callenbach agreed to a one-year trial, and we set up an advisory board that included Deinum; Gavin Lambert, former editor of *Sight and Sound* and by then a script writer in Hollywood; Albert Johnson of Berkeley; Hugh Gray, Paul Jorgensen, and Colin Young[2] of UCLA. Like Farquhar, I included myself, but for a nonpolitical reason, wanting merely to share in the first shaping of editorial policy. Three

2. Young became one of Macgowan's successors as chairman of the theater arts department and later founded the British National Film School in London, of which he is still head.

of those named—Deinum, Johnson, and Young—are still connected with *Film Quarterly,* as the re-born journal was called, although two of them are no longer active.

Unlike most such boards this one actually met each quarter to consider manuscripts and talk about where we were going. To oil the mechanism of discussion, the Press provided Rémy Martin, and the talk was lively. The intellectual sparks flew whenever Deinum and Lambert engaged the same matter. The relation between board and editor became collegial, as the editor called it, with decisions reached by consensus rather than by vote, and so it has continued, with Rémy Martin giving way to plainer potions.

The use of the imprint was approved by the Editorial Committee, and the first issue appeared in the fall of 1958, called volume 12, number 1. As we were making use of the old subvention (for a time), it seemed advisable to continue the old numbering, with the omission of one year in the dating. In his first Editor's Notebook, Callenbach wrote, "*Film Quarterly* is coming in, of course, at a time when Hollywood is passing the end of an era. The great studio machines, which once ground out pictures like sausages for the maw of the block-booking system, have gone the way of the dinosaur." And in the second issue, "Some readers have wondered at the omission of a manifesto. . . . The total continuing effect of the magazine will serve as manifesto enough. . . . For one thing we are in favor of cinematic movies, still believing that film is an art form in itself."

After the trial period revealed that plenty of good material could be had, the new journal went on. Continues on, and still shows no sign of exhaustion, as the old one did. And now, as the founding editor contemplates retirement after thirty-three years on the masthead, enthusiasm appears undiminished, subscription numbers hold firm.[3] But Callenbach has another career to pursue. Beginning with publication of *Ecotopia* (Banyan Tree Books, 1975), he has built himself a wide reputation as author and lecturer on ecological matters.

3. Since I wrote this, Callenbach has retired, joined the editorial board, and been succeeded as editor by Ann Martin.

Callenbach at work. Photo by R. D. Deines.

It happened that the journal came into the film field, as Callenbach says, along with a number of fresh intellectual and artistic movements such as the French New Wave, cinéma vérité, and others, and just before the great explosion of university film studies. Interest soared; writing proliferated. Other film journals followed this one and now, he says, *Film Quarterly* occupies a place near the middle of the road, between the rather esoteric scholarly journals and those more popular.

The critical treatment evolved; the topic remained alive. Long ago I took myself off the editorial board, having served my initial purpose and finding also that changing critical practices had moved beyond my amateur and perhaps old-fashioned interest. And it may be noted that the audience too has changed. Perhaps the greatest number of readers, and certainly of contributors, are now connected with the many university teaching programs that did not exist, most of them, when *Film Quarterly* began publication.

Like other journals of distinctive character, this one has become an extension of the editor's intelligence, imagination, and taste. There has been help and advice from critics and teachers on the advisory board, but the editor is in a very real sense the "onlie begetter." How the journal will evolve under a new editor is hard to predict. It is unlikely, I should think, to move in a popular direction, but there are apt to be pressures toward academic specialization. We may remember what happened to the old *Quarterly* and be wary.

Looking back thirty-three years I wonder that I could have had the nerve, without anyone's approval, to take the old journal's subsidy and use it to gamble on a new journal of quite a different kind. But by happy fortune we put our chips on a right number at the right time, the wheel spun, and the number turned up.

And there has been a second pay-off, a long list of film books, chosen by the same editor with wit and discrimination and designed largely for advanced film studies. Even before *Film Quarterly* led us on, there were a few books: first the Writers' Congress volume mentioned earlier and then in 1951 Raymond Spottiswoode's *Film and Its Techniques*. This began life as a syllabus, put together for a UCLA course by a visiting teacher. Converted into an advanced textbook, it proved the best, almost the only, thing in the field, especially for documentary film, and went through a number of editions. But after the author's accidental death in England, we were never able to find a successor who could keep the book up to date.

A little later we began publishing Rudolf Arnheim, whose interests included film and who has stayed with us ever since, a fine example of author loyalty, producing nearly a dozen excellent books. First of these on our list was *Art and Visual Perception: A Psychology of the Creative Eye* (1954), which quickly became a classic and was followed over the years by books on the psychology of art and related topics. Or one might say on *Visual Thinking,* one of his titles.

In 1957, in our second paperback list, appeared Arnheim's *Film as Art,* a revised edition of a book first printed in Germany in 1932 with the same title, *Film als Kunst,* shortly before the author left that country, a few steps ahead of the Nazis. A translation appeared in London in 1933 but was long out of print in the 1950s although well remembered by film people. For the new edition Arnheim rethought the contents, dropped some parts, and added two pieces written in fascist Italy for an encyclopedia of the cinema, which reached page proofs but never appeared. This is a book of standards, said the author, a study of the basic nature of film as an art. In 1991 it is still in print and used in film courses.

These were forerunners. The main film list came later, paralleling the development of *Film Quarterly,* and it was, I think, the first systematic attempt of any university press to publish books in this field, although Oxford (New York) had a few early titles. After the books had gained a reputation, a number of other presses jumped into the film field, as did some commercial firms and little publishers. There are now more books than anyone can read. More, as Callenbach has written in an appeal for wider reviewing, than are properly noticed in journals other than this one. In the 1990 round-up of film books, good, half good, and not so good, the *Quarterly* listed, annotated, or reviewed more than 130 titles, a remarkable output on a topic that publishers ignored just a few years ago. It is natural to wonder whether *Film Quarterly* brought this about, in part at least, or whether we rode a wave that was already coming in.

I am perhaps the only person who can remember back to the peculiar beginnings in 1944. Since the past is compelling to those who remember it, I may have treated small happenings large and given too little space to greater and continuing ones. But the latter are familiar to those in the know and have little need of my comment. Most of the early publications have long ago been superseded, outgrown, or retired to the shelf, but it is not unreasonable to remember that they once existed, and that without their having been, the new ones would not be. In some genuine sense our many years of publishing about film, the prominence of the Press in this field, together with the hundreds of books and journal issues, all these things sprang— unintended perhaps—out of Sam Farquhar's brief wartime flirtation with Hollywood.

12 London, 1660 and 1960
The Coded Words of Sam Pepys

A t the time when I used to call on them, G. Bell & Sons were an old and old-fashioned family firm. Their publishing list was a motley collection of school books and practical books, graced only by the old Wheatley edition of *Pepys' Diary* and a group of books on chess. They had offices in a building they owned, called York House, on Portugal Street, just off Kings Way. Across the street, improbably enough, was the aggressively modern and left-thinking London School of Economics and the Economist Book Store. More in keeping, a few blocks away and passed when we went to lunch, was the Old Curiosity Shop. There was indeed a Dickensian look about Bells, we thought, as there still was about some other London publishing offices.

The front door led not to a display room with a welcoming or snippy receptionist, as found elsewhere, but to a small shipping room where a few books were laid out on a counter and an old man was doing odd jobs. On learning that I had come to see the managing director, Mr. Glanville, the old man would telephone upstairs—they did have telephones—and Glanville would come tumbling down the back stairs on long legs and lead me up again to the dark library room where we could spread out our papers and, when my eyes had adjusted to the dim light, talk business. More friendly, I thought, than being given vague directions and left to find my way through a rabbit warren of office cubicles, as sometimes happened in London.

When I first visited York House, old Colonel Bell was still alive but inactive, nearly ninety. He had had a long military career in India, Africa, and elsewhere, and was also an expert on divining rods, having published several books on the subject, including *The Elements of Dowsing* and *How to Dowse*. When Bob Zachary (our Los Angeles editor) asked him about his success in finding water, he replied that he had no interest in water but divined for archaeological deposits—artifacts, building foundations, and the like.

At that time the managing director was a Mr. Ready, who died shortly thereafter and was succeeded by Richard Glanville, who had, I think, married into the Bell family. It was Glanville with whom I had dealings for many years and came to know rather well. He seemed formal and reserved, or perhaps merely shy, but was intelligent, friendly, and easy to talk with. I found myself liking him and only slightly uneasy about his casual way with agreements. For several years we had an informal and oral understanding about the American edition of the new Pepys volumes, with nothing on paper except what was implicit in our letters, but I always trusted him and never feared he might deal with someone else behind my back. I would not have trusted many publishers in this way. It was not until 1970, when the first volumes were coming out, that we drew up a written contract.

Meanwhile we talked and corresponded about ways to deal with the two general editors, who were difficult in their different ways, who hated each other and distrusted us. Perhaps they were both miscast. If one were planning from scratch a new edition of a sprightly and irreverent literary masterpiece, one that required both precise transcription and literary flair, it would make sense to hire as textual editor a scholar who is sober, methodical, and patient, and to entrust the general commentary to one with wit, imagination, and a light touch. That the Pepys was done quite the other way around came about by accident. The first thought of a new edition arose as early as 1929; thereafter decisions must have been made—by Magdalene College, Cambridge, owner of the diary, and by Bells—one at a time, with the great end not clearly in sight. If the end result is a wonderful book, as it surely is, the wonder derives mostly from the author himself, although credit enough remains for those who rescued his words from the shorthand manuscript and provided the reader with help on the seventeenth-century setting.

We the publishers understood and respected each other, different as we were, but the editors were always in conflict. On some ticklish matters it came about that I dealt with Will Matthews in California while Glanville dealt with the other editor, Robert Latham, in England. At times I was caught in the middle, as when Matthews demanded that I join him in trying to squeeze more money out of Bells. Both editors felt that a library (in this case Magdalene College) had no business taking a royalty. Royalty should go to them, they thought, in addition to the fees they were getting from Bells. Glanville dealt with them patiently, avoiding fights but never giving way. In one of my letters, praising his delaying tactics, I called him Glanville *cunctator*. Whether he saw himself as a kind of Fabius Maximus, he never said.

If the original fees paid by Bells were quite modest, as they must have been, we may bear in mind that Matthews probably wangled a couple of academic promotions for his part of the work and that Latham turned his into a "living," although perhaps a modest one. He was made Pepys Librarian and a fellow of Magdalene College.

The two editors were both English by origin, although Matthews was not Oxbridge and was quite Americanized. He had studied at Ruskin College, University of London—the working-man's college where students had to work full-time at genuine outside jobs. Will's job had something to do with stenography, I think. When he typed, said Zachary, it sounded like the wind blowing through the trees. As professor of English at UCLA he had multiple interests and talents, his primary field being medieval literature, especially Malory and Chaucer—Pepys' favorite author. He had once written an excellent book on cockney dialect. His work on the history of shorthand systems and his published bibliographies of diaries and autobiographies must have recommended him for the Pepys job.

Matthews was quick at everything he did and also quick-witted and amusing, brilliant and also impatient, always wishing to finish the job in hand and move on to something else. It may be too much to say that he could be a little slap-dash—with the help of his wife Lois he went through the Pepys text five times—but he may sometimes have trusted his memory whereas his partner would have looked up every detail. And Matthews had his emotional ups and downs. In some of the up periods he was wonderfully productive of books and articles, but in these manic moods he could turn on his friends, including me.

Matthews' part of the editorial work was to prepare a complete and accurate text, a million and a quarter words of it, including all the many parts omitted in earlier editions. The difficulties of this I will come to later. He also wrote those parts of the introduction that relate to the text and to the diary as literature, and did the notes that had to do with language and literature.

Latham, the historian, had been hired to assist the Pepys librarian when a revision, not a completely new version, was first planned, and eventually inherited the job of editor. If it was he who suggested Matthews for the textual work, he surely came to regret this advice, for he was quite the opposite kind of scholar—slow, careful, methodical, anxious to control every phase of the project, stretching out the one job to make a life work of it, hoping for a professorship that never came and bitter that it did not. He even redid the index, giving virtually no credit to the man who had been hired to do it volume by volume, so that it was not published until seven years after the last volume of text. Once when Zachary called on him, he was "luxuriating" in a list of more than one hundred coffee houses frequented by Pepys. It may not be unfair to say that he had the soul of an indexer, but one should add that his type of mind is valuable in a work that should be free of error.

If the two men could have admired, or at least accepted, each other's qualities, their different talents—each supplying what the other lacked—might have made the partnership an almost ideal one. But neither would give credit to the other. Each complained to me about the other, Matthews chafing at Latham's deliberate slowness, possessiveness, and lack of imagination, and Latham claiming that he had to correct Matthews' transcription of the shorthand. Reading the introduction, one who knew both of them can read between the lines and see them jockeying for position, competing for credit rather than sharing it. In the long run Latham had the survivor's advantage; Matthews died in 1975 as the last volumes of text were going through the press and before the abridgments were due to come out.

By agreement Latham got the lion's share—two-thirds, I think—of the fee for the big edition, while Matthews was slated to receive a like portion of the fee for the one-volume abridgment. For this work he made a selection just before his death. It went on the shelf, where it may still be. Since his widow died shortly after he did, there was no one to plead its cause. Thereafter Latham edited three different one-volume versions and took full credit.

Samuel Pepys lived through the last two-thirds of the seventeenth century and three years into the eighteenth. Those were not quiet times. Pepys was a boy during the great civil war when Oliver Cromwell became lord protector of England. As a teenager in 1649, he stood in the crowd at Westminster and saw King Charles I lose his head. Eleven years later, as secretary to his cousin, Lord Montagu, he sailed in the squadron that brought Charles II home from exile in Holland, thus restoring the monarchy. It was shortly before this, in January 1660 at the age of twenty-seven, that he began the great diary. He wrote in it nearly every day until he feared for his eyesight nine years later.

The Journal, as Pepys usually called it, was virtually unknown for more than a hundred years after his death. Pepys' own contemporaries knew him as a public servant, a naval administrator. During the diary period he occupied the important government post of Clerk of the Acts to the Navy Board, a group of four officials who had charge of the civil administration of the navy: building and repairing ships, managing the dock yards, purchasing supplies. As clerk, Pepys handled correspondence, negotiated contracts, and generally managed the office. Managed also to feather his own nest, as was the custom of the day, with tips, bribes, and other more or less accepted ways of adding to his personal income. The diary gives, at the end of almost every year, figures on his steadily increasing fortune.

The administration of the navy became Pepys' life work. In 1673, after the diary period, he became secretary of the admiralty, resigning in 1679, when he was accused of treasonable activities and sent briefly to the Tower. But five years later he was back again as King's Secretary for the affairs of the admiralty and continued in that post after Charles II died and was succeeded by the duke of York, a special patron of Pepys, who became James II. As secretary, Pepys was virtually in charge of the admiralty, the operating or sea-going, side of the navy, as distinguished from the civilian service. And it was he, according to biographers, who more than anyone else reorganized and modernized the navy, equipping it to fight the great wars of the eighteenth century. The third volume of Sir Arthur Bryant's biography of Pepys is entitled *The Savior of the Navy* (1938).

After retirement in 1689 Pepys lived as a private person, enjoying and enlarging his collection of books, manuscripts, and music scores, and corresponding with the learned men of the time. Among his friends and acquaintances were the poet John Dryden, who attended Cambridge with him; John Evelyn, the other noted diarist of the day; the architect Christopher Wren, who was building the new St. Paul's cathedral to replace the one burnt in the Great Fire; the poet Rochester, known for his obscene verses; and the scientists Boyle, Hooke, and Newton. It was Pepys, during his tenure as president of the Royal Society, who signed the imprimatur of Newton's *Principia Mathematica*.

Pepys began his book collecting during the diary years, when he first had money to spend, and kept it up all his life, accumulating a considerable library. In the London of that time there were bookshops enough to satisfy all tastes. In 1666, it is said, there were twenty-three of them in St. Paul's Churchyard alone. We may note in passing that this part of London was associated with books for several

hundred years until in 1940 the famous publishing district of Pater-
noster Row, near St. Paul's, was fire-bombed out of existence. When
I first started calling on British publishers in the 1950s, a great devas-
tated area stretched eastward from there, but some firms—such as
Routledge & Kegan Paul—were still housed in surviving buildings
not far away. As the years passed, most publishers moved westward.

By the terms of Pepys' will, his library went first to his nephew
and heir, John Jackson, and then to his old college, Magdalene, Cambridge. By that time there were three thousand volumes and many
more titles—some bound together—in history, science, music, the-
ology, public affairs, plays, and other literature in ancient and modern
languages. Pepys seems to have read easily enough in French and
Spanish, had Latin of course and a smattering of Greek from his
school days. The volumes were housed in twelve large oak presses
(bookcases) and were shelved by size rather than by subject, large
tomes on the bottom shelves and smaller ones above. There they still
are in the same presses, where I saw them several times when I called
on Latham.

The library was housed in the "New Building" at Magdalene,
completed in about 1700 and now called the Pepys Building. For the
next one hundred years and more no one seems to have paid much
attention to six large volumes bound in calf and labeled "Journal." Or
perhaps because they were written in shorthand the viewer glanced
and went on, not taking the trouble to sample. It was not until the
early nineteenth century, when the diary of Pepys' friend John Evelyn
appeared, that the suggestion was made to publish Pepys' journal
also.

A transcription from the shorthand was made by John Smith, an
undergraduate at St. Johns, complete except for some passages considered objectionable. Of this, a selection, about a quarter of the
whole, was published by Lord Braybrook in 1825, 122 years after the
death of the author, and became an immediate success, going through
several editions. Another transcription, this one quite incomplete,
was made by the Reverend Mynors Bright and published in six volumes in 1875. A revision and expansion of this, with notes and com-

Pepys' Library in the house in York Buildings, King Street, 1693.

mentary, was edited by H. B. Wheatley and published by George Bell
and Sons in 1893–99; this became the standard edition until superseded in the 1970s by the Bell-California edition. Although the
Wheatley contained about nine-tenths of the diary, it was less accu-
rately transcribed than the old version by Smith; it was bowdlerized;
it sometimes dropped out passages from oversight or carelessness. If
this was not enough reason for a new and more adequate edition,
there was the small matter of copyright: the old version was going
out of copyright and would become available to all publishers.

Pepys never says why he decided to keep a personal journal but must
have planned it well in advance, because he began on the first day of
January 1660, with a preliminary note on the "condition of the state,"
while the first entry describes his own condition, thus: "Blessed be
God, at the end of the last year I was in good health, without any
sense of my old pain . . . my own private condition very handsome
and esteemed rich, but endeed very poor." The old pain was from

Pepys' Library, Cambridge, 1974. Books and cases are the same.

kidney stones. He had undergone surgery for removal of these—fearfully risky in those days—and every year on 26 March he celebrated with a festival, or at least a dinner, the success of the operation.

After this rather formal beginning the entries come almost daily, some brief but many quite full, even long, and nearly all personal in tone. It has been said that no man ever revealed himself so completely—his desires, noble and petty, his courage and cowardice, his love for books and music and even for his wife, poor wretch, as he called her—a term of affection, says the glossary. Everything that he did or that happened to him, great or petty, happy or shameful, is set down frankly.

Pepys was a great play-goer at a time when Restoration drama was flourishing. He avidly collected money as well as books, and treated himself to the good things in life, including wine, cheeses, and barrels of oysters. He was an amateur musician and an amateur, in a rather different sense, of female charms, indefatigable in his pursuit of shop girls, servant girls, and the occasional matron, one of

Barbara Castlemaine as the Madonna. After Lely.

whom was a carpenter's wife. He never seems to have laid hands on women of higher station, although he wrote admiringly of Nell Gwyn, the actress, and enjoyed a happy dream about Lady Castle-maine—both mistresses of the king.

Other topics of interest are his travels about the city by street and by river; great national events such as the Dutch wars and the return of Charles II; the Great Plague and the Great Fire, both of which Pepys saw and survived. "We find in the delectable wealth of these memoirs ten years of the concrete history of England as seen from a central point by a diligent, assimilating observer." [1]

But the large events, the personal style, and the unashamed frankness of the writing are not sufficient in themselves to account for the fascination of the book. Most important, perhaps, is that Pepys was blessed with a supremely happy temperament, and that he possessed the power of breathing life into what he wrote. He took pleasure in almost everything; each new event was the greatest ever. "His *Diary* wins and holds us as would that of a child greedy for sensation." Pepys writes with gusto even about misfortunes and seems to enjoy repenting his sins. Thus, after an episode with the carpenter's wife (23 January 1665): " . . . back again and to my office, where I did with great content faire a vow to mind my own business and laisser aller les femmes for a month." More later about the mixture of languages.

During the Great Plague of 1665 life for Pepys—as for some others—seems to have been business (and pleasure) almost as usual. He sent his wife to Woolich, down the river, and moved his navy offices to Greenwich, but went into London by boat nearly every day, busy making money and making assignations. So, on 26 July: "I have to set my journal for these four days in order, they being four days of as great content and honor and pleasure to me as ever I hope to live or desire. . . . This day poor Robin Shaw at Bakewell is died . . . the sickness is got into our parish this week; and is endeed everywhere." On the last day of the plague year he reports that his estate has increased from 1,300 to 4,400 pounds.

In general the writing is more lively than poetic, more gossipy than philosophic, but there are some fine flights of style, imbued with strong feeling. After the dream of dalliance with Barbara Castlemaine (15 August 1665) he goes on: "But that since it was a dream and that I took so much pleasure in it, what a happy thing it would be, if when we are in our graves (as Shakespeare resembles it), we could dream,

---

1. This quotation and one in the next paragraph are from E. Legouis and L. Cazamian, *A History of English Literature* (London, 1960), 682 and 683.

and dream but such dreams as this—that then we should not need to be so fearful of death as we are this plague-time."

And of a love less carnal (27 February 1668): " . . . but that which did please me beyond anything in the whole world was the wind-musique when the Angell comes down, which is so sweet that it rav-ished me; and endeed, in a word, did wrap up my soul so that it made me really sick, just as I have formerly been when in love with my wife; that neither then, nor all the evening going home and at home, I was able to think of anything, but remained all night transported, so as I could not believe that ever any music hath that real command over the soul of a man as this did upon me; and makes me resolve to practice wind-music and make my wife do the like." Wind-music is that of the recorder, I think.

But only a few weeks later Pepys was laying siege to the virtue of his wife's new maid, a girl of about fifteen named Deb Willett. The long campaign is described blow-by-blow, and for the first time his wife catches him in flagrante "con my hand sub su coats" (25 October 1668), an event that "occasioned the greatest sorrow to me that ever I knew in this world. . . . I was at a wonderful loss upon it, and the girl also . . . but my wife was struck mute and grew angry." The anger persisted; on the following 12 January she came after him with a pair of red-hot tongs. He talked her into putting them away.

After the plague of 1665 there came the Great Fire of the follow-ing year. Pepys' description of it extends over a number of entries and is one of the glories of the diary. Thus, 4 September: "Sir W Penn and I to Tower-street, and there met the fire . . . coming on in that narrow street, on both sides, in infinite fury. . . . Sir W Batten, not knowing how to remove his wine, did dig a pit in the garden and laid it in there. . . . And in the evening Sir W Penn and I did dig another and put our wine in it, and I my parmazan cheeses. . . . Now begins the practice of blowing up houses in Tower-street, those next the Tower, which at first did frighten people more than anything; but it stopped the fire where it was done."

Neither fire nor plague nor red-hot tongs brought the diary to a close. For a long time Pepys had suffered trouble with his eyes, strained from writing shorthand for long hours by candlelight. At last, fearing that he was going blind, he put an end to the diary in May 1669: "And thus ends all that I doubt I shall ever be able to do with my own eyes in the keeping of my journal, I being not able to do it any longer, having done now so long as to undo my eyes almost every time that I take a pen in hand; and therefore, whatever comes of it, I must forebear. . . . And so I betake myself to that course which is almost as much as to see myself go into my grave—for which, and all the discomforts that will accompany my being blind, the good God prepare me."

But he never went blind. Probably he was suffering from astigmatism. His eyes improved, and he lived another thirty-four years, flourishing in public and in personal life, but without leaving a record of his private thoughts and acts and opinions.

One may presume that Pepys wrote most of the diary in shorthand to foil the prying eyes of wife and friends but not to prevent eventual reading or transcription. The shorthand system used was a rather simple one, known to many educated people. First issued in 1626 as *Short Writing,* by Thomas Shelton, it was later published as *Tachygraphy,* by the Cambridge University Press, and went through more than twenty editions, according to Will Matthews. Pepys probably learned the system while a student at Cambridge.[2]

This shorthand, one of several in vogue in the seventeenth century, used straight and curving lines to indicate consonants, with vowels represented sometimes by the position of the lines following them and sometimes by dots. Since provision is made for only five sounds, long and short vowels are put down in the same way, and there is no separate way of showing diphthongs. Thus words of similar spelling or similar sounds must be identified according to the context. And to the original system Pepys added his own idiosyncrasies, including occasional words in longhand, many of these abbreviated.

2. See Matthews' account of the diary in *The Diary of Samuel Pepys* (1970–83) 1:xli–lxvii.

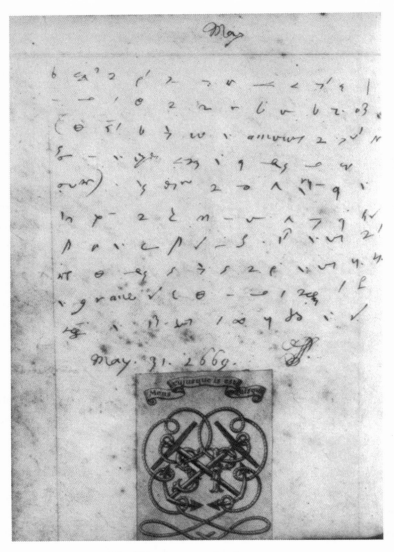

The Diary manuscript, last page.

Thus there is an inherent ambiguity; there can never be an absolutely exact transcription; if there were, it would not be readable. The transcriber can only attempt to determine the intentions of the writer, and in some matters, such as spelling, these cannot always be known.

To the ambiguity of shorthand Pepys added a further disguise, especially in the many erotic passages, printed for the first time in the new edition. He used a kind of lingua franca, as Matthews calls it, a potpourri of English, French, Spanish, Latin, along with a few words of Greek and other languages. Sometimes, when the disguised words are not especially revealing, one gets the impression that he is being more playful than cautious. Thus, describing a grubby little scene with the daughter of a waterman who came to beg the release of his son, pressed into the navy, Pepys uses all five languages mentioned above. But the two Greek words in that alphabet mean only "at another time," when, the writer thinks, he will get further with her. One cannot help suspecting that the girl was instructed to go part way but not too far. Whether the son was released, we are not told (23 August 1665).

But we can be happy—in contradiction to my earlier remarks—that the transcriber, Matthews, was no methodical drudge but a man of wit and imagination. He was also blessed, as I remember, with what we used to call a dirty mind, one attuned to Pepys' own ways of thinking.

On 16 January 1664 Pepys met a Mrs. Lane at Westminster Hall, took her to a place on "the street du roy" and, after some caresses, reports that he tumbled her "sous de la chaise deux times." Here, perhaps, it is possible to question the transcription. The Shelton system can make no distinction between the French *ou* and *u* sounds, and one might expect the preposition *sur* rather than *sous,* on rather than under the chair. But in this case perhaps we need not ask for precision.

We were involved with Sam Pepys and his journal for so very long that I have no sure memory of how it all began. I seem to recall a meeting of the Editorial Committee in the Press library sometime in the 1950s—I think it was—when one of the members, professor of English at UCLA, was called out for a long-distance telephone call. Later that day Will Matthews told me that the call had come from London and that he had been asked to be one of two general editors of a new and (at last) complete edition of a great English literary classic, the diary of Samuel Pepys.

My predatory instincts must have been aroused at once, and I began to wonder whether we could use the UCLA connection as a lever to make ourselves publishers of the Diary—of the American edition, that is, since it was unthinkable that the British would allow their own market to be supplied from a former colony. I learned that literary rights, through inheritance from Pepys, belonged to Magdalene College. For a publisher the college might have gone a few blocks down the street to the Cambridge University Press, but instead they stuck with G. Bell & Sons, the London firm that had sold the Wheatley edition for many years and indeed still had it in print.

The contribution from UCLA was not a minor one: paid leaves of absence for Matthews together with travel grants were surely worth much more in dollars or pounds than Bells would pay him. So at first I thought that Matthews, from his position inside, or halfway inside, might swing the deal for us, but it soon became apparent that he either could not or would not do anything effective, and that I was on my own. So I got on a plane and went to see Bells.

At some point I found that we had another and unexpected advantage. Bells were afraid that an American commercial publisher might play up the sensational aspects of the new and unexpurgated edition, might even advertise in such places as *Playboy* and *Hustler* magazines—unlikely places, you might think, to sell this kind of book. Bells judged that a university press, being almost as conservative as themselves, would not do this. They also told me that on advice of attorneys they felt safe from prosecution if they published the diary absolutely complete, as befitted a great literary work, but might be in trouble if they printed some of the erotic passages and omitted anything else. The age of permissiveness had not yet dawned.

So I went to see Bells and over the next years called on them more times than I can remember. There was no single day of decision, no point when we shook hands and said that we had a deal. Glanville was not playing hard to get, I think, or stalling for better terms; this was merely his way of operating, and I was well advised to go along with it. Early on, memory suggests, I thought to settle the matter by offering to share capital costs long before the books went into production, but the offer was brushed aside. They had money enough; they owned their building. So we just went on discussing various matters such as quantity for the American market, discount from the English price, our need for simultaneous publication and for a comparable retail price to avoid buying around. Glanville never resisted these requests, as some London publishers would have. In time, it was simply understood, if never put into formal words, that we would be joint publishers. In the written agreement, when it was finally drawn up, he accepted my wish for American rights to all shorter editions and other subsidiary publications. It was good to have this spelled out; Glanville retired not long after I did, and the firm was sold to outsiders.

The big edition was published in nine volumes (1970–76) for nine and a fraction years of the diary. Seven years later came volumes 10 and 11, the *Companion* and the *Index,* both put together by Latham. The *Companion,* with contributions by a number of scholars, is a sort of encyclopedia of information about people and places mentioned in the diary, about related historical events and topics of special interest, such as the theater and music, and about Pepys' language. There is also a large glossary of words now obsolete or with changed meanings.

One cannot have everything. The physical books, printed at the Cambridge University plant, appear to be technically perfect but are plain rather than handsome. One could wish that they might have been designed by Ward Ritchie, as were the volumes of our splendid *Sermons of John Donne,* but that was not possible, and we were happy to take what we got. Illustrations are few: maps of London in the seventeenth century, photographs of the diary and of shorthand passages, along with portrait frontispieces in the text volumes.

The one-volume versions are rather different. In 1978, before the big set was complete, came *The Illustrated Pepys: Extracts from the Diary,* a rather thin quarto volume designed by George Rainbird Ltd., the London firm noted for producing lavishly illustrated volumes for publication by various firms. There are many contemporary drawings and paintings, some reproduced in color. There is an endpaper map of London in the 1660s. It is not one of the most attractive Rainbird books—such as those of Alan Moorehead—but is handsome enough.

By 1985, when was published the standard one-volume abridgment, entitled *The Shorter Pepys,* the firm of Bell & Sons had been sold, modernized, and renamed Bell & Hyman. The shorter volume contains more than a thousand pages, probably a larger book than Matthews had intended when he made the first, and discarded, selection.

And in 1988 was published *A Pepys Anthology,* put together by Latham and his wife, Linnet. In this little volume passages from the diary are taken out of chronological order and grouped under topics such as The Husband, The Theatre-goer, The Court, The Navy, The Fire of London, and others. The obvious omissions suggest selection by a mind cleaner, more prosaic, and less imaginative than that of the departed textual editor. Or that of Sam Pepys himself.

13 Nevada in the 1860s
Sam Clemens

It seems unlikely that most textual critics of the Modern Language Association are acquainted with the town of Bodie in the eastern California desert, hard by Mono Lake and the Nevada state line. Nor do many of them know, I think, that textual editing in its American phase may have been born there.[1]

Bodie, like some other mining towns in the old west, was reputed to be an irreligious, riotous, and wicked place. In February 1879 a newspaper in neighboring Nevada reported that a little girl in San Jose, whose family was about to move to the wicked town, had ended her evening prayer with the words: "Good-bye, God; we're going to Bodie in the morning." But the report was wrong, wrote an editor in one of the Bodie papers some days later. The text as printed was corrupt; what the little girl really said was "Good, by God; we're going to Bodie in the morning." It is not often, I think, that a mis-spelled word and a misplaced comma have so corrupted an author's intention. Not often, either, that an editor, restoring the authentic version, has given the reader a text so greatly improved. No critic could call this kind of change mere comma hunting, a charge leveled often enough at textual editing. Editors since that time have some-times pleased the critics, sometimes not.[2]

1. The New Variorum Shakespeare, a rather different sort of thing, may claim precedence by a few years.
2. A librarian colleague, Richard Erickson, and I have striven mightily to ferret out the facts—or folklore—of this story, long known in the region east of the Sierra Nevada. We have located the first citation, worded as here printed, in the

Before we pass on from Bodie, we may remind ourselves that Samuel Langhorne Clemens spent several months prospecting only a few miles to the east in Aurora, called the Esmeralda district in *Roughing It*. This was in 1862, and it was from there that the unsuccessful miner walked a hundred miles or so to Virginia City to begin work on the *Territorial Enterprise,* making that newspaper famous and turning himself into Mark Twain. Aurora, when Clemens lived there, was a considerable town, rich in silver and gold, and the county seat of Mono County, California. But in 1864 along came a party of surveyors, who discovered that the town was actually in Nevada. So Mono County had to find itself a new seat, Bridgeport, which still survives, while Aurora and Bodie have gone the way of Sardis and Petra and become ghost towns. Their structures, built of wood and bricks, have not persisted nearly so well.

Mark Twain, né Clemens, wrote his way to fame in Virginia City, then in San Francisco, in the Sandwich Islands, and on a tour to the Holy Land, and eventually settled down in Connecticut, a celebrated author for the rest of his days. And he seems to have saved every scrap of paper that he ever wrote on, at least in his later years. He was a pack rat, Henry Nash Smith told me. His papers now repose in the Bancroft Library in Berkeley, where a team of textual scholars has been busy for thirty years, editing and publishing his writings in the form that he intended but did not always get in his lifetime, so prone to make changes are editors and printers. Thus Twain in an 1889 letter to his friend William Dean Howells regarding the proofs of *A Connecticut Yankee:* "Yesterday Mr. Hall wrote that the printer's proofreader was improving my punctuation for me, & I telegraphed orders to have him shot without giving him time to pray."

In the 1890s, after Mark Twain's business affairs—including his publishing venture and his backing of a typesetting machine—had collapsed into bankruptcy, the publishing firm of Harpers took over all

---

Nevada Tribune (Carson City) of 10 February 1879, page 2. The second citation still eludes us, but deserves to be authentic and probably is.

his copyrights and in return gave him an annual stipend for the rest of his life. After his death in 1910 his official biographer, Albert Bigelow Paine, acted as "Editor of the Mark Twain Estate," and from the mass of papers published some of Twain's letters, edited to a Victorian taste, as well as a shortened and purified version of the autobiographical dictations. When Paine died in 1937 the papers, property of Twain's surviving daughter Clara, were picked up from Paine's house and from bank vaults and placed in the Widener Library at Harvard, where they were mined for a few books by Paine's successor, Bernard DeVoto. In 1947 Dixon Wecter succeeded DeVoto, and the papers were moved to the Huntington Library in San Marino, but two years later Wecter became professor of history in Berkeley, and the papers followed him, still owned by Clara Clemens Samossoud. That was the final move as far as we can foresee; on her death in 1962 the collection became the property of the University library. In that same year, Henry Nash Smith, successor to Wecter, presided over an agreement between the Twain estate and the University of California Press, whereby the Press, in return for a royalty, gained sole right to publish material from the unpublished writings.

Before that, Smith, like his predecessors, had put together a number of books. One of these, *Mark Twain of the Enterprise,* edited by Smith and Frederick Anderson, was handsomely designed by Adrian Wilson and published by the Press in 1957. Since no complete file of the *Territorial Enterprise* has survived, few examples of Twain's early journalism had been known, but in 1954 the University purchased four scrapbooks in which members of the author's family had pasted clippings from the newspaper. These clippings include news accounts, some factual, some imaginative, spiced up by "no end of seasoning," editorials, dispatches and letters from other towns—all written during the boom times of the Comstock Lode. "Those were the days—those old ones," Twain wrote many years later. "They were so full to the brim with the wine of life; there have been no others like them."[3]

3. Quoted in *Mark Twain of the "Enterprise,"* 3.

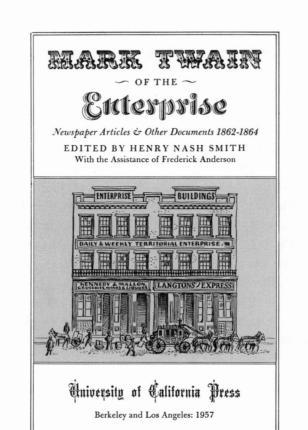

MARK TWAIN
~ OF THE ~
Enterprise

Newspaper Articles & Other Documents 1862-1864

EDITED BY HENRY NASH SMITH
With the Assistance of Frederick Anderson

ENTERPRISE BUILDINGS

DAILY & WEEKLY TERRITORIAL ENTERPRISE.

KENNEDY & MALLON, GROCERIES, WINES & LIQUORS | LANGTONS' EXPRESS

University of California Press

Berkeley and Los Angeles: 1957

Adrian Wilson's title page for *Mark Twain of the Enterprise*.

Shortly after the book was published the telephone rang one day, and my caller announced himself as Lucius Beebe of the *Territorial Enterprise* in Virginia City. I did not know Beebe but knew a little about him—a Boston-bred New York journalist and cafe-society columnist in the *Herald-Tribune,* who had come west in the early 1950s, bought what had to be bought, and re-established the *Enterprise* as a weekly newspaper. It was said to have the largest circulation of any weekly west of the Mississippi River. Beebe, described in one biographical account as "orchidacious," was also a railroad buff and wealthy enough to own a private railway car in which he and his friend Charles Clegg, along with a large dog named Mr. T-Bone, used to ride about the country.

Beebe, sometimes with the help of Clegg, put together and published a number of illustrated books about railroads and about the American west, one of which was entitled *Comstock Commotion* and purported to be—indeed was subtitled—*The Story of the "Territorial Enterprise."* Looking at this book today, written, says the jacket blurb, in "florid, gee-whiz style reminiscent of Bonanza times," one is startled to note that it was published by the now sober Stanford University Press. But that was in 1954 during what might be called Stanford's salad days under Donald P. Bean, before he was succeeded by the intellectual Leon Seltzer and then by the serious Grant Barnes. True to its title but not to its subtitle, the book is a collection of stories about Virginia City and its early inhabitants, with occasional references to the newspaper.

On the telephone Beebe said he had seen our book and would like to serialize it in the *Enterprise redivus.* Before considering the idea—aware of the railway car but not of the Stanford book—I in some way indicated that he must be expecting to pay a fee for the privilege. But no, he was not. He expected permission without payment. I demurred. He grew angry. The conversation came to an end. Our final words are lost, but memory retains those of Smith when I told him the story. "If you let him have it," said Henry, "I'll never speak to you again."

Henry Nash Smith, like the curators before him, was not primarily interested in editing, and in 1963 he stepped aside in favor of his assistant, Fred Anderson. The latter's first selection of unpublished material for a series of books to be known as the Mark Twain Papers suggested a total of twelve volumes. The number was soon raised to fifteen, and by 1981, Anderson's successor, Robert Hirst, estimated thirty-six volumes, including twenty of letters.

Meanwhile a group at the University of Iowa proposed to edit and issue definitive texts of the books Twain published during his lifetime, now about to go out of copyright. An editorial office was set up, and in 1968 the Iowa group contracted to have the books published by California as the Iowa-California Edition of the Works of Mark Twain. So now there were two series or sets, the Works and the Papers, and two editorial offices that did not always see eye to eye. Volume editors chosen for the Iowa books, appointed from universities around the country and of varying degrees of competence, were primarily literary scholars at a time when the tide was beginning to run toward textual editing. In some cases bibliographers were appointed to work alongside the literary editors. Eventually, after more moves than I can know of, Fred Anderson assumed the role of supervising editor for both series, and after his sudden death in 1979 Hirst succeeded to that position. The two series were combined and controlled from Berkeley under the joint title of the Works and Papers of Mark Twain. A total of more than seventy volumes was envisioned. Together with the Mark Twain Library, books with the newly edited texts but without the full apparatus, it appeared that the Press might eventually have on its list nearly one hundred volumes of Samuel Clemens. This may still come to pass, but I cannot see so far ahead.[4]

Brought in by the tide mentioned above was the Center for Editions of American Authors (CEAA), fostered and sponsored by the Modern Language Association. (The demiurge, said Edmund Wilson, was Fredson Bowers of the University of Virginia.) A number

---

4. This brief account, omitting many things, is based largely on Hirst's several applications for federal support and on a letter to me from Henry Nash Smith, 6 November 1985.

of university presses agreed—some had already begun—to publish complete and newly edited editions of classic American authors: Emerson, Hawthorne, Howells, Melville, Thoreau, Twain, Whitman, and perhaps others. The CEAA made grants for editorial work from funds supplied by the National Endowment for the Humanities. Later, applications went directly to the NEH. Textual standards were rigorous; each volume that passed inspection was certified by the MLA with a seal that proclaimed it "An Approved Edition."

But not everyone agreed that this was the right way to republish our classics. In the *New York Review of Books,* 18 January 1968, the critic Lewis Mumford, reviewing two volumes of the Emerson edition published by Harvard, recognized some virtues in the editorial work but said that it was done "by and strictly for" scholars and was unreadable by anyone else. By printing everything in the manuscripts, juvenilia, cancellations, passages rejected by the author, and by sewing the text pages with twenty special diacritical marks—he reprinted one horrifying passage—the editors had blocked the reader's access to Emerson's mind. In this review, entitled "Emerson Behind Barbed Wire," Mumford went on to criticize the current academic establishment. The new editorial practice, he said, "surely has an ominous bearing on the appreciation and teaching of literature. Such technological extravagance and human destitution is of course the fashionable mode of our day. In the present case nothing has been lost by the process—except Emerson." So a literary and cultural scholar on textual scholarship.

There soon came angry replies from a number of editors and from the director of the CEAA, William M. Gibson. Harvard, promised Gibson, intended at a later time to publish Emerson in a "clear text"—jargon for a readable book, said one critic. What was clear enough from Mumford's sample was that this would require a complete resetting of the type. Why variants and apparatus were not put in appendices, away from the reading text, Gibson did not say. This was done in most edited volumes of Mark Twain—among others—making it easy to produce later editions that could be read.

At this point the battle was joined by the feisty Edmund Wilson, then often called our most distinguished literary critic and a confirmed nonacademic. "The editing of the classic American writers," he wrote in a first letter, "has got to be an academic racket that is coming between these writers and the public to which they ought to be accessible." Wilson's anger, never far below the surface, was made hot by the loss of a federal grant that he and some others had expected to get—a grant to start publication of the American classics in handy, readable volumes similar to the French series called the Pléiade editions. The money was about to be granted, he said, when it was "whisked away" and given to the Modern Language Association. In the *New York Review* Wilson then published two long articles (later made into a small book) entitled "The Fruits of the MLA." Those who remember the shape of Wilson's mind and his habit of insulting anyone who crossed him, will have no doubt that the title bore a double meaning.

The "Fruits," long and disorganized, more irritable than cogent, is not one of Wilson's better pieces of writing, but the indictment comes through strongly enough. In the first part he discusses— dissects—the new edition of William Dean Howells' *Their Wedding Journey,* calling it "the reductio ad absurdum of the practices of the MLA." The claim is hard to dispute—a vastly over-edited version of an unimportant work—but perhaps he need not have written of "megalomaniac bibliographers." Later he speaks of the Mark Twain boondoggle, pausing to quote a dictionary definition of the related verb as "to do (and be paid public money for) trivial or unnecessary work." But he believes that Twain's autobiographical writings should be published complete. Wilson then wanders off into a long discussion of the partly published writings of Twain's "dark period" and their biographical importance.

"They order," wrote Lawrence Sterne, "this matter better in France." The author of *A Sentimental Journey* was surely not referring to publishing or even to literature, but the words are fitting enough and we may agree with Edmund Wilson that the Bibliothèque de la Pléiade is superior to any reprint venture in this country or perhaps anywhere

else. Undertaken by the publisher Gallimard, without subsidy so far
as I know, and by now adding up to a couple of hundred volumes,
the series makes available the best works of French literature in handsome, light-weight volumes. I myself prefer to read even smaller
books, one novel or one work at a time rather than omnibus volumes,
but the Pléiade books, even when running to more than a thousand
pages, are clearly printed, flexible, and light enough to go into a briefcase. When truly needed the editorial work has been remarkable; the
piecing together of Proust's great but never quite finished novel required several years of work before publication in 1954 and until recently was the only satisfactory way to read *A la recherche du temps
perdu.*

  After Wilson's death his idea for a similar project was taken up in
1979 by a nonprofit group called Literary Classics of the United
States, Inc. With initial grants from the Ford Foundation and the
NEH, it brought out the first four volumes of the Library of America
in 1982 and by now has issued perhaps fifty volumes in handy and
readable form at reasonable prices. The editing, I gather, is competent but not elaborate. Some texts, without apparatus, have been licensed from CEAA editions, including the Mark Twain.

"It was a dangerously dehumanizing experience to be Mark Twain's
publisher." So Hamlin Hill in the introduction to *Letters to His Publishers,* one of the first two volumes we brought out in the previously
unpublished Papers of Mark Twain in 1967. In the autobiographical
dictations Twain described one publisher as "a tall, lean, skinny,
yellow, toothless, bald-headed, rat-eyed professional liar and scoun-
drel . . . he had the gibbering laughter of an idiot." He called the
same man a "bastard monkey," and elsewhere termed another "a human louse." Among our literary subjects, as I might call them, only
Ezra Pound could match Twain in scurrility.[5] Edmund Wilson comes
in a distant third. What brought on these insults, if I have the moti-
vation right, is that publishers never earned for Twain as much money

5. See, for example, chapter 16, page 1.

as he thought he should get. Late in life, seeking to do better for himself, he went into the publishing business and lost his shirt.

More cautious than some, I suppose, we began publishing books for Twain—including some, perhaps, that he had not wanted published—when he was no longer around to call us names. As noted above, the Papers project, begun by Henry Nash Smith, started editing in 1962 and published the first three books in 1967. Two more came out in 1969, one in 1972, and two—the first two volumes of the *Notebooks and Journals*—in 1975. The parallel Works series began publishing in 1972 with *Roughing It* and in 1973 with *What is Man? and Other Philosophical Writings*. These ten, along with the *"Enterprise"* book of 1957, were all that we published while I was at the Press. The real flowering came in the following years. I should point out also that at one point I turned the Twain project over to Phil Lilienthal to handle for the Press, and that from then on my knowledge of it was not always complete. Lilienthal in turn passed the torch to Bill McClung. This confession of partial ignorance comes late in the story, perhaps. But ignorance has never stopped a writer.

In the group of re-edited Works, all handsome and hefty volumes, *A Connecticut Yankee* and *The Prince and the Pauper* appeared in 1979, the *Tom Sawyer* stories in 1980, two volumes of *Early Tales and Sketches* in 1979 and 1981, and the glorious centerpiece, the one unquestioned masterpiece, *Adventures of Huckleberry Finn,* in 1988. The Mark Twain Library, popular editions without textual apparatus and in paper as well as in cloth, was begun in 1982. By the end of the decade it included seven titles, including *Huckleberry Finn,* issued three years before its parent, the big textual edition.

The latter is, indeed, a most impressive book, nearly a thousand pages containing perhaps everything that anyone might ever want to know regarding Huck Finn and what was written about him. Walter Blair of Chicago, whose *Mark Twain and Huck Finn*—a fine study of the writing of the book—we had published twenty-eight years earlier in 1960, was the literary editor, while Victor Fischer of the Mark Twain Project office established the text, with the help of two colleagues. Under Robert Hirst the Project has tended to rely more and

Jim Sees a Dead Man.

more on the professional editors of the staff and less on outside literary and historical scholars. For textual work this practice would appear efficient but is not apt to silence those who mutter about a Mark Twain factory.

The great novel, including the original illustrations, takes up 362 pages and the literary introduction a few more, while the Reference Material, including textual notes, occupies more than 500 pages. This huge apparatus, which might seem excessive for a minor work of Howells or even a minor work of Mark Twain, may well be right for the scholarly edition of the most celebrated novel in American literature. Some parts, such as the maps of the Mississippi River as it was in antebellum days, the explanatory notes, and the glossary, will be of use to any reader whose interest is more than casual. The text itself, the reason for the whole endeavor, has been carefully restored, insofar as possible, to what was written and wanted by Mark Twain.

In the new text one entire chapter, omitted from the first edition for practical publishing reasons, has been put back, and thousands of smaller corrections have been made from the most authentic surviving documents, of which the most important was one-half of the author's original manuscript, now in a library in Buffalo. The other half, unfortunately, was lost one hundred years ago. Or so it was thought.

I used to tease my classical friends by suggesting that a day may come when a mound will be uncovered in Egypt or excavators will chip their way into an ancient library in Herculaneum, and at once, in the twinkling of an eye, the long shelves of carefully edited Oxford Classical Texts, the Teubner and Budé texts, will all be rendered obsolete. A happy day, of course, for those of us who would like to read the lyrics of Sappho and Archilochos, now known only in fragments, the missing dramas of Aeschylus and others, the lost historical books— but think of all the long work to be done over again!

The splendid *Huckleberry Finn* edition, based mainly on the surviving half of the author's manuscript, was completed and published in 1988. In the fall of 1990 a California woman, getting around at last to sorting the inherited papers of her grandfather, opened the lid of an old steamer-trunk, and there—Eureka!—was the other half-manuscript of *Huckleberry Finn*. We need not be concerned here with legal title to the find, now being argued in the courts, but how was the news greeted in the academic world? The find is "just beyond anyone's dream," said general editor Bob Hirst, as quoted in one newspaper, while volume editor Walter Blair, quoted in another paper, said that such a discovery, after a lifetime of writing about *Huck Finn,* was "a scholar's worst nightmare." Dream or nightmare or both? Surely, editorial feelings must be mixed, each editor sharing the expressed reaction of the other. Hirst estimates that it will take three or four years to revise the 1988 book.

Of the projects within the Project, the largest, perhaps, is that of publishing a complete edition of the correspondence of Mark Twain— his nearly ten thousand letters and letter fragments. At first the letters were published in discrete groups such as *Letters to His Publishers* (1967) and *Correspondence with H. H. Rogers* (1969), but Anderson and later Hirst decided that all the letters should be published together in one chronological sequence. This change of direction, only one of several as the project has proceeded, seems to have had something to do with the transition from literary and historical editors to textual editors or bibliographers. This set within a set, including full annotation and a selection of letters written to Mark Twain, will make twenty or more thick volumes. After more than a decade of work, after throwing in the first typesetting and starting over again, the editors and publishers brought out the first volume in 1988, the second in 1990, and the third in 1992.

During the period between the two settings of type, a new method of transcription was devised, called "plain text" to distinguish it from "clear text," unencumbered and readable, and from "genetic text," everything included. It makes use of the newest typographical means and allows the inclusion of canceled words, corrected mistakes, and the several idiosyncrasies of Twain's style without rendering the text unreadable, like the barb-wired text of the Emerson edition. The annotation of letters is full, even elaborate—"wonderfully generous and detailed," wrote one critic, while another declared it done "to a degree unprecedented . . . in American literary scholarship." Interspersed between letters is what amounts to a running biography for the period covered.

Praise was general but sometimes qualified or grudging. "There is also something slightly mad," wrote the *TLS* reviewer, "in its display of research, which is at once so punctilious and so unbridled." And he then went on to justify the excess by asserting that Mark Twain, more than anyone else, symbolizes nineteenth-century America, speaks for it. But one wonders, will it be possible to find time enough and money enough to do seventeen more volumes on this scale? The Endowment people have expressed doubt, the Project's executive committee has asked for changes, and in his 1990 application Hirst speaks of "leaner annotation" and of using selectivity in the later volumes.

It is not for a mere publisher, let alone a retired one with literary rather than textual tastes, to question editorial practices, but—but I find it not easy to appreciate the arguments for completeness or inclusiveness, arguments sometimes made in relation to the Twain and other editions, believing that discrimination between the important and the unimportant is part of the editorial task. This is true, I be-

lieve, even if the editing has to be done over again to the tastes of a
later generation—as it has been said that each generation must have
its own translation of Homer. It may be vain to seek permanence or
perfection. To include everything, every scrap and fragment, every
mistake crossed out and corrected, may obviate one kind of criticism
but can make an edition as unwieldy as the collection of manuscripts
whose place it is usurping. Some rethinking appears to be going on
at the Bancroft Library.

I—one individual—also have doubts about the ethics of printing
what an author has rejected, crossed out, and decided not to print.
Such ethical scruples are, perhaps, old-fashioned, an outmoded kind
of decency, since this practice now appears common among scholars.
One of our early Mark Twain editors, Franklin R. Rogers, editor of
Satires and Burlesques (1967), seems to have had a guilty conscience
when he wrote in his introduction: "It should always be with some
misgivings that an editor presents to the public materials which the
author had discarded. . . . By resurrecting them, the editor risks ex-
posing the author to the adverse criticism which he wished to avoid."
Rogers then seeks to quiet his conscience by asserting that the cancellations and discards will be useful to scholars who wish to study
the creative process. Why this handful of scholars should not work
from the manuscripts or from copies of them, and why the author's
"garbage" should be put before all readers, he does not say. The "mi-
nutiae of scholarship," wrote Lewis Mumford, are now recorded with
"scrupulous non-selectivity."[6]

Enough of quibbles. "Dogs bark, but the caravan moves on," says an
Arab proverb. The Mark Twain project may not be perfect—in its
very effort to achieve perfection—but it is one of the great editorial
endeavors, achievements, of our time. We of the Press in my time,
along with those who have come after us, are pleased and happy to

6. Discrimination is essential. The writer of a letter may sometimes cross out a
word or phrase lightly, intending it to remain readable. Thus, possibly, on page
197 of the third volume of *Letters*.

have these books on our list and to display them in our catalogues. When I first came to the Press it was no cause for pride that all our literary books were secondary studies, that we could offer for sale no great works of original literature. Change has come with the years: first John Donne, then John Dryden, then the great *Diary* of Dryden's friend, Samuel Pepys. And now Mark Twain, eventually all of Mark Twain, not only in scholarly editions but thereafter in "clear text" editions for the reading public. We have come a considerable distance.

There was a year, not long before I retired, when we were bringing out both Pepys, in the first uncensored version, and Mark Twain. It even occurred to us in our new-found pride that we might make a splash by advertising the two great sets together, classics of English and American literature. What other university press could do the like? To dress up a brochure we had the original illustrations of *Huck Finn* as well as numerous likenesses of Mark Twain, including one photograph of the young writer, bare to the waist long before he lost his shirt in the publishing business. For the Pepys there were other riches to choose from, including fine oil portraits of the mistresses of Charles II, Nell Gwyn and Barbara Castlemaine, posed in candid Restoration style.

As Harlan Kessel and I discussed the possible plan—not too seriously, perhaps—we thought we might exhibit on one page Mark Twain without his shirt, and on the facing page Nell Gwyn without hers. The brochure might not sell books, we knew, but it could improve our standing with booksellers.

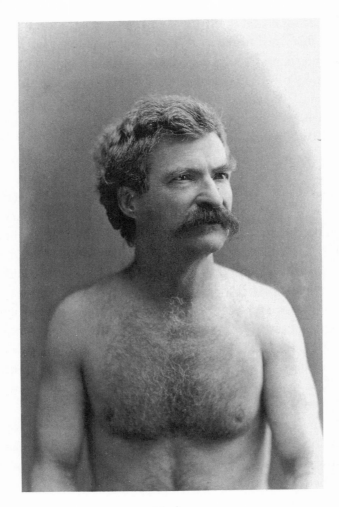

Mark.

Nell.

14 In Any Language but English
Poetry at the Press

The godfather—so to speak—of our literary translation list was an unemployed professor of English, whose first versions from Rilke had been published by the Press in 1940, shortly before he was thrown out of the University. There were a few earlier translations, but they were all single shots, leading to nothing further.[1] The Rilke too might have led nowhere had it not been for a fortuitous meeting several years later.

Works of scholarly research make up the proper diet of a university press, but for those with a taste for books of imagination the meal goes down better after an apéritif and with wine, great or *ordinaire*. Believing that we should not seek to be what we are not and compete with commercial firms for new literary works, we looked about us and saw that literary classics, in translation or in collected editions, were proper to our function. And that we could do as well with them as could anyone else.

In 1940 I was working at the California State Library in Sacramento, where all new books came over my desk. One day there arrived a slender volume entitled *Rainer Maria Rilke: Fifty Selected Poems with Translations by C. F. MacIntyre*. Whether it was Farquhar's

---

1. Farquhar's very first book, in 1933, was Henry H. Hart's *The Hundred Names*, translations of Chinese poetry. And Dorothy Prall Radin's version of *Eugene Onegin* came out in 1937. The first went through several printings; the second did less well.

graceful design or the first lines of verse or the frontispiece that caught my eye, I no longer know, but I found myself reading back and forth across the double-page spreads from English to German, taken with the English (and the discursive notes) and so led deeper into the originals. Early and minor Rilke, critics may say, but more pleasing to some of us than the later, more mystical things.

In the book is a poem about a children's merry-go-round, with the refrain: "Und dann und wann ein weisser Elefant." The frontispiece to that edition, unfortunately omitted from some reprints, is a line drawing of a simple merry-go-round with the elephant looming front and center. Looking at it then, I could not foresee that fifteen years later I would be walking through the Jardin du Luxembourg with the translator, that he would lead me past some trees, around a corner, then stop and say, "There it is." And there it was, almost surely the same diminutive carousel that Rilke had seen some fifty years before when he was working in Paris as secretary to Auguste Rodin. It looked homemade, primitive, charming, quite unlike the large and brassy machines of my own childhood.[2] This little pilgrimage was typical of MacIntyre. He used also to make sentimental journeys to the graves of his favorite poets, pouring wine on those whose occupants, like Paul Verlaine, might appreciate it.

But I get ahead of myself. In late 1944 I moved to the University Press and before long was looking around for books that might add sparkle to our list. My old library school classmate Larry Powell, then librarian at UCLA, said, "Why don't you go see MacIntyre. He has a trunk full of manuscripts, including more translations." After studying under MacIntyre at Occidental College, and taking inspiration from him, Powell had kept track of his down-sloping academic career—from Oxy to UCLA, where he ran afoul of the dominant lady in the English department, and then to Berkeley, where he fared no better and was eased out into the cold. The story is that he was traded like a baseball player from one university to another. Whether Mac's

2. Marian MacIntyre tells me that the carousel was still there in the spring of 1992.

Das Karussell.

trouble stemmed primarily from his behavior with girl students, which might have passed unnoticed twenty-five years later, or whether he had got himself in the wrong milieu—teacher and translator in a university that prized hard research—this I do not know. Both may have been true.

I found MacIntyre living alone and working in a small house at the top of the Berkeley hills, next door to our chief editor Harold Small, who got along with his eccentric neighbor but had not thought of asking for further manuscripts. He worked on them happily enough when I brought them in. From that beginning and over the next several years we published seven or eight more books by MacIntyre— more Rilke, Baudelaire, Verlaine, Mallarmé, Corbière, a symbolist anthology.

By the time this was done we had got into the habit of translations, and people had come to think of us as publishers of foreign poetry in English. Manuscripts began coming in. So a program was begun, one that has produced well over a hundred volumes from ancient and modern languages, some of them considered masterpieces of translation. Perhaps it is understandable then why I sometimes think of MacIntyre as the godfather of all these books, although he had little or nothing to do with those that came after him. With him we got off to a running start and never looked back.

Mac constructed his own mythology of the poet (himself) as outlaw or outsider, a myth, partly true, that survives among his old students, such as Powell and Ward Ritchie. He sometimes thought of himself as a sort of latter-day François Villon, or rather the romantic Anglo-American notion of Villon as lovable rogue, something he never was. Mac's sins, of course, were peccadillos compared to those of his great exemplar. His worst, perhaps, was one he confessed to me: that he had shot a horse that got in his way one dark night on a Mexican road. Pale sin, if true, beside those of his predecessor, who is known to have robbed a church and knifed a priest. And fate was kinder to Mac; exiled from the University, he found the good life, and a handsome new wife, in Paris. Exiled and driven from Paris five hundred years earlier, Villon is likely to have found—no one knows—violent death on the open road or cold death in a provincial prison.

It may be that Mac was wilder in his youth, before I met him, than he was later, but I knew him through most of his time as outsider. Behind the rebel facade lurked a family man manqué. In his unpublished novel on the life of Tristan Corbière, which he let me read, the sex scenes—based presumably on experiences with female students—were rather unreal, while the scenes of son with parents were truly felt and convincing. I once took a new acquaintance to meet Mac in Paris. "Don't," advised Mac the libertine. "She's too nice a girl."

In the nonviolent Berkeley of the late 1940s Mac proclaimed his urge to slug President Sproul, who had failed to over-rule the English department's denial of tenure. For fear he might encounter Sproul and be tempted, Mac refused to cross the University campus, coming round-about to our offices. When he needed a book from the University library, it was fetched by Editor Small. I don't know whether the threat to slug would have been carried out or not. Mac had an obligation to his boasts and he possessed a temper, as the horse incident shows.

The poet had his little games with the editor, most of them consisting of sly insertions into manuscripts. On one occasion Small, puzzling over an undocumented quotation from Anatole France and thinking it rang not quite right, accused Mac of making it up. I thought it might amuse you, said the latter. The passage, as I remember, had something to do with a *chameau:* the name of the enemy professor mentioned above was Campbell. In the first Rilke, unnoticed at the time but clear now to one who knew the perpetrator, there is printed something similar in the note to "Das Karussel," the merry-go-round poem.

In the same book, in the commentary on a poem about Leda: "For an example of a much more modern version I am indebted to Count Brunetto of Agrigento, not only for his permission to use one of his unpublished poems, but also for his help in getting it into

English of a sort one stormy day in his villa by the Mediterranean."
There follows a sixteen-line poem about the careless girl and her swan
lover. Again something rings wrong, and I doubt the existence of
Count Brunetto, wondering whether the poem might be one of
Mac's own, slipped past the editorial eye. It is now too late to accuse
him, and too late also to ask Small whether he guessed at the decep-
tion and let it pass. But that was his first encounter with Mac, before
skepticism set in.

But games are games, diversions from serious work, and Mac-
Intyre never allowed them to corrupt his admirable translator's conscience. He might occasionally make mistakes but never knowingly
did he falsify a line or add to the meaning or subtract from it, although substitute images might sometimes be necessary. Some French
and German poets go well into English; others are recalcitrant. Some
were more suitable to the translator's talents than were others. Some
manuscripts remained in the trunk. Most of the finished volumes
were well received by critics and other poets, such as Louise Bogan,
who then wrote poetry criticism for the *New Yorker*. The 1940 Rilke
went into our very first paperback list in 1956 and is still selling more
than fifty years after first publication.

There is an unhappy story about one unfinished translation. In
1955, when Mac and I were in the Rheinland, the toast of the German
literary scene was a Franco-German poet named Georg, or Georges,
Forestier, who was supposed to be serving in the French Foreign
Legion in Indochina, from where he sent back tender and nostalgic
poems in what was surely good German verse. German booksellers
told us that he was considered the best poet in the language since
Rilke. So we bought the books and, once back in Paris, Mac sat down
to translate them, working late at night with a bottle of red wine at
his elbow, while I dozed on a couch across the room, and Marian
slept in the bedroom. So far so good, but one afternoon in a cafe in
Montparnasse I picked a French newspaper from the rack and there
read the confession of an editor in a German publishing house, who
had written the poems and invented the character of the legionnaire

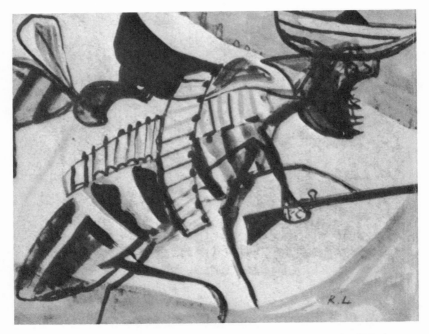

Drawing by Rico Lebrun for cover of Azuela's *Two Novels of Mexico.*

author. Mac read and looked a bit sick but soon recovered and downed a cognac in honor of a kindred spirit.

Literary translations, we thought, added luster to the list and shook some of the stuffiness out of our reputation, but the sales were modest except for Rilke, who was then in fashion. So we did only one or two a year until—happy change—the paperback revolution showed us that literary classics could be sold if the books looked not too formal and the prices were low enough. After that we stepped up the pace and brought out many more. The first experimental paperback list of five titles in 1956 included two translations, the Rilke and also *Two Novels of Mexico,* by Mariano Azuela, translated by Lesley Byrd Simpson. The latter book was doubly experimental, a paperback original at a time when originals were thought to be risky ventures. At about the same time we did three translations from early Spanish literature by Simpson: *The Celestina, The Poem of the Cid,* and *Little*

Sermons on Sin, by Alfonso Martínez de Toledo—all paperbacks and all in addition to Simpson's many versions of Latin American historical works, financed on the Rockefeller Foundation grant and described in an earlier chapter.

The success of the paperbacks along with the example of the Latin American program suggested that we try a few modern Spanish things. Encouraged by Luis Monguió, member of the Editorial Committee and native of Tarragona, I commissioned the American poet Ben Belitt to translate *Juan de Mairena,* a philosophical prose work by Antonio Machado, considered by some to be the finest modern Spanish poet. That was in 1963, and three years later we brought out Rafael Alberti's *Selected Poems,* also translated by Belitt. And ten years after that Alberti's autobiography, *The Lost Grove,* translated by Gabriel Berns of the Santa Cruz faculty. There were other Spanish books, including a couple of novels by Ramón Pérez de Ayala.

In Chapter 8 I have written about Helen Caldwell, teacher of Latin at UCLA, lover of the Portuguese language, and prodigious translator of the novels of J. M. Machado de Assis, the Brazilian master. The first of these came out in 1960, the last in 1984, a few years before her death. Most of our other books from Brazil, and there were quite a number of them, were not literary. An exception was *The Rogues' Trial,* by Ariano Suassuna, the only separate play we published at the time. It never got the attention it deserved. When I was in Lima for the Ford Foundation I went to see the widow of César Vallejo, the noted modern Peruvian poet, again prompted by Monguió, who had written a book about Vallejo. She was known to be difficult, and my request for rights was rebuffed. Others must have been more successful later because in 1978 the Press published *The Complete Posthumous Poetry,* translated by Clayton Eshleman and José Rubia Barcia. It won the National Book Award for translation.

Possibly our most praised translations have been from the ancient languages. I cannot say which came first, but the first to create a stir was Mary Barnard's *Sappho,* which was part of our third paperback list in early 1958 and has sold more than 100,000 copies. Many years later, after retirement, I edited for the Press her autobiography, *As-*

sault on Mount Helicon (1984), pleased to learn that she came from, and now lived in, Vancouver, Washington, a few miles down the Columbia River from where I was raised. And she was born just one day after I was—delivered by the same stork, she once suggested.

As a young and hopeful poet, Mary tells in the autobiography, she felt isolated in the Pacific Northwest, then far from the known literary circles. Where could she find help and advice? She went over the list of poets she had read. Then looking up the address in *Who's Who,* she wrote out of the blue to Ezra Pound, remembering his reputation for helping other writers. To her request there came from Rapallo one of Pound's eccentric postcards. That was in 1933, and for the next few years they corresponded, with Pound, the mentor, setting a training regimen that included the writing of sapphics in English. Later, in New York, Mary became friends with W. C. Williams, Marianne Moore, and other writers of the time but gave up poetry, wrote stories, and earned her living.

But in 1951, at home once more for slow recovery from a critical illness, she took up her Greek again, rusty from neglect, read Homer, and began the serious effort to put Sappho's poems and fragments into English verse that would convey something of the quality of the original. Sending a few of the first trials to Pound in St. Elizabeths, she got this reply: "Yuz—vury nize—only grump iz yu didn't git to it 20 years ago." But he offered criticisms, and she kept on trying, with the enforced patience of one confined to bed, striving to attain what she finds in the original, the underlying cadence of the speaking voice. Pound wrote, quoting Fordie—Ford Maddox Ford—"40 ways to say anything," and Mary thinks she may have done forty versions of some of the fragments.[3]

And in the end she got it better, many think, than anyone ever had. Dudley Fitts, in the introduction to the published book, speaks of "the direct purity of diction and versification." Of one remarkable passage he says, "Like the Greek, it is stripped and hard, awkward with the fine awkwardness of truth. . . . It is exact translation; but in

3. Quotations from Barnard's *Assault on Mount Helicon,* 282–83.

its composition, the spacing, the arrangement of stresses, it is also high art. This, one thinks, is what Sappho must have been like."

> Some say a cavalry corps,
> some infantry, some, again,
> will maintain that the swift oars
>
> of our fleet are the finest
> sight on dark earth; but I say
> that whatever one loves, is.

After years of work it was the old story of being turned down by any number of publishers who said that Sappho would not sell. But in paperback—when the manuscript came to us—we thought it would, and so it has. And has been widely appreciated. In *Hudson Review* Burton Raffel wrote, "Sappho now enjoys as nearly perfect an English translation as one can find, a great translation, an immensely moving translation."

In the beginning I sponsored most of our literary translations, being the editor most interested, but others soon got into the spirit of the thing. Lucie Dobbie worked on a number of books, as did Phil Lilienthal and others. After Bob Zachary came to the Los Angeles office in 1959, just as I was about to get embroiled in Latin American matters, he sponsored more and more varied translations than did anyone else, and from many languages—continuing in French and German but working from originals in Italian, medieval Irish, modern Hebrew, Anglo-Saxon, Ancient Egyptian, Welsh, Provençal, and others I forget.

But for his greatest successes he went back to Greek and Latin, as befitted his own classical education. Allen Mandelbaum's *Aeneid* (1971) won the National Book Award. Bernard Knox called it a brilliant translation, and Bill Anderson, the Berkeley Latinist, wrote that it "comes closer to the impossible goal of perfection than any of the numerous efforts that have poured out of American and British presses since World War II." In a de luxe edition ten years after the first and after quoting the shades of Virgil and Statius from the *Purgatory,* Mandelbaum asked himself: "Is translation but shade embracing shade—though with enough love to make one forget the emptiness of shades?" Later, after Bob and I had both retired, Stan Holwitz sponsored Mandelbaum's *Divine Comedy* (three volumes, 1980–82) and *The Odyssey* (1990). The Press published in cloth; paperbacks were done commercially.

The same is true of Peter Whigham's *Poems of Catullus* (1969). Influenced, like Mary Barnard, by the prosody of Ezra Pound, Whigham, says Zachary, "tested himself for twenty years against Catullus." Of these versions Cyril Connelly wrote, "He brings back his translations as something that actually happened to him, like Noah's dove with the olive." And Hugh Kenner said that they are "not only a reclamation of the past but a book for young poets to study." Kenner, who was then teaching at Santa Barbara, brought Whigham to the University for several years of teaching, off and on, both there and in Berkeley, but poet and multiversity were on "osculating curves," as Zachary put it, not likely to touch for long. Whigham lived the life of a poet, supporting himself in various ways, sometimes as a bit player in odd movies—he was a trained actor—and sometimes as a fry cook.

His *Poems of Meleager,* done with Peter Jay and including the Greek text, came out in 1975. And in 1987 I finished editing a book that Zachary had started and did not stay around to finish: *Epigrams of Martial Englished by Diverse Hands,* chosen by J. P. Sullivan and Whigham, who did many of the translations. When Whigham was killed in an auto accident later that year, it was Zachary who spoke the funeral elegy.

"Greek lyric . . . ," once wrote W. R. Johnson, "exists for us only in shards and tatters."[4] The poems of Archilochos, soldier-poet from the island of Paros in the seventh century B.C., two hundred years before the great classical age of Athens, are even more fragmentary than those of his near contemporary Sappho, existing only in the quotations of grammarians and on scraps of papyrus from Alexandria. No extant poem is complete although there are some rather long

4. In *The Idea of Lyric* (Berkeley and Los Angeles, 1982), 25.

fragments, long enough to reveal unusual qualities. Again through Hugh Kenner, Zachary got in touch with Guy Davenport, teacher, artist, and essayist in Lexington, Kentucky, and in 1964 brought out his *Carmina Archilochi: The Fragments of Archilochus*. So little known was this perhaps first lyric poet of the West that when Davenport's first versions showed up in a magazine he was thought by many to have amused himself by inventing a Greek. And in a rather different sense—perhaps like Pound inventing China in *Cathay*[5]—Davenport has constructed for the Greekless reader a book and a poet that were not there before. Working from the Budé text of Lasserre and Bonnard, he put into English every fragment, including those of a single word, which may be viewed as we view a lone pottery shard, although perhaps less concretely. The longer pieces reveal, in Kenner's words, "a very ancient, unclassically recalcitrant poet, fitfully to be heard cursing his fate." And sometimes extolling his love.

There were many more books, and from more languages than I can mention here. In one year (1974) there was a collection from modern Arabic and another from Hispano-Arabic. There was a witty version of Christian Morgenstern's Galgenlieder (gallows songs, 1963) by Max Knight, one of our editors. And in 1983, after my time, *Postwar Polish Poetry*, by Czeslaw Milosz, winner of the Nobel prize. And indeed, translations have continued unabated, a happy and semischolarly part of the publishing list. And a much larger part than MacIntyre, Small, and I could have foreseen when in the late 1940s we began trying out the market for Rilke, Baudelaire, and the like.

Translation is, of course and by definition, impossible. It need not betray (*traduttore/traditore*) but can never equal the original. A "translation" may turn out to be better than the original, as Fitzgerald's *Rubaiyat* is said to be, but then it is not translation but a parallel work on the same topic. To equal the original in meaning and tone a new version would have to be—like that of *Don Quijote* in Jorge Luis Borges' story—reconstructed word for word in the original language.

5. Kenner's figure, after Eliot, in *The Pound Era* (1971), 192.

From *Carmina Archilochi*.

But no one need be deterred by impossibilities; credit in Heaven and gratitude below may be earned by striving to come ever closer to an ideal. And some of the strivings, including some of ours, are close enough in letter and spirit to serve the half educated—most of us. One who does not read Latin may find a satisfying part of Virgil in Mandelbaum's *Aeneid*. Or in Dryden's, for that matter, if one's taste is not too uncompromisingly modern for rhyming couplets.

This is not the place for a treatise on theories of translation, even were I capable of such, but it may be well to say a word about what we were thinking when we published approximations of Ovid, Laforgue, Issa, and others. We were not inclined to quarrel with a number of received opinions: that every age must redo Homer to its own taste; that no one should try to "improve" the original; that a literal version, words without spirit, is perhaps the least accurate of all versions. Thus the interlinear translation of the New Testament can save much dictionary thumbing, but no one would call it King James. To these we may add a thought less widely accepted: that a genius who can perceive and transmit the tone and feel of the original may be

forgiven some inexactnesses. But there are not many geniuses—
Pound in *Cathay*, perhaps, but few others.

"The translator must, somehow, see into the author's thought,
beyond the words." Thus Mariano Azuela to Lesley Byrd Simpson,
who wished to translate Azuela's sketches of the Mexican Revolution.
Simpson writes that he piled up discarded versions for many years,
while his knowledge of Mexico grew, until he could allow himself to
think that he was not too far from Don Mariano's thought.[6]

From the beginning we decided that, whenever feasible, we
would publish bilingual editions of translated poetry: original printed
opposite the translation, thus two books in one and a service to the
reader who knows something of the original language and can read
the two versions together, enjoying the translation and becoming
more familiar with the original—as I had done with the 1940 Rilke.
This practice was clearly useful with the major European languages
but perhaps less so with most others. Egalitarians may bristle, but the
consideration was always a practical one: would the number of
readers served justify the added work and cost? For a time I wanted
to redo Mary Barnard's *Sappho* with the Greek beside the English,
but could never quite convince myself that the gain would be worth
the effort, especially since the choice of Greek text would have been
troublesome. The cost of printing non-Roman alphabets and the
great length of some works, such as the ancient epics, both precluded
bilingual treatment if the books were to be sold to students at reasonable prices.

6. Quoted from Simpson's preface to his version of Azuela's *Two Novels of Mexico*,
published in our first paperback list in 1956.

15 The Poetry-Hating Director

To be published by the University Press a poet must write in any language other than English. So complained some English-writing poets on the University faculty, implying a strange kind of prejudice. That there was reason—of a kind, at least—behind such an unreasonable practice I shall attempt to show. And the claim was only partly true, as could be seen when we published the collected poems of Kenneth Burke, Louis Zukovsky, and others. We were restricting ourselves to classics and semi-classics, to works that had already made their reputation, and declining to compete with other houses for the work of new poets—and new fiction writers.

Some university presses saw the matter differently, hoping to strike a blow for new poetry—always difficult to publish commercially although not impossible. The two presses best known for poetry, Yale and Wesleyan, were turning the selection over to well-known older poets, even Auden at one time. The Yale series of younger poets brought out one volume a year, if I remember aright. Wesleyan did more. I once examined the Indiana list of about twenty volumes and judged it to be only half successful: no great critical acclaim and no book selling more than four hundred copies. Chicago did a few books by poets of some reputation, including one by our translator, Ben Belitt, who first offered it to us.

The Editorial Committee minutes show that publication of creative writing had been discussed as early as 1938 and perhaps before then. In that year the Committee debated and with some reluctance approved publication of a volume that included about thirty pages of original poems along with a collection of translations from the Sanskrit. But this was a memorial volume for a recently deceased professor and was in no way a precedent.[1] I remember being approached, probably in the 1950s, first by Josephine Miles and later by Tom Parkinson, both poets—as well as critics—in the Berkeley English department. But there was no concerted push until 1966, when a group of poets from several campuses mounted a campaign that had to be considered seriously. At that time there was talk—as there often is—of redefining the function of the University; it should take responsibility, some said, for encouraging the creative arts. Creative work should have the same legitimacy as other kinds of "research" and be used for promotion in the same way. During the Easter break that year an all-University conference was held in Davis on the University and the arts. Suggestions were called for, and one, of course, was for the publication of poetry.

Meanwhile, the Editorial Committee, accepting similar arguments from composers in the music departments, had set up a monograph series for the publication of contemporary scores. Like other series it was limited to work from faculty members and was distributed mostly by exchange. Not an ideal provision, perhaps, but there was no other.

That summer, shortly before going on leave, Leonard Nathan, a poet who taught in the speech department at Berkeley, wrote to President Kerr, proposing as one of the planned series of centennial publications an anthology of poetry by University authors. He followed this up with a longer letter to Mortimer Starr of Davis, then northern chairman of the Editorial Committee, spelling out the arguments mentioned above and suggesting that the anthology might be followed by a regular program of poetry publication. The Committee, as committees will, appointed a subcommittee to study and investigate, but informed Nathan's group that it would not consider

1. Arthur William Ryder, *Original Poems Together with Translations from the Sanskrit* (1939).

a centennial anthology, since that would look like a house organ, a self-honoring device.

There followed several months of study and discussion, during which the subcommittee interviewed poets and poets buttonholed Committee members. In November the subcommittee's report, written by Ralph Rader of Berkeley,[2] firmly rejected the idea of a monograph series, limited to in-house poets, while leaving to the director the decision on a book program open to all. The University is not obligated to publish what it promotes for, they said. Rejecting the comparison with the new music series, they noted that there was no place at all to publish contemporary music, while poetry was regularly, if not readily, published by commercial firms and small presses. Poetry, being personal, subjective, and emotional, could not be judged by the Committee in the way it judged scholarly work. Moreover, the best University poets would not publish in such a restricted series; we could expect only the second best.

As for books of poetry, it may appear that the Committee passed the buck to the director, but it is hard to see what else they could have done, since they could not tell him how to invest the risk funds for which he was responsible. They could encourage, and this the report did in a rather equivocal way. The Committee's role was to pass judgment; they would work with the director in determining the nature of a poetry program and in setting up a selecting mechanism. And the Committee did not blink at the practical problems, some of them more serious, said the director, than the anticipated but moderate financial loss—for example, a huge influx of manuscripts that would use up much editorial time.

The surviving papers do not show what happened after that, and my memory is as empty as the files. I know, of course, what did not happen—we did not publish poetry—but whether there was ever a statement to the Committee or to the poets, I do not know. Probably the matter was handled little by little and with no big announcement.

2. The other two members were Donald Heiney of Irvine, a successful writer of fiction, and Hugh Kenner, the noted critic, then at Santa Barbara.

Possibly the Committee's action, rejecting a basic part of the poets' proposal and throwing the rest back into my lap, was sufficient discouragement. One of the proposers—which one I do not remember—had referred to me as the "poetry-hating director."

At a small university, like Wesleyan, or even at a great but not large one like Chicago, one could appoint an outside judge or panel of judges and abide by the choices without getting into much trouble, but I could never imagine how to deal with thirty or forty poets within the University of California, who could act as a body in promoting a program but who might be less of one mind when choices were made amongst them or when outside poets were preferred to them. And the dealing would take up much time and provide—what benefits would it provide?

Ah, there was the rub. Publishing poetry might be a boon to local poets, useful even to other poets, but it would do little or nothing, I thought, for the Press. Elsewhere I have written that a book should be good or it should sell. From the perhaps narrow point of view of the Press, it should add something to our reputation or should earn a few dollars to help other books. In this little equation money was the least factor. I could have found funds for a few small books each year. Often enough we would risk loss or take a deliberate loss, but only when the book was one to be proud of, one that in the long run would help make us a better press. But the chance of getting truly distinguished, internationally known, writers always seemed remote. A good translation would put Sappho or Catullus or Baudelaire on our list, but how much literary distinction would the local poets bring us, admired as they might be in some circles? It would be better, we thought, to wait and perhaps do the collected works of the happy— i.e., successful—few. I may add that the publication of poetry, in my view, is best seen as a personal endeavor. The publisher should take pleasure in exercising judgment, in promoting work he or she believes in, seeking to make literary reputations. This is feasible in a private firm, large or small, but not at a large public press.

Doubt looms even larger when we consider original fiction. In this a university press may be of humble service to a few writers but will never do anything for itself. It is not possible to move outside one's area of competence—area of acceptance by the book trade—and get any but second-choice manuscripts. If, by some stroke of fortune, a successful novel lands on the list, the author will, and quite rightly, take his next book to a commercial firm. There is no way to win—and I don't like no-win games.

But a press, some will say, is only part of a larger organization and should work for the benefit of the whole university and not for itself. I used to hear this argument when the printing department wanted to control our manufacturing work—at their prices. It is an argument for bureaucracy, when the only salvation is to act as unbureaucratically as possible—argument for a service agency rather than a true press. I have discussed that matter elsewhere.[3] Here it is sufficient to say that a press can best serve its university by striving to become a great press.

3. "The Service Agency and the Publishing House," *Scholarly Publishing* (Toronto), January 1976, pp. 121–27.

16 A Few Pounds of Lit Crit

The angry professor asked: "Why do you publish only books about Ezra Pound in American literature?" This accusation of prejudice, more than the one about poetry in English, took me by surprise. I mentioned the huge Mark Twain series and books about Melville and Wharton by colleagues of the accuser. But the Twain, he said, was an editing project and the others were only two and were published quite some while before.[1] I could have mentioned, but did not, that my own personal taste happened to be more Proustian than Poundian—pure American that I am and, like Pound, born in the state of Idaho. Nor did I think to point out that we had no special reason to favor an author who once wrote: "Piracy is lesser sin than the continued blithering of University presses, the whole foetid lot of 'em, men with NO human curiosity, gorillas, primitive congeries of protoplasmic cells without conning towers, without nervous organisms more developed than that of amoebas."[2]

We had never consciously thought to put together a list in American literature, or in English literature for that matter. Other areas had to be worked at, we thought, whereas there would always be submis-

---

1. Leon Howard, *Herman Melville: A Biography* (1951), and Blake Nevius, *Edith Wharton: A Study of Her Fiction* (1953).
2. In *Guide to Kulchur* (London, 1938), 147. Pound was writing about the lack of bilingual editions of Chinese classics and noted that one edition may have been pirated.

sions from the large English departments, and all we needed do was to choose the better ones. Not entirely true, I can see now, looking back, but enough true to make some practical sense of our attitude. And in literature, as in other fields, one thing leads to another, one book brings in other books. So if we then had a group of books on Pound, it was largely because we had published the first one in 1955.

Our critic had, unknown to me, submitted a manuscript that got unfavorable readings and was declined—perhaps a mistake on our part, because he was quite intelligent. Thereafter we became better acquainted; he came on the Editorial Committee and saw how we worked, saw that we were publishers, hence generalists, and that personal preferences played little part in fashioning the book list. Over the years, and in one way or another, we managed to make friends of several who came to us as enemies. A term on the Editorial Committee could be hugely enlightening.

Our first Pound book was written by John Espey, another UCLA colleague of the critic. Entitled *Ezra Pound's Mauberley: A Study in Composition,* it surprised both author and publisher by attracting much critical attention. It later went into paperback and is still in print. The author, wrote one reviewer, "amasses a whole album of new perceptions and . . . new validations."

One thing led to another, and from that point on it is easy to see connections. By the time the next manuscript came in, Espey was on the Editorial Committee and he made so many useful suggestions to the authors that they asked us to put his name on the title page as third author. *An Annotated Index to the Cantos of Ezra Pound,* by John Edwards and William Vasse, came out in 1957, perhaps the first reference book to that difficult poem.[3] If we had known then how Pound studies would grow and flourish, we might have set the book in type instead of reproducing it from typewritten copy, after inserting Greek and Chinese characters by hand. And it was surely the existence of this WPA project—as Pound is said to have called the book—that

3. About this same time Edwards, then on the Berkeley faculty, brought the manuscript of Mary Barnard's *Sappho* to us.

several years later led K. K. Ruthven to send us from the University
of Canterbury in New Zealand the manuscript of his *A Guide to Ezra
Pound's Personae (1926)*, published in 1969.

The book that seems to have put the stamp on us as Poundian
publishers came out in 1971 and was described later by a hostile critic
as "the Bible" of the Pound industry. Although a bible may seem
more suitable to a cult than to an industry, the critic—if I have it
right, and the article is not at hand—was firing a broad salvo at the
host of scholars, here and abroad, who by then were working on
Pound and his *Cantos*. Literary "industries"—Joyce industry, Twain
industry, and others—are apt to spring up when an author's works
are voluminous, complex, and obscure enough to provide endless material for study and disagreement.[4]

And when the author himself is complex and contradictory—
when he is kind and generous to friends and others, helping unknown
and distant writers like Mary Barnard, but writes viciously of those
who cross him, when he remains very American but broadcasts treasonable hate against his country, when he espouses weird economic
theories and yet provides the clear intelligence that guides the rebirth
of poetry in our century—when he is all of these things and more,
then there are apt to be as many detractors as disciples. Liberal critics,
like the one mentioned above, are often unable to separate poetics
from politics. And even without the corruption of politics, many of
us appear unable to deal with public figures who are not all of one
piece. Thus, and in regard to another matter, one of our editors, brilliant but sometimes stubborn, once condemned the introduction to a
book, calling the famous writer (not Pound) a charlatan. To which I
could only reply: "Yes, but what you are forgetting, Grant, is that one
can be a charlatan and a genius at the same time." The contradictions
in Pound have led to violent words among the intellectuals, such as
those thrown about when *The Pisan Cantos* were awarded the Bollin-
gen prize by the Library of Congress in 1949. By now, one hopes, the
past has retreated, the rage is mostly dissipated, and it is possible to

4. The Mark Twain case is rather different, as we have seen in another chapter.

deal sympathetically with a great but flawed man. A few could do so twenty years ago.

One day Hugh Kenner, recently come on to the Editorial Committee, sent me an issue of a little magazine, containing his article "The Invention of China." He could not have known that *Cathay*— especially "The River Merchant's Wife" but also the other poems in that small volume—happened to be the work of Pound that most appealed to me. I was then too lazy, or too involved in other things, to have read my way through the *Cantos*—something I might have told the accuser mentioned above—but had been struck by some of the shorter poems. Presumably Kenner sent the article as a courtesy, but I swallowed as if it had been bait, wrote back my pleasure, and asked whether the piece might be part of a book and, if so, could we publish for him. Yes, it was a book, said he, but was contracted to an eastern publisher, who had given a royalty advance—but now seemed unenthusiastic. So the ball was in my court, and I offered to double the advance, so that he could buy his way out of the contract and have something left over for wine or computer ware. Not a usual university-press practice but justified this time, I thought.

As *The Pound Era* begins—in Jamesean and unacademic prose— it is June 1914 and Henry James is strolling down a street in Chelsea with his niece, and there they run into Ezra Pound and his wife Dorothy Shakespear. From then on this long book is a mixture of literary and personal history, literary and social criticism, explication of key verses, evocation of people and places. Altogether perhaps a recreation of a *temps perdu,* a gone world, not very long gone but quite unlike our present world, a literary age, with Ezra Pound at the center, others revolving around him—James, Ford, Eliot, Lewis, Moore, Williams, and even Joyce. Literary criticism become literature, a rare thing.

Because of this book, and others that were coming in or being offered by London publishers—one thing leads to another—I went to the Pound conference at the University of Maine in 1975, a mixed gathering of scholars and disciples, presided over by the eminent entrepreneur of Orono, ringmaster of Poundian affairs, editor of *Pai-*

deuma, Carroll F. Terrell. I was rather out of place, knowing less about Pound than anyone present, nodding blankly at mention of Malatesta or Omar or Brunnenburg. I did know something about Montségur, the little mountain in Provence where Pound once went in his pursuit of the troubadour lyric, but no one spoke of it. I gave a short talk about publishing and, with the help of Kenner, signed up a few projects for the Press. Terry himself, from his central position in the great web of Pound studies, undertook to compile a new guide to the *Cantos,* replacing the now outdated *Annotated Index.* It was eventually published in two volumes.[5] And at Orono I met Louis Zukovsky, poet and friend of Pound, and arranged to publish for the first time in one volume his long poem *"A."* Original poetry but not new and unknown, the culmination of a life's work. Later the Press published the collected poems of Charles Olson, Robert Creeley, and others.

Why we went to Montségur, Bob Zachary and I, is no longer clear to me. I seldom go on literary or other pilgrimages, having made a few and come away empty-handed. Driving near Chartres one day a few years earlier, I saw the name Illiers[6] on a road sign and swung the car around. In the town I happened to coincide with a small group being shown through the house of Tante Léonie. And I walked outside the town and along the little river, trying to *see* the two *côtés,* or ways. It was all pleasant enough on an autumn afternoon, but no ghosts were there. The simple bedroom must have been like any other of the time. The hawthorns were not so different from hawthorns in Berkeley. In the town there was a bakery shop called Les Madeleines, and I suppose one could have bought some, like a proper tourist, but I did not go in. The little church was not the church of Combray, although it had made its contribution along with others.

I should have known—perhaps I did know—that I would find nothing I had not brought with me. I could not see with the eyes of

5. Carroll F. Terrell, *A Companion to the Cantos of Ezra Pound* (1980–84).
6. Now renamed Illiers-Combray, I believe.

On the way to Montségur. Zachary at Cahors.

a child a hundred years before, or with the inner eye of the man that child became and whose words could make the reader see. The *clef* to a *roman* of second or third level—New York intellectuals writing about each other—may be useful or at least curious, but the key to a great novel is not so easily come by. What the great writer adds to the model or to the skeleton is virtually everything. It was Proust himself, as I have noted before, who wrote that the work of art is made not by the quotidian self but by a secret or inner self that may have little or no connection with the artist's daily life. So much for most literary biography.

But Montségur is not Combray, is a historical rather than a literary site, with the history made a little more attractive by Pound's interest. Still, why did we go? We happened to be driving in France; Kenner must have mentioned Montségur as a place to go, or we remembered it from *The Pound Era;* I had read Zoé Oldenbourg's great historical novel *The Corner-Stone (La pierre angulaire)*, with its vivid

Montségur.

scenes of the Albigensian Crusade, the bloody religious wars in which the northern French put down the southern French in the thirteenth century. And eventually drove out the southern French language, Langue d'oc or Provençal, the tongue in which the troubadours wrote their lyric poetry, so important to Dante and much later to Ezra Pound in his search for the source of lyricism in the West.

In southern France one goes to Foix and then south and east toward the Pyrénées. At the top of a pass on local highway D9 one parks and climbs a steep rocky trail, called a *sentier pénible* by the green Michelin, to the roofless stone temple at the top of the mountain. Here in 1244 some two hundred Albigensians—heretics to the great church—were besieged and eventually burned on the plain below.

Pound went there in 1919 with his wife Dorothy, and Kenner followed while writing *The Pound Era*, as his photographs in the book show (pages 333–34). Both had the good sense to go in the summer; Zachary and I arrived in late January. More knowledgeable than I about Pound and other matters, Bob the indoorsman was less at home on the mountainside. I remember that the upward scramble almost did him in. As we sat on the stone remains at the top, the coldest wind I have ever felt came down off the Pyrénées above. My tired and freezing companion suggested that the Albigensians had surrendered not from hunger or military weakness but because burning at the stake would provide a few moments of warmth. That burning was almost the end of the Albigensian heresy. Provençal poetry died about the same time.

Only a fraction of our books of lit crit, and lit hist and lit ref, were about Ezra Pound or even about modernist literature. Others ran into the hundreds, but none, from Malory and Chaucer down to the present, grouped themselves in quite the same way or came with such personal overtones, and none caused us to scramble up even small mountains. Over the years and without pain or complaint we put together a large clutch of books about that other hero of modernism, James Joyce, including three lexicons to the Gaelic, the German, and the classical words in *Finnegans Wake*. In 1966 Kenneth Burke, once called by W. H. Auden "the most brilliant and suggestive critic now writing in America," spent a term as Regents Professor on the Santa Barbara campus, and again one thing led to another. Zachary became Burke's personal editor, and after a few years the Press had in print almost the complete writings of Burke, critical, philosophical, and imaginative. None of them ever sold very well, I believe, but they added luster and substance to the list.

I7 Mega Biblion
Exposing the Press to Art History

Before there was art history there was art. Whether art will survive art history is a question for others to ponder. Art history, in its full scholarly manifestation, came late to the Press. Indeed it came late to American universities, at least to this one. In about 1938, when I was working in the University library in Berkeley, one task assigned me was to work with a young professor, recently come from Heidelberg, to build up a collection of books by art historians. Since we were buying basic and standard works, we must have been starting pretty much from scratch. The young professor was Walter Horn, who twenty-five years later was to become general editor of our book series California Studies in the History of Art and who will show up again in the latter part of this chapter. Before then we published quite a number of art books of other kinds.

When I first came to the Press in 1944, the closest thing we had to a best-seller was a book by Erle Loran entitled *Cézanne's Composition: Analysis of His Form with Diagrams and Photographs of His Motifs* (1943). As a very young artist Loran had lived for more than two years in Cézanne's studio in Aix-en-Provence, painting in the country round-about once frequented by the older artist. Whenever he recognized a landscape or a road or a building that Cézanne had painted, he photographed it. In a 1930 article he seems to have been the first to think of juxtaposing photographs and reproductions of paintings to note changes and study the mystery of Cézanne's form. The book, when it came to be written later, went far beyond that beginning, with diagrams analyzing the structure of the paintings. The purpose of the study was broad. Cézanne, said Loran, was "convenient to use as the fountainhead for modern concepts of space organization." A glance at the reproductions, photographs of motifs, and diagrams will show how useful the book is to painters and art students.

It was our best-seller, I said, but we had no books to sell. Printing paper was rationed in wartime, and we could not get what we needed to reprint a book not judged essential to the war effort. But before long we did; the book was reprinted many times, was revised for second and third editions, and is in print fifty years after first publication.

In 1948 we brought out a book that was much more specifically about the teaching of art: *The Unfolding of Artistic Activity,* by Henry Schaefer-Simmern, with a foreword by John Dewey. The book was based on an experiment financed by the Russell Sage Foundation "for the purpose of showing by actual case histories the development of the creative potentialities in men and women in business and the professions, and in institutionalized delinquents and mental defectives; that is, in persons not devoted to the arts." When I questioned the key word in the title, suggesting something less awkward, the author would have none of it. "It is I, Henry," he said, "I who do the unfolding." But in his preface he speaks of "an art education which will encourage the natural unfolding of artistic activity as an inherent quality of man."

He ran a successful art school in Berkeley, quite unconnected with the University and attended largely, I seem to remember, by housewives. Some said, rather unkindly, that he taught students to do primitive art. The very attractive illustrations in his book may seem to bear this out, but no harm in that, we thought. Although Henry's stiff and rather pompous manner turned off many people, especially in the University, we knew him well enough to look past the manner but were amused to learn that he had been born plain Henry (perhaps Heinrich) Schaefer. Preferring something less ordi-

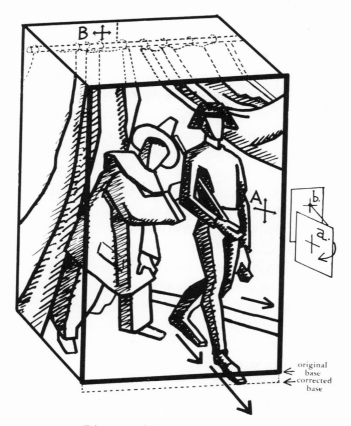

Diagram of Cézanne's *Mardi Gras*.

nary, he added the name of the small town on the Rhine, Simmern, where he was born. Double names can be acquired in various ways.

A good and helpful book, it was reprinted and used for many years, years during which Henry worked on another and larger book that he never finished. In the meantime he brought in his friend Rudolf Arnheim, the great scholar and theorist in the psychology of art, who wrote books—and we published them—for the next thirty years and more, beginning with *Art and Visual Perception* (1954), still a standard work. Subtitled *A Psychology of the Creative Eye,* this book describes the visual process that takes place when people create—or look at—works of art and explains how the eye organizes visual material according to psychological laws. In a later volume, *Visual Thinking* (1969), Arnheim argues that all thinking (not just thinking related to visual experiences) is basically perceptive in nature and that the ancient distinction between perceiving and reasoning is false and misleading. Arnheim was also one of the first important film critics; in a still read early book, *Film as Art,* he made a strong case for the superior qualities of the silent film.

While we were still dealing with Schaefer-Simmern, there walked in the front door a tall man, carrying under his arm a portfolio of striking photographs of the art works of the Haida, the Kwakiutl, the Tsimshian, and other related tribes of the Pacific northwest—art now well enough known but then familiar to only a few and published only in monographs. Robert Bruce Inverarity had spent many of his early Seattle years visiting the wooded and rainy coast between there and Alaska, studying these peoples and their arts. He now proposed a book that would begin with a brief study of the society and culture and would then display the rich variety of the art—not just totem poles, the one form known to many. There would also be a study of the symbols and their meaning. *Art of the Northwest Coast Indians* (1950) is one of our early books that pioneered a little-known topic and did this so well that it has been selling ever since—usefully selling. A photograph in the *British Columbia Magazine,* fall 1976, shows a young Indian carver at work in a village on the Skeena River, and in front of him, as source study, is a well-worn copy of our book. Before that I had observed the new totem poles of Bill Read and others going up in Vancouver and Victoria, and had bought a pair of Read's silver earrings for my wife. So the author, and even perhaps the publisher, may claim some part in the contemporary rebirth of a great Indian art style.

Inverarity, then teaching in Los Angeles, is anthropologist, painter, photographer, and something of a genius in acquiring and displaying not only works of art but also large and small objects of material culture. He moved on to establish a folk art museum in Santa Fe, a regional museum in the Adirondacks, and then revitalized the

Indian carver at Ksan with book as model (*British Columbia Magazine,* Fall 1976).

maritime museum in Philadelphia. When the time came for retirement, Bruce sold his own collection of northwest art to the British Museum. On one of my last working visits to London I was pleased to attend an exhibition of the Inverarity Collection.

In those early days, as I have remembered in another chapter, some of us were pleased to leaven our scholarly list with translations from a number of foreign literatures. Mere adornment, some may call it, since scholarly books had always to be the largest and the basic part of what we published, but translations were appropriate, they gave us variety, and they helped to get attention from booksellers, who tended to shy away from university press books. Art books could serve the same purposes, and they made our daily work more interesting.

Several of us became particularly attracted to the writings of artists about their own work. At that time I was listening to the talk of

Rico Lebrun, an artist who knew how to make clear what he and others were trying to do. And in this interest we were encouraged by a member of the Editorial Committee, Michel Loève, a mathematician who could out-talk professors of French literature in their own field and who could probably have done the same to professors of modern art, had there been any on the Committee. After that kind of performance he would apologize to me, saying that he had the advantage of knowing little about the subject.[1]

And we were publishing in 1952 an anthology entitled *The Creative Process,* compiled by Brewster Ghiselin of the University of Utah. A collection of short accounts by mathematicians, musicians, artists, writers, inventors, and others, all commenting on the mysterious and sporadic way in which the human mind works, or does not work, in the creation of new things. The subject is too large and too complex for description here, but a comment or two may not be out of place. Nowadays we hear about the left and right sides of the brain, terms not common then. Long ago poets talked about inspiration. In the seventeenth century Blaise Pascal wrote about the *esprit de finesse,* in which the mind goes directly from problem to solution, without (apparently) following the logical steps of geometric reasoning. That passage is not in Ghiselin's book, nor is Proust's account of the involuntary memory, out of which his own huge books were written, but there are many other striking things. One that has stuck in my memory is Henri Poincaré's description of mathematical creation and the reciprocal roles played by the conscious and unconscious minds. After long mental work had failed to solve the problem before him, he would sometimes put the matter out of mind—or so he thought—and go off on a trip. Then unexpectedly and from nowhere—once as he stepped onto an omnibus—the solution might suddenly appear in his head.

Before we brought out Ghiselin's book, it had been turned down by any number of commercial publishers, who could see no market

1. See Chapter 9, note 5.

for it. Afterwards it came to the attention of two imaginative paperback editors, Arabella Porter and Victor Weybright of New American Library. They bought paperback rights from us, and for many years the book was available on popular stands for fifty cents or thereabouts. The Press now has its own paperback edition. Publishing, we like to say, is a kind of gambling.

Out of the same interest came a little book of our own, *Art and Artist* (1956), in which we ourselves put together a number of pieces by present-day artists, writing about their own work. The authors were a mixed lot, some well-known, others not, and included Henry Moore; Jean Renoir and Cesare Zavatini, the film directors; W. Eugene Smith, the photographer; and Rico Lebrun, whose talk about the need for a place to publish such writings had suggested the book. Several of us took an interest, including Michel Loève, mentioned above, and Rita Carroll of the staff. It was an attractive little volume, and if there had been a real need for it, or a strong response to it, we might have tried to make it an annual publication. But the impulse faded, and there were other and more urgent things to do.

We did, however, bring out a volume of Lebrun's *Drawings* (1961), together with a collection of his writings. A man of great emotional power, deeply affected by human suffering, fascinated also by color and line, he was then rather famous for his huge triptych of the Crucifixion, now at Syracuse University, and his many related studies of contemporary men and women, centurions, animals, crosses, and other objects. In his talk, in his lectures, he was highly literate and perhaps more eloquent and compelling than any other artist I had heard. It was natural, then, to think that he could write a kind of intellectual autobiography; and he himself was quite taken with the idea.

He tried but could not do it. After a time I came to see that his great talent for words and thoughts, for seeing and understanding the work of others as well as his own, along with his sense of humor and the ability to turn a phrase—that this talent might be called lyrical in nature, suited to the sentence or the paragraph, to the shorter passage, individual, discrete, but not to the organized discourse that

Lebrun, *Woman Leaning on a Staff.*

makes a book. After all, he was a painter, who portrayed individual objects or scenes, not an ordered world.

So, since he was known as a great draftsman, we decided to do a book of drawings, together with brief writings about himself as artist and about the nature of drawing. But getting these on paper was a problem; his talent was also oral. So in the end I sat at his typewriter in Los Angeles while he paced the floor and dictated his thoughts about this matter or that. Between topics, and when inspiration receded, we teased it back with coffee, wine, and conversation. In this way quite a lot of oral wisdom was given the quasi-permanence of written words. These I carried home, had retyped, and sent to him.

What did he do then? He did what a bad editor is supposed to do—revised the life out of his words, made them stiff and stilted, more reasonable, less idiosyncratic, less personal. Fortunately I had kept a copy and could try to save him from himself—editor telling author to leave happy imperfection alone, to retain insights in their first fresh form, preserve them from artful revision. For many weeks we fought—vehemently, as friends will—over these few pages, face to face for a time and then by letter while he was at the American Academy in Rome. The book appeared in 1961 (three years before his death), with a foreword by the art critic James Thrall Soby, and went through two printings.

Of himself, Lebrun wrote: "The real drama is in the fact that personal drama produces nothing of merit whatsoever. Many professors have struggled even harder than Cézanne, and for the wrong reasons. In a superior civilization some day, we should have a Pantheon for them. 'He was an ass and toiled as if he had the obligations of a hero.' Who knows how many of us may yet belong to that legion?"

Of his native Naples, forever a part of him: "At every dawn our street, like all others, slowly emerged from visceral darkness into peach-and-brass light, shrouded in miasmic smells and heavenly fragrances, festooned by immaculate laundry hanging everywhere on lines like angels electrocuted by the sun."

Of another kind of line, that of the draftsman: "I use a line, I suppose, as a lifeline to hang on to against the risk of being washed overboard."

And of the Crucifixion, his great subject for several years: "This was a period in which I could go from one picture to another as a speaker goes from one phrase to another—the wood of the Cross, the ladder, the signs, the nails, the hammer, the uniforms of slaughter, the black of mourning. I think it was Melville who had given me the courage to do this when he wrote about the spade, the lance, the tow-rope. . . .

"After Christ was taken down and the Golgotha scaffold scrubbed with whitewash, someone discovered that without the irrelevant trivia of blood and pain the Cross made a composition of 'significant horizontals and verticals.' This meant nothing at all to Mary the Mother. Her sight had been made unsophisticated by experience."

In the meantime, in the 1950s, we essayed still other kinds of art books, too many titles for mention here. The director of the new UCLA art gallery, Fred Wight, had embarked on an ambitious program of showing the work of the best contemporary painters, and for each show he put together a small but handsome volume, with critical appraisals and excellent color illustrations. There were books on Hans Hoffman, John Marin, Morris Graves, Arthur G. Dove, and perhaps others I forget. Quite different was *Children's Art,* by Miriam Lindstrom of the De Young Museum, wife of my old Stanford classmate Charles Lindstrom. Published in 1957 as one of our first paperbacks, the book was for many years a staple of that list, and is still in print.

During our early and amateur years we consorted with Art; in the 1960s, growing old, we found ourselves entangled in a more serious affair, with Art History. Which of my sins brought this fate down upon us is not clear. Perhaps the sin of Ambition.

Ten years after we began publishing our large series of books in art history, I wrote to another press director who had asked advice about undertaking a similar venture: "If you are prepared to deal with short print runs, long production times, much care and expense in producing good illustrations, and an outlandish amount of editorial attention, then the field of art history is open to you, and may God go with you." To the list of tribulations I might have added dealing with foundations, artists, and general editors. They, of course, may have had their thoughts about dealing with me.

The series California Studies in the History of Art now includes more than twenty-five titles, many in more than one volume, all of them large, some of them great. Among the great are *The Plan of St.*

Gall, by Walter Horn and Ernest Born; *Corinthian Vase-Painting of the Archaic Period,* by D. A. Amyx; and my own choice for finest book of all, Jean Bony's *French Gothic Architecture of the Twelfth and Thirteenth Centuries.* The Horn and Born will be considered in a moment. Amyx's volumes were described in an earlier chapter. Bony's great work provides the only satisfactory account I have ever read of how Gothic architecture developed from or arose out of Romanesque. "The past must be relived," writes Bony, "as what it was when it was happening: as a sequence of distinct and unforeseen presents." Among other fine things is a revealing comparison of two great cathedrals, Bourges and Chartres.

The three books just mentioned, in seven volumes and weighing perhaps forty pounds, were all taken in during my time but published after I retired. The two dozen books of the series, many of them distinguished works of scholarship, all handsomely illustrated, amount to a considerable publishing achievement. One has to be proud of them. Perhaps, perhaps, they are worth the pain and trouble occasioned to me and to the Press.

Our old correspondence file, now sadly incomplete, does not make clear how or why we began this large undertaking. Our very first book of this kind, never meant to lead anywhere, came out in 1953: Alfred Frankenstein's *After the Hunt: William Harnett and Other American Still Life Painters 1870–1900.* Years later a revised edition went appropriately into the big series. Then in 1957 a Mellon Foundation grant—one given to all university presses—was burning a hole in our pocket, and we spent much of it on *German Expressionist Painting,* by Peter Selz, then teaching at Pomona College.[2] This was the first general book in English on a period of painting that has since been much written about.

No surviving papers document the leap of our minds from these individual books to the rather grandiose idea of a big series in art history. Ambition, I have said. Princeton and Yale had produced

2. It was Selz who arranged for Lebrun to paint a large outdoor mural on one of the Pomona College buildings.

some imposing sets. It seems likely that the first impulse toward a series came from Rita Carroll, who was then our art and medical editor and who had been designer of the book by Selz. A surviving memorandum of January 1960 shows that we were considering a number of art manuscripts and that she and I had approached Walter Horn of the art department in Berkeley, asking him to become general editor of a book series. After some hesitation, he agreed and, for better or for worse, we were on our way. Three years later Rita departed the Press, leaving the art books in my lap, alas, with no one to relieve me. In the 1970s Lorna Price, working for us at first and then for the art department, saw the books through the Press.

The first two books, both of moderate size, came out in 1962: *The Birth of Landscape Painting in China,* by Michael Sullivan of London, and *Portraits by Degas,* by Jean Sutherland Boggs of the Riverside campus. Neither of these, nor the third book, *Leonardo da Vinci on Painting,* by Carlo Pedretti of UCLA, was especially difficult to produce, and the illustrations were mostly in black and white. After that the books became larger, the problems more complex, the costs greater. To support the series we solicited a grant from the Kress Foundation, and in 1965 were given $100,000, a considerable sum more than twenty-five years ago. The money was used over a period of years, during which the Foundation took a close interest in our progress, requiring annual reports and much correspondence with Mary Davis, assistant to the president and later executive vice-president. She took a special interest in our illustrations, they needing improvement, she thought. At that time the older art historians had little faith in color reproduction, preferring the greater accuracy of black and white, but younger scholars were demanding color.

In this part of our story, the pièce de résistance, the magnum opus, the casus belli, was a book entitled *The Plan of St. Gall,* with text by our general editor, Walter Horn, and visual material by Ernest Born, a San Francisco architect. The reader with a taste for academic warfare may turn to Jim Clark's account, at the end of this book, of a ludicrous but crucial battle, perhaps the second most sanguinary

Abbey Grange, Beaulieu St. Leonards.

in the history of the Press. It would not do for me to retell what Clark has told in a way I cannot—with an even hand—but perhaps I may add a few touches to the background along with an opinion or two.

In the 1960 memo mentioned above I reported from a meeting with Horn that he was working on two books, a large one on medieval three-aisled halls or barns and a small one on the plan of St. Gall, a ninth-century vellum manuscript, on which is drawn the building plan of a model monastic community. In the years that followed, and in ways not clear to me, the two books switched places or switched dimensions. The large one, or a part of it, became a thin published volume in 1965, and we shall see what happened to the smaller book.

When published, the large-book-become-thin was entitled *The Barns of the Abbey of Beaulieu and Its Granges of Great Coxwell and Beaulieu St. Leonards.* On the dust jacket we called it "a study in medieval survival: two Cistercian abbey-barns in England dating from the first half of the 13th century." It is a remarkable volume, perhaps as handsome as any put out by the Press. In retrospect it may also be seen as a trial run for the small-book-become-large. Ernest Born's balanced folio pages, diagrams, and above all his magnificent shaded drawings of interiors and exteriors—these come close to taking one's breath away, and not from the physical effort of holding them up. This book, as they say about some buildings, was constructed on a human scale.

The St. Gall manuscript, then limited to the "guest and service structures" of the plan, was said in 1960 to be in semifinal draft, about 150 pages in length. When approved by the Editorial Committee and accepted by me in 1967, it came to several hundred typed pages, about right for a single quarto volume. As the work moved through the production process during the next twelve years, we paused every now and then to call for new estimates of size and cost, and each time discovered that new sections had been added, along with a few dozen new diagrams and drawings. Expansion seems to have been engineered more by Born, the artist and designer, than by Horn, the author, who may not have had much control toward the end. When published on Christmas Day 1979, three years after I retired, the book had become three huge folio volumes; each of the nearly one thousand printed pages was equal to three or four ordinary book pages. The reader could not easily hold up even one of the volumes; this may be the only three-lectern book the Press will ever publish. And all this served to interpret the lines and words on one side of a sheet of vellum measuring 30½ × 44 inches.

In my skeptical and perhaps scatterbrained way, I sometimes wonder how a research scholar can work on the same project decade after decade and retain faith in its intellectual importance. Perhaps some do not, and that is why their books are never completed. But we can also observe an opposite phenomenon. As the years go by the object or document for study may swell and expand in importance until—until, for example, "The Plan of St. Gall is . . . one of the most fascinating creations of the human mind . . . one of the greatest humanistic statements of the Western Mind."[3] Or until it becomes "a book, over which shines a star, below which one may read *Fiat lux*."[4]

In the book itself, on page 53, is the less grand assertion that the Plan is "a document of paradigmatic significance drawn up in the [Carolingian] palace itself under the eyes of the country's leading bishops and abbots." Even this was called "wanton hyperbole" in the *Times Literary Supplement*. The reviewer there went on to praise Born's drawings but to judge the design of the book too grandiose and confused to be successful.[5]

This much said, I should add that she found much to admire in the volumes, and that the other reviews, or most of them, made up a chorus of praise. We can be confident, I like to think, that *The Plan of St. Gall* is a great book, although it may be—as a famous writer once said of his own novel—that the pedestal is too large for the statue.[6]

What, then, did this "monument"—a term that irritated Horn but pleased Born—cost the Press in money and in good health? In the battle so well described by Jim Clark, did we suffer a defeat or manage a kind of stalemate? It is not easy to say. The authors and I and those who came after me raised subsidies totaling more than $150,000 against a manufacturing cost of over twice that much; the book sold out the entire edition at a price that varied; but the overhead cost of staff time can never be calculated. After I retired the new production manager, Chet Grycz, spent most of his time for three years on this one project. And the influence on the Press of this huge work of art seems—here I speculate—to have helped bring about a kind of bibliographic intoxication, resulting in publication of a number of large, handsome, and high-priced volumes of a kind that appeal (or do not appeal) to book collectors. Not all of these sold, and their

3. Horn to Frugé, 30 October 1973.
4. Born to Horn, 6 December 1973.
5. Rosamond McKittrick in the issue of 26 December 1980, page 1470.
6. Flaubert of *Salammbô*. I quote from memory.

piling up in the inventory contributed to the financial crisis of the mid 1980s. No accurate assessment can be made. The Press suffered but survived.

Moral: Having escaped disaster, more or less, I may now try to extract a message from this last little story. When one feels the tug of ambition, or observes it tugging on someone else, it is well to remember that ambition needs to be curbed by the sterner stuff of tight control.

18 The Book as Artifact
Design and Printing

Some years ago a great eastern university constructed a new library building, a tall and garish tower with pseudo-Gothic excrescences. The librarian, it is said, threatened to post a sign by the front door announcing, "The Library is on the inside." As we have seen a few pages back, some readers have similar thoughts about books that are too imposing for their contents or too fancy.

How should the frame relate to the picture, the package to the contents? Or should the physical book be considered a package? The publisher may assume so, but to devotees of the Art of the Book the printing and binding may seem more significant than the words within. Few authors are as collectible as some printers. After my retirement dinner in 1977 one of our great book designers wrote to another: "I was amazed that none of the speakers mentioned the design or physical qualities of the books, only their ever increasing numbers, their scholarly virtues, and their achieving 'best seller' status. . . . I should have leapt up and told them what I thought their major importance was. But the wine had flowed too freely."[1]

More on this topic later. Here it is sufficient to note that many of us, printers and publishers alike, may agree that the design of a book should be appropriate to the matter within. If the book is a genuine

---

1. Adrian Wilson to Ward Ritchie, quoted by the latter in *Hoja Volante,* November 1979, p. 7.

book, something more than mere information, it ought to be attractive, even handsome, and its size and shape should invite the reader inside. This does not always come to pass.

Printing at the University of California Press began in the shop of Old Mr. Flinn, as he was known—Joseph W. Flinn, an immigrant journeyman who came to Berkeley as University printer more than a century ago in 1887 and stayed for the better part of half a century. It appears that he ran an efficient shop and served well the needs of the University for announcements and other official work, but gave less attention to the faculty's research publications, which began coming out in 1893.

In 1932, when Flinn was ready to retire after forty-five years on the job,[2] he had survived complaints from the Press and the Editorial Committee, complaints about slow schedules, lack of special fonts, and the undistinguished appearance of the printed page as he produced it. The plant's work had the nondescript look of public printing, designed for utility—or rather, not designed at all—and with no attempt to please, or even to ease, the reader. Some books of more than usual size or distinction, such as the works of Palóu and Anza, edited by Herbert E. Bolton, were printed elsewhere and financed by Sidney M. Ehrman. But not every faculty member could call down an angel.

The lack of aesthetic concern must have been galling to many in Berkeley in the twenties and early thirties, years of typographic splendor just across the bay in San Francisco. With Flinn ready to leave at last, the faculty manager of the Press, George Calhoun, recommended to President Sproul that the printing office be expanded in a way to permit the printing of fine books in the Harvard and Princeton tradition, and Robert P. Utter, a member of the Editorial Committee, wrote that "any plan for the future . . . should include a typographical

2. Flinn's record for long service was eventually surpassed by a young woman whom he hired in about 1920 and who stayed on at printing office and Press for forty-nine years. This was Hazel Niehaus, who was Farquhar's office manager in the 1940s and who, after separation of the two departments, managed the University monograph series for the Press.

expert who should be more than a mechanic." In 1932 Samuel T. Farquhar was appointed superintendent of the printing office, and a year
later was made manager of the Press. The two organizations were
combined and for the next sixteen years functioned together as the
University of California Press.

Farquhar was neither mechanic nor practical printer. He was an educated man with an enthusiasm for fine books and a taste for classical
literature. He had worked in the advertising business, had been a
printing salesman, and from 1927 to 1932 was a partner in the printing
firm of Johnck & Seeger. For a time in the late 1920s he wrote a
weekly essay in the *San Francisco Chronicle* about finely printed books,
particularly those of John Henry Nash, the Grabhorns, Taylor & Taylor, and other Bay Area craftsmen. And he was one of the founding
members of the Roxburghe Club of San Francisco, formed in 1928 as
a forum for discussion of fine books. His knowledge of printing was
broad and historical, that of an executive rather than a hands-on journeyman. But few journeymen, if any, could match his knowledge of
printing types and printing papers.

Although a bibliophile, Farquhar was no mere collector. Wishing
to make fine books and not just look at them, he set out to transform
the Press into one of the great scholarly presses of this country, both
as printer and as publisher. The first of these ambitions he accomplished in full measure but the second had to come after his time.
Printing was his true love, and it was in the design and production of
well-printed books that he gained his great successes. Even in this he
had too much good sense and understood too clearly the nature of
the University to play the Grabhorn game of limited editions for
book collectors—except now and then and with one hand. But he
was determined to establish a standard of attractive and dignified
printing that would, in his words, serve "the clear transmission of
thought from author to reader."[3] In this he had a lasting success.
Although his distinctive design style passed away with him, the ideal

3. *Catalogue: University of California Publications 1893–1943*, vii.

that nourished it still holds at the Press more than forty years later. And many of his books are still admired.

As befitted his love for Virgil, Horace, and other ancient writers, Farquhar's taste was classical. He strove for balance, restraint, harmony. "The fundamental principle which governs us all in the production of any printing," he wrote as early as 1934, "is that of simplicity and legibility. It is particularly necessary to avoid all distractions to the eye when producing work of a scholarly character. Ornamentation is not taboo but is avoided."[4]

One may wonder about the later association of Farquhar and Amadeo Tommasini as joint designers. Some have ventured to call Tommasini the creator and to surmise that Farquhar rode on his back, contributing only advice. But the evidence says otherwise, and so do my five years of observing them together. The distinctive design style of the Press was established between 1932 and 1938, before Tommasini came to work as assistant foreman (later foreman) of the composing room. That style was spare, restrained, classical, as I have said, whereas Tommasini was by nature flamboyant, flowery, a lover of decoration. He learned to work with Farquhar, as did Fred E. Ross before him. Ross and Tommasini were the hands-on co-designers, but it was Farquhar who directed and controlled—the architect if not the artisan. The style was his creation.

And a distinctive style it truly was. In the early 1940s, before my time at the Press, I used to claim that I could identify a University of California Press book across the room. And I could, four times out of five. The typical title page was perfectly spaced and nicely balanced, usually centered, with nearly always a small something in red, sometimes a device but more often a word or two of the title itself. The double-page spread of text was high at the top, pulled slightly to the center in the classical proportions.

In embryo this style may be seen in a small souvenir book pro-

4. *Pacific Printer and Publisher,* December 1934, p. 33.

duced for an early meeting of the Roxburghe Club in 1928: *Of Studies,* by Francis Bacon. "This book," says the colophon, "has been designed and the type handset by Samuel T. Farquhar. It is his first work of type composition." The title page is perhaps a little too spare, but at the Press several years later the style was worked out, refined, made suitable to the books in hand. An early example, not entirely typical, is *The Hundred Names* (1933), and in 1934 came the large and splendidly complex volume of Newton's *Principia.* Or one may observe four small and stylistically related books, all published in 1937: *Eugene Onegin, 'Ware Sherman, The Life and Adventures of George Nidever,* and *A Historical, Political, and Natural Description of California by Pedro Fages.*

In those days, and for twenty or more years thereafter, the chief competition for fine book design and printing was the annual show of the Fifty Books of the Year, chosen for artistic and technical excellence by the American Institute of Graphic Arts. The University Press had its first success in the show of 1936 for books published in 1935, placing two titles, *The Dancer's Quest* and *Byways in Bookland.* The first of these was a little unusual in that title page and cover carried freehand drawings by the author, Elizabeth Selden, but these were placed in perfect balance, and the rest of the book is a clear example of the Farquhar style. The second title, *Byways in Bookland,* was a small book printed for the Book Arts Club, a student organization sponsored by the Press and the school of librarianship—that is, by Farquhar and Professor Della J. Sisler.

Both books were designed by Farquhar and Fred Ross, whom Farquhar had brought in from his old firm of Johnck & Seeger and made foreman of the composing room. The same two men were also responsible for the next four books chosen for the AIGA shows of 1938 and 1939, thus six books in four years, a remarkable record. The reputation of the Press for fine books was now established. The next book to succeed in the competition, after the sudden death of Ross, was *A Scotch Paisano,* by Susanna Bryant Dakin, chosen in 1940 and credited to Farquhar and Tommasini. Over the following seven years

BYWAYS
IN BOOKLAND

By James Westfall Thompson

The Book Arts Club
of the University of California
Berkeley, 1935

THE DANCER'S QUEST

Essays on the Aesthetic of the Contemporary Dance

BY ELIZABETH SELDEN

UNIVERSITY OF CALIFORNIA PRESS
BERKELEY · CALIFORNIA · 1935

five more prize books were credited to the same team, listed in that order, with Frederic W. Goudy sharing the credit for one of them. There were three others with Tommasini's name in first place, as well as one credited to Goudy and Farquhar. Credits, as I remember, were apportioned with care. After 1947 there were no other AIGA prizes until the free-lance system was set up in the early 1950s, after Farquhar's death.

As his health deteriorated in the late 1940s, he came to take a less active role in design as in other things. Tommasini was given the title of designer in 1946; he would set up something, pull proofs, and bring them in for consultation. Sometimes Farquhar would approve and might tell Tommy to take full credit. At other times he would curb the impulse to decorate with type ornaments. I remember hearing him say, "Take that crap off the title page, Tommy."

One may wonder whether the dominance of Farquhar was the making of Tommy as designer or whether instead it was inhibiting, so that he never fully developed a style of his own, which would have been more ornamental and quite different from that of his mentor. Both things could be true. Tommy was quick, inventive, skillful, but he also adapted well to what was required of him, as many of his title pages show. What he might have done on his own is impossible to say.[5]

Ward Ritchie, in his Zamorano Club talk of a few years ago, makes much of the brief presence at the Press of two notable local printers, Wilder Bentley, whom I never knew, and William Everson, whom I did.[6] But to the best of my knowledge, neither man had anything to do with the making of books at the Press. Bentley was Farquhar's first sales manager in the early 1930s but did not last long; surely man and job were not right for each other.

5. One may look at Tommy's Thirty, a series of small books printed privately and sent out as Christmas keepsakes. They show little or no evidence of Farquhar's classical influence.
6. *Hoja Volante,* November 1979.

In the late 1940s, before he became Brother Antoninus, Everson put in a brief stint as our night janitor. He chose the job, he told me, because it required no mental effort, leaving his head clear for poetry. Ritchie says that he spent happy night interludes looking over the type in the composing room. This may be so although I never observed it, but I do remember another kind of interlude. In those days of ambition I often used to work alone in my office until late in the evening. When Bill became bored with sweeping the offices down the hall, he would park his broom outside my door, take a chair beside my desk, and help me drink the beer that I brought along to make night work more palatable. I remember some happy conversations. Shortly thereafter Bill left to seek salvation in another way of life. When next I saw him, more than a quarter of a century had passed. I was serving on the board of his Lime Kiln Press in Santa Cruz, we were both bearded, he more luxuriantly than I, and our active careers were running to a close.

After Farquhar's sudden death in 1949 the design system, along with nearly everything else, had to change. But before that there occurred several notable events of a typographical nature. The first of these began with a suggestion by Regent Edward A. Dickson that the University should have a typeface for its own exclusive use. President Sproul spoke to Farquhar, and Farquhar in late 1936 wrote an exploratory letter to Frederic W. Goudy, the most distinguished type designer of the day. Goudy was interested, an agreement was made, and the matrices were eventually delivered sometime in 1939. Known during the design period as Californian, the type was officially christened University of California Old Style.

In the beginning Dickson suggested, and Farquhar recommended to Sproul, that the new type be used exclusively by a small printing plant to be established in the garage of the Clark Library in Los Angeles. But that plant never came into being, and the face came to the Press in Berkeley. For the first book in the new type, and also as the University's contribution to celebration of the five hundredth anniversary of the invention of printing, Farquhar proposed that

Goudy himself should put together a volume of his writings on type design and type production along with historical and philosophic comments and, in particular, an account of the planning and cutting of the California type.

Goudy came to Berkeley to design the book and supervise its production. It appeared on time in 1940 and was entitled *Typologia: Studies in Type Design and Type Making, with Comments on the Invention of Typography, the First Types, Legibility, and Fine Printing*. A bit of a mouthful and something of a hodgepodge perhaps, but physically a fine example of a classical letterpress book, set handsomely in monotype, with ligatures, and the presswork crisp, the lines perfectly backed up. Chosen as one of the Fifty Books of the Year, it also elicited praise from some of the famous printers of the day. Carl Rollins of Yale wrote, "The type I think almost the best that Fred has ever done." And of the book itself Bruce Rogers wrote, "Every detail seems to me admirably and beautifully correlated:—paper, type, ink, and dimensions all seem made for each other, and the binding is discreetly gay." Except perhaps for the gaiety, not apparent to my eye, this is a clear statement of the Farquhar ideal. Whether Rogers had in mind the regular edition in cloth or the limited edition in leather and vellum, I cannot know.

The book itself, fine as it is, may seem a little over-formal, even austere, to those of us accustomed to the lighter touch of Ward Ritchie or Adrian Wilson or the Grabhorns. We may prefer another Farquhar-Goudy collaboration, the second book done in California Old Style, Goudy's *The Alphabet and Elements of Lettering* (1942). This over-size volume is formal enough but has a more open and happy look.

To the best of my knowledge, the type was used for only one other full-length letterpress book, *The Letter and the Spirit* (1943), a collection of addresses by Monroe E. Deutsch, vice-president and provost of the University. And that was virtually the end of the affair. It is saddening to think that such art and ambition never led to the great use contemplated, that so much has come to so little. What did come next was World War II, with its own imperious needs, and after that the postwar world had little quotidian use for fine typographical luxuries. At the Press publishing began to take precedence over printing and required efficient manufacture. Printing wages doubled almost overnight, and for one reason or another the University plant lost its competitive edge. California Old Style was cut only for monotype, and monotype was too expensive—at least in our plant—for use in books. And the Goudy fonts did not have the special characters and accents needed for most scholarly work. So we possessed our own handsome and exclusive typeface but were not able to use it— except on rare occasions and for small things.

Since then linotype has followed monotype to the junkyard—or to the private printer's basement—and letterpress printing has disappeared from commercial and university shops. For a time California Old Style was licensed to the Monotype Company for general sale under the earlier name of Californian, but that company has not survived. The matrices are now stored with M & H Type in San Francisco, and type is occasionally set for small books of appropriate nature, such as James D. Hart's *Fine Printing: The San Francisco Tradition,* printed at the Arion Press and published by the Library of Congress in 1985.[7]

In the centennial year of 1968 there was produced *The University of California: A Pictorial History,* by Albert G. Pickerell and May Dornin. Although the Press imprint was not used, the Press managed the production and marketing of a big book that was mostly photographs, with little text, and that came to us with the design largely done. This was Dave Comstock's first year at the Press, and it was he who suggested the use of California Old Style, with the type being set in the University plant. Repro proofs were pulled, pasted up with

7. Set in U. of C. Old Style, an earlier version of this chapter was designed by Bruce N. Washbish, printed by the Anchor & Acorn Press in Petaluma, and published in 1991 by Western Heritage Press of Berkeley as a keepsake for the Zamorano Club of Los Angeles and the Roxburghe Club of San Francisco.

Typologia

STUDIES IN TYPE DESIGN & TYPE MAKING

WITH COMMENTS ON THE INVENTION OF
TYPOGRAPHY · THE FIRST TYPES
LEGIBILITY AND FINE
PRINTING

FREDERIC W. GOUDY, L.H.D., LITT.D.

∴

BERKELEY AND LOS ANGELES
UNIVERSITY OF CALIFORNIA PRESS
1940

ABCDJ
EFGHI
KLMQ
NOS&

DESIGNS FOR UNIVERSITY OF CALIFORNIA OLD STYLE
REDUCED FROM THE 2½-INCH WORK PATTERNS

the illustrations, and the book was, of course, printed by offset. This appropriate use of the University's own typeface might have been made clear in a colophon, but was not.

A few years ago the International Typeface Corporation of New York revived the face in a digitalized version for electronic composition under the name of Berkeley Old Style. And quite recently, I am informed, the face has been made available on computer software. So what was once special and exclusive is now available to any compositor for the price of the diskette. But of course it is not quite the same thing. The weight of strokes was changed, and elements from other Goudy faces were, I think, incorporated. If the result is something less than genuine Goudy, perhaps there is no help for that. My eye, in looking at the samples, finds something of the cragginess of the original in the larger sizes, but in the smaller ones, such as the 10-point, everything looks smoothed out; the individual character is less apparent. Some prefer it that way, no doubt, but one wonders whether the distinctive character of a face cut for letterpress can ever survive electronic approximation and the flatness of offset. Or is it part of a gone world? Change was foreseeable as Goudy and Farquhar worked in 1940, but no one could have known where it was going or how fast.

In that same year of 1940—celebrated as the five hundredth anniversary of the invention of printing—the Press moved into its new building at Oxford and Center streets, said then to be the most efficient as well as the handsomest printing plant in the country. And work was going forward on another book, quite different from the Goudys but judged by some, including Farquhar, to be the most beautiful ever put out in Berkeley: *Ceremonial Costumes of the Pueblo Indians,* by Virginia More Roediger (1941). Designed by Farquhar and Tommasini, in that order, the book has a lighter touch than usual, influenced perhaps by the author's handsome watercolor paintings, or perhaps it is a rare example of influence going both ways to a happy result. There are forty color plates printed from rubber blocks, some of which went through the press thirteen times for that many colors. The printing of this book, begun and destroyed in Nazi Germany, taken up again in Los Angeles, and eventually accomplished in Berkeley, has been vividly described by Harlan Kessel.[8]

1940, then, was something of an *annus mirabilis* for Farquhar as printer, a culmination, a high point never to be reached again, although there was a moment of glory five years later. After the attack on Pearl Harbor aesthetic and scholarly matters had to stand aside, and for the next few years the Press dedicated itself largely to the war effort. Publishing energy went mostly into a long series of Japanese-language textbooks, some of them licensed by the Navy—approved piracy from Japanese editions—and printed outside our plant, which then had no offset presses.

The moment of glory came in June 1945, when the Government Printing Office asked the Press to act as technical adviser and then as chief compositor and printer of the United Nations Charter. The story of this prodigious effort, most of it crowded into three days and nights, has been told by Farquhar in a handsome little book entitled *Printing the United Nations Charter* (1946). The book carries no design credit but has all the look of a joint effort. Although the title page is rather flashy, with the United Nations symbol printed in blue and stamped in gold, the book is chaste enough otherwise except for blue type ornaments on the chapter openings. I judge it to be Farquhar in spirit with details by Tommasini.

The United Nations Charter itself was not, of course, a Press publication, but we did what we could to make it ours. That was my first year at the Press, and I can still remember Farquhar's excitement when he told me his plan, sprung to mind on a sleepless night, to publish a facsimile edition. We had the type for the English, French, and Spanish versions, as well as clean proofs for offset printing (at Stanford) of the Russian and Chinese. The edition of a thousand copies in two volumes, published in late 1945 at a high price, sold out

8. *California Printing . . . Part III* (Book Club of California, 1987), 21–23.

**УСТАВ
ОРГАНИЗАЦИИ ОБ'ЕДИНЕННЫХ НАЦИЙ**

и

СТАТУТ МЕЖДУНАРОДНОГО СУДА

САН-ФРАНЦИСКО · 1945

quickly. In the Fifty Books of the Year catalogue the designers are listed as Tommasini, C. A. Ruebsam of the Government Printing Office, and Farquhar—a work of collaboration with credits carefully and generously apportioned, as they were for the original Charter.[9]

After Farquhar's death in 1949 Press and printing department were separated once more after sixteen happy and unhappy years together. The ensuing conflict went far beyond the two departments, becoming

9. *Printing the United Nations Charter,* 47–48.

PRINTING THE
UNITED NATIONS
CHARTER

By Samuel T. Farquhar

UNIVERSITY OF CALIFORNIA PRESS

Berkeley and Los Angeles · 1946

a civil war between the University faculty and the University business office. The world of the late forties was not that of the late thirties. The faculty now wanted scholarly publishing, with or without crafts-manship. And craftsmen at sky-high wages were an anomaly that no university publisher could afford.

In a more rational world Farquhar and I might have made an ideal combination. And we did, I think, for a while. He was a biblio-phile, a lover of fine printing with an intelligent appreciation of schol-arly publishing but no great passion for it. I had an appreciation, without great passion, for clean and handsome typography, while my ambition was to build a publishing house like those at some of the great private universities. In his last years we divided the work pretty much in this way and got along quite well, thinking alike on most matters and sharing our tastes for the Greek language, good whiskey, and the back roads of California. He himself was wise enough to see that the University was changing, that our future had to lie with the Editorial Committee of the academic senate. There were others who could not see—a story told in earlier chapters.

Farquhar's death, of course, was the end of the old design team. Tommasini was made superintendent of the plant under a new print-ing manager, brought in from another University department. I was in charge of the Press, now separated from the plant. We asked Tommy to design some of our books, and he did so, working alone of course. Having grumbled at Farquhar's strictures, he would never have accepted mine, and I had no wish to play co-designer. There were now too many books for any one designer or any one printer, and many of them had to be printed outside the University plant. As a further complication, and as part of the continuing civil war, the Press was accused of wishing to tear down the high standards set by Farquhar.

So an entirely new scheme was needed, and it was then that we decided to use free-lance designers, assigning books individually to the best people we could find, understanding as we did so that the use of many designers meant the abandoning of a single and distinctive house style. The Farquhar style, I thought, could not be carried on without him, and perhaps it had run its course, as such things do. We could, however, continue to respect his ideal of attractive books that would serve "the clear transmission of thought." This would have to be done in a variety of styles, variety appropriate to the hundred or more books a year that we expected to be publishing before long.

Although I had no ambition to be designer or co-designer, I did intend to exert some control over what we were getting. In order to save time for other urgent matters, I asked one person in production—at first Rita Carroll and later Jane Hart—to help me deal with designers, and the latter were asked to prepare hand-drawn layouts of all the important parts of the book—text, title, chapter openings, cover—as well as to provide specifications for type, paper, cloth, and the like. None of this had been necessary when these things were decided day by day in the plant, but we had to be clear and plain when getting bids from outside printers. The layouts we went over with some care, judging appearance, appropriateness and, so far as we could, the practical problems that might arise. Often enough I asked for changes but not for specifics, as Farquhar once did.

Feeling some urgency to show that we were not biblio-barbarians, that we knew a book from a government document, we cast our net for the best designers within reach. As the first of these, and our surest bet, we chose Ward Ritchie of Los Angeles. In skill and reputation he was on a par with the finest private printers in California or elsewhere, and he was more businesslike than most. One could hardly ask the great loners, such as Ed Grabhorn or Saul Marks, to provide layouts suitable to the commercial printers we had to use, but Ward was at home in both worlds and could provide what we needed. Over the next few years he designed about seventy-five books for us, including such great sets as *The Sermons of John Donne,* in ten volumes, and six of his books were chosen among the Fifty Books of the Year. One could say that we hit the jackpot on the first pull. Furthermore, we had eight prize books by various designers in the three years 1951–53.

Several of these were designed by John B. Goetz, a young south-

The Christian Century
in Japan
1549-1650

by C. R. Boxer, *Camões Professor of
Portuguese, King's College, University
of London. Published by the
University of California Press,
Berkeley and Los Angeles, and the
Cambridge University Press, London*
1951

Two by Ritchie.

CHEROKEE
DANCE
AND DRAMA

by

Frank G. Speck and Leonard Broom
in Collaboration with Will West Long

University of California Press
Berkeley and Los Angeles
1951

GALILEO GALILEI

Dialogue Concerning
the Two Chief World
Systems—Ptolemaic &
Copernican *translated
by Stillman Drake, fore-
word by Albert Einstein*

UNIVERSITY OF CALIFORNIA PRESS
BERKELEY AND LOS ANGELES 1953

Design by John B. Goetz.

erner with New York experience who had moved to San Francisco
and came looking for work. This he found first as a free-lance designer and then as head of our production department, where he designed books with one hand and bought printing and binding with
the other, all with great flair and skill.

Along with the three professionals, Goetz, Ritchie, and Tommasini, we gave design work to others less experienced but promising;
these included Marion Jackson (now Marion Brucker) as well as our
two design assistants. One day the first of these, Rita Carroll, came
in with samples of theater programs printed for the Interplayers in
San Francisco by one of their members, and she suggested that we
ask him to try his hand at designing a book for us. This was, I think,

George Altman
Ralph Freud
Kenneth Macgowan
William Melnitz

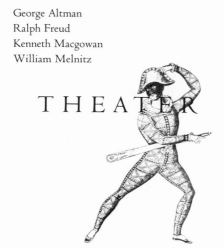

THEATER   PICTORIAL

*A History of World Theater
as Recorded in Drawings, Paintings,
Engravings, and Photographs*

UNIVERSITY OF CALIFORNIA PRESS   *Berkeley and Los Angeles 1953*

Design by Adrian Wilson.

Adrian Wilson's first commission for book design. At that time he was not yet accustomed to drawing the layout sheets that we needed, but he carried off some of those prepared by Ritchie and Tommasini and made a quick adjustment. For this first book, he admitted later, he set up some of the lines in type, pulled proofs, and traced from the proofs to the layout sheets.[10]

We were delighted with the result and so, I think, was he. From then on Adrian did one book after another for us, at least five in that year of 1951, and one of these, *Herman Melville,* was chosen for the Fifty Books of the Year. He himself was most pleased, perhaps, by *Theater Pictorial* (1953), appropriate to his own theater background,

10. *The Work and Play of Adrian Wilson* (Austin, 1983), 35–36.

and by *Morris Graves* (1956), the handsome catalogue of a retrospec-
tive exhibit at the UCLA Art Gallery. Adrian had known Graves (as
well as Bill Everson) at a pacifist internment camp in Waldport, Oregon, during World War II at a time when Graves' paintings were
going for twenty-five dollars or less.

In that same year, 1956, Adrian came to work for us under John
Goetz in the production department. There his design work continued at the same high level but, unlike Goetz, he never seemed comfortable in the office environment, with the constant give and take,
some of it rancorous, that goes on in a large organization of talented
but often difficult people. Press and printing department were legally
separated, but the University had left us rubbing against each other
in Farquhar's building, planned for every-day consultation of editors
and printers. Relations were never easy until the Press moved down
the street in 1962. Before then Adrian, who needed to work inde-
pendently, set off for a period of study in Europe. On his return he
took up free-lance work again and designed books for us off and on
through the 1960s.

Before that decade was far along the publishing list had grown so
greatly in numbers and complexity that I found it impossible to continue a close interest in the editing and design of each book. Authority had to be spread, with general rather than specific control. First,
we set up the sponsoring editor system, with each sponsor acting to
some extent as a small publisher within the larger organization, each
controlling his or her own list of books. This meant, among other
things, that the sponsor could call for the kind of design wanted, had
something to say about the choice of designer, and passed editorial
judgment on the layouts, as I had once done for the entire list.

There followed a similar division of work in production. Conrad
Mollath, by then manager of that department, was a skillful printing
executive with no great interest in aesthetic form. Under his system
several production-designers each had charge, under general direction, of twenty or thirty books at a time. Some of them—notably

Dave Comstock and William Snyder—did the design themselves for some of their books while hiring outside designers for the others, in consultation with the sponsoring editors, as noted above. The woods, we found, were full of capable free-lancers who were willing to provide layouts for our modest fees. This decentralized system worked well, giving us quick and competent design on standard books as well as more elaborate treatment when that was called for.

This was, however, a time of difficulty and confusion—because a time of transition—in the production of scholarly books. Linotype setting was giving way to photocomposition as letterpress had already given way to offset printing, and with more problems. The first faces devised (not designed) for photosetting were probably more graceless than anything used in the more than five hundred years of printing from metal; some horrendous pages were produced. Thus in Greek composition, which one thought might have been managed easily enough (and was later on) the accents floated here and there above the line, like flyspecks.

But the springing up of small photocomposition firms enabled us to pull typesetting, so called, out of the large printing houses and even out of the production department. In the Los Angeles office the managing editor, James Kubeck, began buying design and composition as well as editing (nearly all done outside the office) and then sending camera-ready copy to Berkeley. A similar but more complex system was set up in Berkeley a year later. This plan of work has survived in part, with changes to meet new conditions. At the time I was pleased with the saving in both speed and cost.

About the same time in the 1970s Mollath conducted an experiment in OCR, optical character recognition, where the copy is typed with codes and then is read by a machine and converted into camera-ready copy. But this method, usable enough for simple newspaper copy, proved unable to cope with the complexities of scholarly writing. And it was, in any event, an interim technology. Eventually, the new digital composing machines were adapted to scholarly work and drove out other methods.

In the early 1970s Dave Comstock reversed the move made by John Goetz twenty years before, leaving the office to become a freelance designer and producer of books for us and other publishers. The two men had a number of qualities in common, qualities endearing to a publisher—a fine eye and hand for design along with quickness and adaptability to modern machines. We may admire the craftsmanship of Goudy and Farquhar, may even wish that the world had not changed away from it, but publishing is a financially desperate business, especially scholarly publishing, and one must struggle to survive. Or to put it another way, craftsmanship now resides with the private printer—long may he live and print!—while the publisher must seek aesthetic salvation in good design and the best printing available from commercial firms.

After retirement at the end of 1976 I no longer participated in these matters but could observe from a discreet distance. Mollath retired at about the same time, and was succeeded by Czeslaw Jan Grycz, a man with strong feelings about the aesthetic side of printing and binding. With the help of Bill Snyder he began making the design assignments and controlling the appearance of the published books. But the pressures were great, and he brought in an art director, Steve Renick, who began dealing with outside designers as well as working directly on some of the art books and other large projects.

In order to handle the growing list of new books and reprints—more than one for every working day of the year—ten or twelve standardized text layouts were set up and given to the editors as well as to typesetting houses; thus editors could once more choose appropriate formats and work with typesetters in somewhat the way that Jim Kubeck pioneered in the 1970s. Grycz, Renick, and others spent much time on the relatively few books that called for special treatment. Wolfgang Lederer, a free-lancer, designed a number of distinctive and handsome volumes, including the several small books in the Biblioteca Italiana, a collection of bilingual editions of Italian classics. Their clean and almost classical look would have pleased Farquhar.

In the previous chapter I devoted a few appropriate words to the largest of the specially demanding books, *The Plan of St. Gall*, designed by Ernest Born, which in my time devoured years and strained patience. Book and designer outlasted me; production work went on for three years after I was gone. Grycz spent a large part of that time coaxing layouts and drawings from Born, who could never be hurried, and dealing with printers and binders.

No other book, however monumental, could be allowed to take up so much time and energy, but there followed several projects of lesser size, illustrated classics such as the trade edition of Andrew Hoyem's Arion Press *Moby Dick* (1979, 1981), with woodcut illustrations by Barry Moser, and other facsimile editions of private press books. There were two Press originals, designed at least partially as works of art. *The University of California / Sotheby Book of California Wine* (1984), published jointly with the London auction house and designed by Ernest Born, is a sort of coffee-table (or wine-cabinet) book that was perhaps more appropriate to Sotheby than to the Press. More suitable were the three quarto volumes of Allen Mandelbaum's new verse translation of the *Divine Comedy* (1980, 1982), designed by Moser and Grycz.

When Grycz went off in pursuit of his new love, computer technology, he was succeeded by Anthony Crouch, whose initial training came in his native England and who then emigrated to Canada, where he worked at McGill-Queens University Press and then became director of publishing for the Nova Scotia government. Happily for the Press, Crouch has a foot in both camps, traditional and contemporary, combining a taste for the old printing heritage with an appreciation of current technology.

Although private press books no longer tempt the editors, every year sees a number of large art books and other illustrated books of appropriate character. In 1989 there came *Spanish Cities of the Golden Age: The Views of Anton van den Wyngaerde* edited by Richard L. Kagan, a square folio volume with forty double fold-outs in color of the works of the sixteenth-century artist. Designed by Steve Renick, the book was produced in Barcelona along with a Spanish edition done at the same time. Printing was done from camera-ready copy prepared in Berkeley. It is one of the most magnificent books ever published at the Press. Other big and handsome books included, in 1990, Allen Mandelbaum's translation of *The Odyssey,* with engravings by Marialuisa de Romans, and *My Tibet,* with text by the Dalai Lama and remarkable color prints by the wilderness photographer Galen Rowell.

Other books too numerous to be listed here were designed by staff members and free-lancers. Many book jackets and paperback covers are now designed efficiently on the Macintosh computer and sent to the printer on a disk. Reprints in cloth and in paper are so many that they require the full-time attention of a reprint coordinator. I remember, in the late forties or early fifties, when we put through our first reprints, thinking we were beginning to act like real publishers.

Past and present have a way of coming together. In 1991, fifty years after first publication, the Press brought out a fine new edition of Virginia More Roediger's *Ceremonial Costumes of the Pueblo Indians,* once called by Farquhar the most beautiful book ever published in Berkeley. Although the jacket, to my eye, is a little garish, that is perhaps the fashion of the day. And if jacket and cloth cover seem slightly heavy for the light and graceful interior, that interior has lost nothing. The forty color plates, originally printed from hand-cut rubber blocks and now reproduced by offset in Hong Kong, match the original plates quite well. After half a century it is good to have this splendid volume—planned by those old co-designers Farquhar and Tommasini—once more on the publishing list.

In 1903, thirty years before Farquhar, the very first book of the Press was a handsome facsimile of the Codex Magliabechiano, entitled *The Book of the Life of the Ancient Mexicans.*[11] For 1992 the Press

11. Described in Chapter 10.

has announced the Codex Mendoza, another sixteenth-century Aztec document, reproduced in color facsimile together with translation and interpretive material. We may note, with amused pleasure, that the four large volumes are being printed on the stock of 90-pound paper left over from producing the St. Gall book.

19 Anybody Can Write a Book, but . . .

I n that furniture store in Oregon in the Great Depression of the 1930s I learned about my talent as a salesman. To customers I could talk up the virtues of sofa or bed or washing machine, but they, the customers, usually got away without putting down cash or signing contracts. You have to "close" the sale, said the manager, before they get out the front door. So I went back to doing the office work with one hand and driving the delivery truck to distant farms and to mill towns across the river.

There were other things to learn. My first task of the morning was to count the cash from the day before and balance it against sales slips and payment receipts. One morning there were a few dollars too much cash; counting and recounting I got the same result. After a while the manager strolled by, looking concerned. "Troubles?" he asked. "Too much cash," I said and told him the amount. Wandering off, he spent some time rearranging the merchandise, then strode back with the sudden light of memory on his face. He had sold a lamp the day before, he said, and for precisely the excess amount; he must have forgotten to write it down.

That was one of my naïve days: I believed what he told me. But a couple of weeks later, when this little episode was played out a second time, even a slow learner could begin to see what kind of trap he had been setting for me. On the third occasion there was no need to walk through all the steps, and I said, "Jack, tell me what you sold for $5.95, and I will write out a slip." The temptation may be compared to my weekly salary of $15.00. So he knew that I knew, but the little game was replayed from time to time, never openly discussed.

At the University Press a decade later, we seldom dealt with cash, but I was more at ease with one part of the sales manager's job than with the other. Catalogues, brochures, letters, reports, these were handled easily enough. But I can still remember standing for ten minutes on the sidewalk outside the Pickwick Book Store in Hollywood, summing up the nerve to go inside and confront the owner and buyer, Louis Epstein. To the personal difficulty was added the fact that we had very little that he might want to stock. He and other buyers were polite—most of the time—going through the list to find a few items for their shelves. It was then, perhaps, that I decided we should always bring out a few trade books or regional books—not many but enough to make ourselves welcome in the stores. Later, when we had a salable paperback list, this little problem went away.

In those early days we produced handsome books, and only then began to think about what to do with them. One day the messenger would drop a new book on my desk—quite unexpectedly sometimes—and it was time to consider whether anyone might want to buy it, whether we should send out a mailing piece. It is hard to imagine that we could have been so amateurish, but our kind of publishing in those days consisted of one part editing and two parts manufacture, as it still did many years later in some of the old-fashioned university presses that I visited in South America.

I exaggerate a little. In 1937 Bill Garrett sold 285 copies before publication of Lionel A. Walford's *Marine Game Fishes of the Pacific Coast,* a large book with color plates, and lamented that there were no other such salable books on the list. In 1944, with the war still on, we had a few steady sellers on the backlist along with a sure military market for our Japanese-language textbooks. But the latter required little or no promotion, and it was promotion that was then an afterthought and not a planned part of the publishing process. How we got from that primitive state to the complex and aggressive selling organization set up by Harlan Kessel, with a network of sales representatives and with books stocked in New York, London, Sydney,

New Delhi, Tokyo, and Mexico City—I am not sure that I know. Let me go back a ways and come forward again.[1]

In 1933, when Sam Farquhar began the general book program at what was before then a monograph press, his first sales manager was a man named Wilder Bentley, later well known as a fine printer. He did not last long; Farquhar must have seen the error quickly. Next came William A. Garrett, who knew how to sell books and complained that the printing plant produced them at its own convenience and without regard to selling seasons—a problem that persisted for many years. In 1941 Garrett moved to the Sather Gate Book Shop in Berkeley and was for a short time succeeded by Leura Dorothy Bevis, coming from another bookshop, Dawson's in Los Angeles, and bringing with her a strong interest in rare books and fine printing; it was she who wrote the first issues of our newsletter, *The Pierian Spring*, described in an earlier chapter. Dorothy joined the Coast Guard in 1942 and was followed at the Press by Lydia Park, wife of the noted local painter David Park. And then, in the fall of 1944 I became the next, but not the last, of the amateur sales managers—amateurs at that job if not in other respects.

Having learned a little about myself, I had agreed to do this work with the understanding that I would shift to more general duties as assistant manager of the Press when Dorothy came back from the wars. She never came back, preferring a teaching career, and Farquhar found a new sales manager fresh out of the navy, Thompson Webb, Jr. A year or so later I made what may have been the first of my manipulations, moving Webb to the editorial department and giving the sales job to Albert J. Biggins, a former glider pilot, who had done well with direct mail.[2] He and Bill Garrett were perhaps the only two in this little parade of sales people who possessed what I used to call the killer instinct for selling. Biggins got along well with booksellers, understood promotion, and spent several years with us in the 1950s,

1. Not all the stocking arrangements survive, but they were all useful at the time.
2. The double experience must have helped Webb become director of the University of Wisconsin Press, where he stayed for many years.

then came back for a couple of years in the early 1960s, but was perhaps a little rough around the edges for a university press.

It is Biggins who has given me, from beyond the grave, the title for this chapter. Anybody, he used to say, can write a book, but it takes a genius to sell one.[3]

In the interval between his two stints at the Press, the department was held together by Virginia Bunting, who had supervised other activities for us and was an excellent manager but not sales minded. When she inherited some money and retired to Carmel, it seemed time—past time, some might say—to go professional. In December of 1960 I hired Donald W. Brown, then sales and promotion manager at Columbia University Press and later American distributor of Penguin Books, to survey our needs and recommend a course of action that would do justice to our growing list of books, including the paperback list that we had started in 1956.[4] The primary need, said Brown, was for a professional sales and promotion manager, but it was not until a couple of years later that we managed to find Harlan Kessel, or perhaps he found us, and at last we had a sales program to match the editorial one.

But first we had to do something about the three thousand miles that stretched out between us and the great center of publishing, wholesaling, reviewing, publicity, book clubs, of everything that had to do with the book business. Viewed from the 1990s, this problem may not seem overwhelming, but in those days the west coast was a publishing desert and we a small oasis in it. A trip east took the better part of a week. In his report Don Brown said that we could never compete with the great eastern presses unless we had a presence in New York—a small publicity office and books stocked nearby for quick delivery to wholesalers and eastern stores. To book people in New York we would always be country cousins, visitors from the provinces, not taken seriously until they could call us across town or

---

3. He may have had the idea, if not the words, from Stanley Unwin's *The Truth about Publishing,* but Biggins used the expression often and made it his own.
4. See Chapter 6.

David Hales and Susan Frugé in Sausalito, 1964.

become familiar with us as they did with people from Columbia, Yale, Harvard, Princeton. Perhaps it was the New Yorkers who were provincial, but the power lay with them.

How we got the University bureaucrats (before the Board of Control) to let us set up a New York office is not shown in the surviving files and has slipped past memory. But we could always claim that we were merely stationing a regular employee there, along with a part-time secretary. We found a large, bare room on West 45th Street, not far from the Algonquin Hotel, where I used to stay in one of their dingy rooms, accepting upstairs squalor for the splendid lobby-bar and the taste of their French onion soup. This was after the glory days of Ross, Gibbs, Parker, Arno, Hokinson, and Thurber, when the *New Yorker* made the reputation that it has been living on ever since. I once saw Thurber at a table across the room.

As New York manager we hired a melancholy Australian named David Hales. Along with his taste for literature and philosophy, David had managed to make acquaintance with all the useful people in the book business. He did little direct selling but could talk to reviewers, wholesalers, publicity people. He delivered proofs of new trade books, met visiting publishers from England, entertained (modestly) our own authors when they came to New York. He never looked or acted like a publicity agent but turned out to be more effective than the two bright young men who were next to hold this job. For our books he got attention that we could never have obtained from distant California, and after we took the Sierra Club into our office, it was David who wangled the Carey-Thomas publishing award for the Club's series of exhibit-format books. (We ourselves did not win this award until years later—for *The Plan of St. Gall,* which I might not have proposed for this kind of prize.)

There were those among other presses who questioned the wisdom of spending money on a New York office, but it was surely a necessary part of pulling ourselves up by our bootstraps, and its value for publicity still seems worthwhile after thirty years. And we always asked Harlan Kessel to absorb the cost in the 15 percent or 16 percent of sales income that we allowed him for operating his department.

Only a few years ago I had to defend the idea of New York warehousing to my friend Jack Schulman, the great wizard of university press finance, who wanted to believe it an added expense. But we had no building cost, paid no rent, paid no salaries, paid only a percentage of invoice value, and that percentage was lower than we could ever manage in California, with our high state personnel costs. And there were many peripheral benefits. Books printed and bound in the east—most books—were shipped more cheaply to New York than to California. Bulk shipments to London cost much less in freight and were faster. And when we had a warehouse strike in Richmond in 1971 it was shipping from New York that saved us.

I have forgotten how we got acquainted with Joe Batiato and his Abetta Book Service in Brooklyn; nor do I know whether the name of the company was a pun meant to sound Italian-American or whether it was merely devised to make the first page of the telephone directory, but I shall always be grateful for the service we got. We were very lucky. Had we gone with a big company, controlled by commercial publishers, as we had to do in London, there would have been endless dissatisfaction. But Abetta was a family firm, and we came to feel like part of the family. There developed a kind of devotion to our interests, only partly because we were for a long time the largest customer. Once when Lloyd Lyman, our assistant director, told Batiato that we were having trouble in Berkeley, Joe offered to come out and take care of our enemies. A fine Italian joke, of course, but it showed a kind of loyalty, something that we treasured for many years. When Harlan Kessel left the Press in 1985, Joe came all the way from Brooklyn to attend the retirement dinner.

This happy relationship lasted for thirty years. At the beginning of 1992 California and Princeton university presses joined in setting up a new and modern shipping service in Ewing, New Jersey. But that is another story.

Another story also is our venture in London. When I was young in the publishing business, all the American university presses of any size were represented in Great Britain by either Oxford or Cambridge. Three of us (Chicago, California, and Duke) were with the latter, and the rest with Oxford. The Cambridge imprint went on the verso of all our title pages. They held stock of most books at Bentley House, their handsome building on Euston Road in London, set British publication dates, and advertised as much as the potential sale made feasible.[5]

But in the 1960s the American presses suffered from growing pains, feeling the ambition to represent themselves in Britain and on the Continent. The first to break loose were Chicago, Columbia, and Yale, who opened a joint office in London, known as CCY. Another group followed; some of us waited. We were then selling on the Continent

---

5. It was then felt by both Oxford and Cambridge that the selling part of their businesses needed to be conducted from London. Later, both changed their minds, or conditions changed. Cambridge sold the Euston Road building and constructed a new building in Cambridge, close to the new printing plant.

through an informal group of seven presses known as IBEG (International Book Export Group) with headquarters at Princeton, and two salesmen in Europe, including a young German named Wolfgang Wingerter.

In England we held off, not ready to go it alone and feeling some loyalty to Cambridge in a contract that went back to 1923. But Cambridge was preparing (along with Oxford) to bring out the long-awaited New English Bible, with an anticipated first-year sale of a million copies or more, and felt they should clear the decks by dropping their American and other foreign clients. It was also a time of change in this country. The seven presses in the IBEG group began to go off in several directions. The three remaining presses—California, Johns Hopkins, and Cornell—decided to stay together and set up in London.

In early 1969 we opened for business in quarters on Brook Street, a good location in Mayfair but less elegant than the address might suggest. We were near Hanover Square, at the lesser end of a not very long street; at the other end were Grosvenor Square and the American embassy. Each of the three presses had to establish a limited company under English law, and the three of us set up a fourth and wholly owned service company under the old name of IBEG. Since each of the limited companies had to have one English director, we were able to maintain a measure of continuity by choosing Dick David, old friend and by then head of the Cambridge University Press.

The three American directors—Harold Ingle of Hopkins, Roger Howley of Cornell, and I—were directors of IBEG and had to oversee the business from a distance, not an easy thing to do.[6] Twice a year we met in London with our British directors and the manager; once a year, in late winter or early spring, we brought the manager

6. Much of the setting up and some of the later management fell to Jack Goellner and Tom McFarland of Johns Hopkins and Lloyd Lyman of California. Later McFarland succeeded Lyman at California. Lyman recently retired as director at Texas A & M University Press. Goellner is now director at Hopkins and McFarland at the University Press of New England.

Trevor Brown and Lloyd Lyman in Mendocino, 1973.

to this country, meeting usually in places like Death Valley or Mendocino—for the benefit of our chilled eastern colleagues. In London we worked very hard, often until seven or eight in the evening, and allowed ourselves the one indulgence of dinner at the best restaurants we could find.

Mistakes were made, the first being our initial choice of a manager. In spite of his commercial background, he proved quite unable to cope with the problems of what was essentially a small commercial business, and we had to buy him off with the company car, a Rover 2000—something we could never have done in California, where the bureaucrats would have tied us in knots. In London we could use our best judgment; in California there was the rule book, to be obeyed or outwitted. That the Rover 2000 symbol meant more to our man than anything else says something about what we found wrong with him.

So we bought a cheaper car and hired a new manager, Trevor Brown, who had worked for CCY, knew something about the American presses, and was acquainted with booksellers in several parts of the world. With him we gradually worked out a trusting relationship and, in spite of difficulties, the office lasted, even prospered, for fifteen years, about half of them in my time and half thereafter. Sales went up rapidly in the markets we served, Britain, the Continent, Africa; a particular success, I seem to remember, were the many adoptions for our paperbacks. We never wanted the office to make profits, taxable in the UK, allowing it only a 50 percent discount and asking it to pay freight and many other expenses. In any event, it was always difficult to keep track of our British-American finances as the pound and dollar fluctuated against each other.

Later, with improvements in surface and air freight, the Press tried to avoid the troublesome British warehouses by shipping from New Jersey, but this proved too slow for British and continental stores—of first importance as the library market declined—and stocking in the UK has begun again. Selling for California and Princeton is now done by the same Wolfgang Wingerter, who sold for the original IBEG so many years ago. For a brief time, Oxford replaced London as part of the imprint. Trevor Brown now manages selling for a number of other American presses. Other London arrangements are too varied to describe here. They shift with the years; groups dissolve and reform themselves. It is not quite musical chairs, but some of the good people go from one set of presses to another.

In 1961 we began to implement the recommendations of Don Brown. And in 1962 we moved at last away from the printing department to the sixth floor of the Farm Bureau building—on the same Berkeley street but with the name changed—after a jog—from Oxford to Fulton. The gain was in spirit as well as in space. We could now *see* that we were no longer part of a printing plant. Thirty years had passed since the two departments had been joined in unfortunate wedlock.

Shortly after that move Harlan Kessel came back to California and joined the Press. He had started a career in the book business at the Emporium store in Stonestown, San Francisco, moved downtown and there rose to become buyer for all the Emporium stores. In about 1958, when we were severing our official connection with the printing department, but before we had moved, Harlan went to New York and there spent five years working for the publishing houses of

Kessel with books. Photo by Suzanne Wu.

Putnam and Macmillan. He might have remained there, but at that time the big conglomerates were beginning to swallow up the better trade publishing firms, a change not pleasing to people with bookish and intellectual interests, among them Harlan. The time was right for another move. He had conquered the eastern provinces and was ready to pack up his books and return to his alma mater.

He did not come into a going sales organization—as his several successors have done—but had to create one, had to invent a part of the Press, a part to match the editorial organization that we had spent so much time putting together. So he had as large a share as anyone in the joint effort to transform the Press from what it was to what it has become.

Again I exaggerate but not very much. We amateurs had begun and nourished a paperback list, more a selling than an editorial step. We had secured a beachhead in New York. In 1961 we had managed with success our first hardback best-seller, *Ishi in Two Worlds,* matching print runs to the on-going sales, neither too much nor too little. Joe Biggins, the least amateurish of us, did an especially good job with the book stores. But still we had no integrated organization for planning publicity, exhibits, reviews, mail and space advertising, store selling, and all the rest of it. It was Harlan who put all this together, made it work, made it a central part of the publishing process. If I am not mistaken, nearly thirty years later the sales organization still functions pretty much in the way he planned it.

As the editorial mind is flawed without some feel for the market, so the best sales and promotion people must have an editorial sense. How do the two parties talk together if they don't speak the same language? If there is too sharp a difference in the thinking, in the *kind* of thinking, then the group planning of new books becomes chaotic; the beleaguered director must choose between extremes or invent compromises. With Harlan we never had this trouble: he was a lover of books, not of merchandise; when we disagreed, as people always do, the gaps in thinking were bridgeable. He knew the difference between a trade book, with some kind of general market, and a book of narrower appeal, and did not urge trade discounts when they

Kessel with two editors, Susan Peters and William J. McClung. Photo by Suzanne Wu.

would do little good. He did not overplay his hand, never went over-board for imaginary best-sellers, as some scholarly publishers some-times do, but neither did he underplay those books that had a special market or a kind of popular appeal.

A measure of Harlan's combined sales and editorial sense is that some of our best long-time authors made a habit of coming to see him rather than anyone else. If I spotted Lesley Simpson—the hero of our Latin American and Spanish list—in the hall, he was not com-ing to see me. When Lesley had an idea for a new translation or new paperback, perhaps from another publisher's list, he took it to Har-lan. And it was Harlan who thought to plan a silver anniversary edition of Simpson's *Many Mexicos,* a mere ploy to my way of thinking, but one that sold many books.

A number of happy accidents, or accidental happenings, beginnings that led happily on for twenty or thirty years, are a part of this story. One was our delay in looking for a professional marketing manager, a delay that eventually made the timing right for Harlan Kessel to come to the Press. Perhaps that gives me the excuse I need to close this chapter with a story about our wittiest critic, our finest sales manager, and three dogs.

During most of the time that my wife and I lived in Berkeley, we kept cats and not dogs. When a friend came to the front door with a dog, Susan would say, "You can't bring that dog in here; this is a cat house." But there came a day when our last great brown cat, Moshi, went to join the Big Burmese in the Sky, and we decided to replace him with a dog. A big dog; Berkeley was no longer the safe and pleasant place of earlier years.

First intimation of change came in Santa Barbara, when Hugh and Mary Anne Kenner introduced me to the redoubtable Thomas—a quarter German shepherd, a quarter malamute, and the other half Alaskan wolf. Once you had shaken hands with Thomas, you were a friend of the family. Those who were not friends were well advised to keep their distance. A profile of Thomas and a record of his sayings are now part of American literature.[7]

But by the time we were dog-ready, all the Kenners had moved to Baltimore, where I sometimes visited and took Thomas for a walk. Or he took me for a walk, said an observer. Back in California the Kessels lived with a German shepherd, and Harlan said, "Why don't you get one like ours?" I said, "That's all right for you, but we don't have a yard big enough for a shepherd to run in." Harlan then told me that shepherds, no matter how big, are house dogs. They don't like the outdoors. And he proved as right about dogs as he was about

7. In Hugh Kenner, *Mazes* (1989), 317–20.

Lash La Rue and mistress.

books. House dogs they are. Lap dogs they would like to be if they could get away with it.

So Harlan and Esther went with us across the hills to a kennel near Livermore and helped us pick out a big red and black pup. His name was Lash La Rue, after the old-time movie star. Although he tore up the basement the first night, chewed his way through doors and fences, grew to weigh 125 pounds, and frightened many people, he was at heart a gentle soul. The only person he ever bit was Harlan.

All four of us made the mistake of taking Rue into the Kessel house, the domain of Kiam, asking the two dogs to tolerate each other. They seemed to at first, but Kiam bided his time, chose a favorable moment on an inside stairway, and attacked. Rue counterattacked. Harlan got in the way, and there ensued a visit to the hospital. I should add that Rue was forgiving, bore no grudge, and in later years always wagged his tail when Aunt Esther and Uncle Harlan came to visit.

20 The Bird That Was Overdue for Evolution
And Other Tales of the Financial Wars

I take it as a warning that some of my most intelligent friends do not get through their thick heads the rather obvious distinction between operating and capital accounts, between expensing an expense and capitalizing it. Nor do they always see that one may finish the year with a black figure on the bottom line while preserving a fine fat loss on the balance sheet. What is not understood becomes a bore. A warning, then, that I must go easy on financial explanations in the stories that follow even though financial needs—some of them desperate—lay close beneath actions that upset many people.

I should sympathize with these puzzled friends, since I too am thick-headed about similar if larger matters—how one can buy a corporation with its own assets; how it is possible to pile one money-losing company on top of another and still another to create a huge financial empire like those we read about in the papers (for example that of the late Robert Maxwell, who not long ago was found floating in the sea off the Canary Islands and near his yacht). Since we financial dunderheads are siblings under the skin, perhaps I can appease the others with a vulgar little tale about a time when the great Captain Maxwell called on me in Berkeley.

That must have been in the early 1960s, because our offices were still in Sam Farquhar's handsome printing building on Oxford Street. Maxwell had not yet acquired his newspaper holdings but he controlled a number of companies including the Pergamon Press, a publishing house based in Oxford, I think, with a large international list of scientific books and journals. And he had already earned the hatred of those London publishers for whom he had lost money in the Simpkin Marshall affair of the 1950s. It was salt in their wounds that they had been bilked, as they saw it, by one who was not even a genuine Englishman—a transplanted Czech.[1]

He called one day, wanted to visit the Press, and arrived in the late afternoon with a very young man—too green for us to hire—whom he introduced as manager of his California office. Where the office was, or was going to be, I fail to recall. Nor do I remember much of the conversation, except that he was prepared to take over this distant province—about as distant perhaps as was Britain to the Romans of Caesar's day. Our university was rich in scientific talent; its professors could add to the riches of the Pergamon list. He offered me $1,000 a year—or was it a month?—to act as his agent. Even multiplied by the inflation of thirty years, it was not a princely fee or bribe. And I wondered afterwards how I would have gone about collecting it.

When he was ready to leave, after closing time when everyone else was gone, he asked for the men's room, and I directed him to our handsome curving stairway to the second floor. Where he went on that floor I do not know, but after he and his acolyte had departed the janitor came down to my office and asked who was the strange man: "He pissed all over the floor."

So that is what he thought of us and our piddling affairs. He, the great man, went on to financial fame and to death in Spanish waters, where the lesser fish may have nibbled on him. We—when the floor had dried next day—could laugh at ourselves and go on with the

---

1. Simpkin Marshall was a large wholesale firm that lost its huge stock of books in the fire-bombing of London. Maxwell purchased the firm and ran it into bankruptcy without any apparent loss to himself. Among the outraged losers was Harold Macmillan, the future prime minister.

business of keeping our small enterprise afloat. The problems were complex enough for us.

For its first forty years the Press lived like any simple University department on an annual appropriation. When one year's fund was spent, that was it until next year. The small income from sales was not put against the cost of publications issued; it merely went into the University's general fund. If the Press was ever to be a publishing house and not a mere service agency, all this had to be changed. But within change lay the seeds of trouble.

Under Sam Farquhar in 1933 there was set up the General Publications program for publishing books at risk. It was given a few thousand dollars of start-up money, which, along with funds Farquhar could attract from outside, was supposed to revolve, with sales income from earlier books providing investment funds for later ones. And in a general way it did revolve.

The General Publications, which amounted to a kind of business, were set up parallel to the older Scientific Publications, entirely non-commercial and funded on the state appropriation. But with one staff to operate both programs, it was inevitable that the two should become mixed together in ways that only a few people understood. And into this mixture was stirred another ingredient, the printing department, which was much larger than publishing and was also profitable. With the approval of President Sproul, a number of publishing expenses came to be paid from printing surpluses.

By the time I arrived in 1944 there were, I think, five separate publishing budgets, funded in different ways. Thus Farquhar had a good deal of flexibility; when need arose he could split a salary between two budgets and could make other manipulations to assure that all budgets were kept healthy and within bounds. I write this without intending the slightest kind of criticism. In the position he found himself there was nothing else he could do to keep president and faculty happy, his publishing program alive, and his print shop healthy. He and Hazel Niehaus, his office manager, understood the budgets, whether anyone else did or not. So I too learned to understand and manipulate them for the good of the Press. It may have been then that I prepared myself, without knowing it, for some later and larger manipulations, also for the good of the Press.

After the war the happy equilibrium lost its balance. The publishing side of the Press, as noticed in earlier chapters, became too big and too ambitious for easy co-existence with the printing plant. The latter, in the inflationary postwar years, lost its competitive edge and hence its ability to help finance publishing and at the same time satisfy its other University customers. After Farquhar's death in 1949 and the separation of the two departments, the accounts had to be pulled apart. And at about the same time we were finding out that you cannot operate a publishing business with institutional accounts that divide expenses not by publishing function, as everyone else did, but by such unhelpful state categories as salaries, general assistance, supplies, equipment, and facilities. We pushed for change; the University resisted. It was not until sometime in the 1970s that we finally got the accounts set up the way they needed to be.

There was a time when the University kept our accounts in its old way, the state way, while we kept a separate set of books in the publishing way, hoping that the two sets of totals could be reconciled at the end of the year. Much extra work, of course, and that leads me to comment on the university services that are given to a press and often thought of as hidden subsidies. Disservices they have been called in a term I should have invented but did not, although I used to argue that university services *cost* us money. The purchasing office got in our way, lost us time; we could buy printing better without them. The personnel department cost us untold extra work. For this, Lord help us, they forced us to pay too much—well beyond publishing standards—for several kinds of work and allowed not enough to some critical positions. Over the years of my time, with huge effort and the help of the Board of Control, we managed to hump some of these "services" off our backs, but in a bureaucracy Personnel is a burden that cannot be shed. In a state university, at least in ours, there is no free ride or free lunch. Possibly rent, when you can get it, but that is not enough to offset the bureaucratic make-work.

I used to say to our Board of Control, set up in 1961 with three top University vice-presidents along with senior faculty members: "Please be a true board of governors. Make the decisions. Draw up a set of rules, and we will live by them, but keep the bureaucrats away from us." This never came to pass, and I still wonder why a board of high University officers cannot take over small authority as well as large and simply make the Press off limits to the service departments. As justification there is this: unlike other activities the Press has no captive customers within the University; no faculty members are required to bring in manuscripts; no one, no library must buy the published books; the Press must make its way by attracting free authors and by selling books on the open market. Is it fitting, then, that the Press should be a captive customer of other University departments? I regret that I never found the time or the eloquence to make this case to the Board.

Nevertheless, the Board was wonderful; in the fifteen years that I worked with them, they always understood and encouraged and helped. I will come later to some of their larger actions, without which we could never have built the financial base that underlies the Press of today. Here a smaller act will illustrate some of the unkind remarks above. We used to wrap packages in Richmond and truck them to Berkeley, where an office known as the mailing division would affix postage at a surcharge to us of 25 percent. Ridiculous, you will say, and easy enough to fix: buy a postage meter. But how could we buy a meter when a branch of the purchasing department was operating this little boondoggle? It took a vote of the Board of Control and then the stern intervention of its chairman, senior vice-president Harry Wellman, before we got our meter. The first order, signed by a lesser vice-president, was stonewalled.

Robert Townsend, the man who was famous for revitalizing the Avis Rent-a-Car company and other businesses, once published a book telling how he did it. Among his recipes for running an efficient business was to "fire the whole personnel department" and set up a one-person "people" office. And after that, fire the whole purchasing department. "They cost ten dollars in zeal for every dollar they save through purchasing acumen. . . . They'd hire Einstein and then turn down his requisition for a blackboard."[2]

For a number of years after 1933 the Press's use of investment funds was so small that it could lie hidden in the University's large capital account. When a new book was published, the University simply advanced the manufacturing cost, set the amount up in an inventory account, and recouped the money when the copies were sold. No one saw need to consider the Press investment separately. But as the backlist grew, and the invested amount—covering inventory and receivables—began to approach the million mark, there was set up for us a separate account known as Regents' Capital. And in a series of good years in the late 1950s and early 1960s, we regularly made operating surpluses that could be added each year to the capital account. We were, in a sense, earning the investment funds needed to enlarge the publishing list.

But of course we were doing so with the help of an operating subsidy, contained within the annual state appropriation, and before long state auditors began to take an interest. Soon they were closing in on us, acting to recoup that part of the surplus judged to result from use of the subsidy. So the state was not going to provide capital or help us earn it. It took us six years to find it elsewhere.

In 1963, when we first asked help of the Board of Control, we had $560,000 in the capital account, but most of this was "earned" and the state was after it and was also chopping the subsidy that helped us do the earning. We were moving backwards, being squeezed ever tighter. During the next several years the Board kept us alive by making a number of upward adjustments in the regents' part of the fund

2. *Up the Organization* (New York, 1970). His reasons, not quite the same as mine, are compelling.

and arranging a line of credit for further use, with interest at the prime rate.

Board members must have been convinced that we knew what we were doing, because in 1968 they asked for a five-year projection and decided to go to the regents for a permanent solution. At the regents' meeting we had the support of chancellors Murphy of UCLA and Mrak of Davis, and of President Hitch, a former member of the Board of Control. But the prime mover, the chief intelligence behind the action, was Graeme (Jim) Bannerman, the new financial vice-president, who believed us, saw the need clearly, and made sure that action was taken. It was also Bannerman who saw to it that we were finally given a set of accounts that helped rather than hindered management. These two actions, taken in his short time at the University, made possible the transformation of our financial condition. Some part of the Press ought to be named for him.[3]

Our regents' capital fund of a half-million dollars was now made permanent and without interest, and in addition there was set up a University Press Fund of several million dollars, the income from which we were allowed to take each year as an addition to working capital. This was a kind of endowment, something that I had discussed with Chancellor Murphy a few years earlier. He must have spoken up for it to the regents.

In just a few years after that, by June 1976, the end of my last full business year, we had accumulated earnings of $710,000, after the subsidized part had been withdrawn by the state. From this we had purchased a small building on Durant Avenue for $130,000 and had set up a building reserve of $354,000.[4] To round out the capital picture, we also had the old regents' fund, now $550,000, and accumulated endowment funds of $1,363,000. By that time we were working without an operating subsidy, unless some of the University "ser-

3. He died suddenly while playing golf.
4. Several years later, the Durant building, appreciated in value, was used to help pay for the new Press building on Berkeley Way.

vices" may be counted as such. And we were writing off all plant cost
so that no future losses were hidden in the inventory account. All
these things were made possible by a Board of Control that believed
in what we were doing.

Plant cost, in publishing language, is all the production cost of a
book before it goes to press—editing, composition, and the like, everything except paper, presswork, and binding. It is good financial practice, common in commercial publishing, to write this off (expense it)
at the time of publication or sooner. Carrying it in inventory post-
pones putting it in the expense accounts and can mislead management by making the operating figures look better than they are.

The sad demonstration came soon enough. After I retired and
with changes on the Board of Control, the University auditors demanded that the plant cost policy be changed and that these costs go
into the inventory—that is, be capitalized rather than expensed. This
they had wanted for several years, but we had managed to fight them
off. From this and other encounters I gained the reputation among
service departments of being irascible and difficult. Perhaps this was
so—such traits grow along with one's years. But perhaps this story
has shown that the battles were necessary. On this particular occasion
a service department confronted a new Board and new Press management not yet accustomed to university in-fighting, and got its way.
The inventory started swelling almost at once.

The Board of Control must have been napping. As one reads the
minutes of the next several years it is apparent that the Board, with
an inexperienced chairman, Donald Swain, and without the financial
acumen of old member Loren Furtado—indeed with no financial officer for some while—failed to see what was coming. The old Board,
with Angus Taylor in the chair and Furtado watching the accounts,
would surely have recognized the danger. When the crunch came, a
two-million dollar loss had to be swallowed in the inventory account.

It is pleasant to write that decline was stopped and health restored. With a new chairman, William Frazer, a new financial subcommittee chaired by Earl Cheit, a professor in the business school
at Berkeley, and with its first outside member, Jack Schulman, former

director of Cambridge University Press, New York, the Board took hold once more and now provides genuine financial guidance. Director Jim Clark was given a new financial officer, Christina Olton, and a new assistant director, Lynne Withey, the three of them making a management team that could lead the Press out of the wilderness. A seven-year plan of recovery, devised by Olton and the Board's finance committee, is being followed successfully and one can look ahead with confidence once more.

But such things were not dreamed of in 1970. With investment capital assured, we found ourselves turning to the other set of accounts, the operating ones, and the state subsidy that helped us pay expenses. We could never be sure that the state, in one of its periodic drives toward economy, would not decide to eliminate this and leave us high and dry. A warning had come in fiscal year 1966 when about $100,000 was suddenly lopped from the amount. That year we must have had a good list, and Harlan Kessel surely did a splendid job of promotion, because we came up with a sales increase of 31 percent and finished the year with only a small operating loss of about $15,000, the only such loss I can remember in more than twenty-five years. Indeed, we might have finished triumphantly in the black by juggling the inventory write-off, but that would hardly have been wise. Better to protect the future. Better also not to let anyone think that we had not needed the subsidy.

By strenuous work with the University budget office and with state officials, we managed to get the cut restored for the following year. But in the year after that the knife was wielded again, and we could now see the handwriting on the wall. A general subsidy would never be safe from Sacramento officials who had little or no understanding of scholarly publishing. We had to get ourselves into a safer position.

Here I must draw a distinction between a general or operating subsidy and title subsidies for individual books. The first helps to support the basic operation of a press while the second, much more easy to justify, is used to cover the loss on certain books that are expensive to produce and sell few copies. No matter how efficient the basic operation, some books cannot possibly pay their own way from sales. Our title subsidies came from the Scientific Account, controlled by the Editorial Committee, and from outside sources.

The annual state appropriation to the Press amounted to about half a million dollars, but only part of this was used to help cover operating expenses for book publishing, our chief concern. Also included were funds to cover the editing and handling cost of the Editorial Committee's no-commercial publications, the series monographs, and the cost of several scholarly journals. If the entire appropriation were considered a publishing subsidy and suddenly withdrawn, the latter two programs would be destroyed, or their costs would be dumped on top of book publishing, an extra load that could bring down the entire structure. So we cut a deal with the Board of Control: if they would give us three years to do the job, we would work off the operating subsidy for books and would also bring the entire appropriation account to zero. Some of the monies saved might be used for other University purposes.[5]

First, this big account had to be pulled apart. In a series of benign manipulations, the cost of editing monographs and the loss on scholarly journals were transferred to the Editorial Committee's budget, along with, of course, money to cover them from our state appropriation. We judged that the Committee's fund—quite separate from ours and termed a cost of faculty research—would be safer than our account from state depredations. The Committee was happy enough; it lost nothing and gained the power to make or break journals.[6]

With those little moves under our belt, we could look at our main set of accounts, now clearly related to book publishing, with no other matters to confuse. The operating subsidy had become considerably smaller but was still a hefty sum, well into six figures. To eliminate

5. The Press budget was part of a larger University category called Organized Research. Within this the University had some flexibility.
6. They could always grant or refuse the imprint but never before had had the power to finance a new journal or de-finance an old one.

this and operate at the break-even point—the only secure way to go—we had to increase sales or reduce expenses or both. Both, surely, because we could not expect sales to go up 31 percent every year, although our new capital funds allowed us to publish a larger number of books. We gained something by raising prices, especially of the backlist, but that was not enough. We had to whittle on the expense accounts.

To guide us in this we had one splendid tool, the operating ratios developed by Jack Schulman and others for the Association of American University Presses. These were contained in composite or group operating statements, expressed only in percentages of sales. When net sales were set at 100 percent, and manufacturing and royalty costs were deducted in the upper half of the statement, the remainder, plus or minus 50 percent, became the gross margin, out of which all the operating expenses had to come if one were to break even. There was a percentage figure for each department or publishing function—so much for paying editors, so much for running the sales department, and the like. I simplify, perhaps over-simplify, for the sake of those friends mentioned some pages back. If they are still unhappy, they can jump a few paragraphs.

Separate ratios were compiled for small and for large presses, and the large-press figures, the ones that concerned us, were divided between presses losing money and those breaking even. We turned our eyes to the break-even ratios and compared our costs to those of other presses. Good news and bad news. We were pretty well off in the upper half of the statement because we had kept the inventory slim and healthy, writing values down each year and allowing no plant cost to inflate them. So we had a good gross margin for covering expenses.

The bad news came further down the page. We had controlled the largest expense, sales and promotion, by telling Harlan Kessel that he could spend 15 percent of income or perhaps 16 percent, because we were striving for sales increases, and no more, spend it any way he judged best. I might add that he had to cover the New York office and pay the paperback editor, who worked for him. Our overhead costs for administration, business office, and production department were roughly comparable with industry figures. But two expenses, editorial and warehousing, were out of line; only if we could bring them down would we have a shot at breaking even. This bringing down—the work of two or three years—cost us pain and commotion: the employees' union accused us of "racism, sexism, and union busting"; I was portrayed as an old bird with half its feathers gone; a strike was called.

One might have thought, at first glance, that editorial costs were high because we maintained two editorial offices, in Berkeley and in Los Angeles, but analysis showed that this was not so. It took no more editors to do the work in two places than in one. There was no duplication of effort, only a small extra office expense, a low price to pay for demonstrating that we were a statewide and not a Berkeley operation—not to mention more efficient manuscript solicitation. The trouble lay elsewhere.

We also employed two kinds of editors. When I first came to the Press in 1944, the editors were all copyeditors or manuscript editors, who worked on manuscripts after they had been taken in and approved by the Editorial Committee. Later, it became clear that we had to go out after better manuscripts if we were to become book publishers of stature, and we began hiring acquisition editors, the first of whom was brought from New York and placed in the Los Angeles office. Others followed, in both offices, and by the time expenses had to be trimmed there were two editorial staffs, sponsoring (acquisition) editors and copyeditors.

There was of course nothing wrong in this. Trade publishers and some large scholarly presses were organized in this way, with the two functions kept separate. But copyediting, as practiced in American scholarly presses—as opposed to the practice in other countries—was and often still is elaborate, thorough, and slow, amounting sometimes to rewriting. (Because professors cannot write, some say. And when they can, should be made to conform to something called house style.) And our difficulty was compounded by the University's personnel system, which forced us to pay copyediting salaries that were much higher than those paid in trade publishing and by our eastern competitors.

It was clear that we could not go on in this way if we were to bring our costs into line and compete with the other large presses. It seems likely, I now think, that the existence of an operating subsidy had allowed us to become careless with this expense, even while trying to run a tight ship in most other respects. I should add that what we managed to do about the subsidy would be more difficult today, might even be impossible now that the average scholarly book sells fewer copies than it did in my time. But one should always bear in mind that the regular use of a general or operating subsidy is a kind of crutch; one gets used to it, as we had done, and depends on it, fighting not quite so hard to trim expenses when they can be paid with given money. In the early 1970s we knew that the crutch was going to be pulled out from under us and we had to learn how to walk without it.

Copyediting is essential, but not too much of it. "The good copyeditor is a rare creature," writes Judith Butcher, chief subeditor at Cambridge University Press, and then goes on to praise "the judgment not to waste his firm's time or antagonize the author by making unnecessary changes."[7] In an earlier chapter I have pointed out the fallacy of seeking to ensure the quality of a book list by heavy editing. By that time it is too late; quality must be sought earlier by sponsoring editors who do their job properly, without expecting the copyeditors to clean up after them. We had thought about this matter from time to time, but only now did we come up hard against it. Our practice was mixed; at times we let ourselves do too much of the author's work or tried to make good books out of middling ones—a common enough practice among university presses.

From then on, it would be nice to say that the faults were all corrected; we took in only clean manuscripts and put them swiftly through the editing stage. Of course this was not so. But we had made a change in our thinking, instructing the sponsors to do a more

7. In *Copy-editing: The Cambridge Handbook* (ca. 1975), 2.

thorough job with their authors and not plan on heavy revision. And had asked that copyediting be held to what it ought to be—editing but not recasting. We had decided to put our money where the benefits were—in acquisition.

In-house editing was costing too much. The cure was simple but not easy: we eliminated the copyediting staff and had the work done by free-lancers on the outside. If that sounds hasty or harsh, it was neither. The change was made over two years, first in Berkeley and then in Los Angeles, and we either kept the best people on the staff or arranged futures for them. In Berkeley Susan Peters had shown that she could handle twice as many manuscripts as did others, and her authors were the happiest—she gave the help they needed but did little violence to their syntax. So she survived and was put in charge of supervising the free-lance work. In Los Angeles the quick and efficient Jim Kubeck took over a similar role. A few years later, as described elsewhere, he began buying composition as well as editing.

We wondered at first whether we could find enough free-lance editors in our part of the world, where publishing was not a big industry, but there was never a shortage; their number was legion. And with them we could control the cost, as we never could with in-house work. The latter was done on the salary roll and—as our old chief editor used to say—it would take as long as it would take. With free-lancers it was simpler: we paid by fee, agreed upon in advance. A quick editor could make good money; a slow one did not cost us extra. Quality, controlled by Peters and Kubeck, was kept high. I thought about kicking myself for not taking the step years earlier.

In reducing the staff it was feasible to eliminate some positions, after giving rather long notice to the people who held them. But we could not in conscience do this to a number of senior editors, who had been with the Press for many years, who had developed their skills, and could do the most difficult kind of revision—just the kind of work that we no longer wanted to pay for. One was asked to retire and given free-lance work to fatten a good pension. But there remained three others, all in Berkeley, and we really had no place for them under the new system. And could not afford to carry their salaries. Once more benign manipulation was called for.

A number of academic departments, whose professors turned out much research, wanted editors on their staffs but had no budgetary provision for them. When I offered the gift of a position and the money to pay for it—money from a subsidy that we expected to lose but that they could manage to keep—it was not difficult to strike a deal, especially when the chief budget officer, a member of the Board of Control, approved. There were no losers within the University: we cleared our budget; the departments, which did not have to make their own way, were happy to enlarge theirs; the employees were protected. At least one of them managed to wangle a promotion out of the deal.

In this way Joel Walters went to the college of agriculture, Max Knight to the department of anthropology, and Lorna Price to art history. For this largess I exacted a small price, objected to by no one. The gift editors, it was agreed, would spend part of their time editing manuscripts that came to us from the three departments. In the field of art history this side benefit was not small; even well-written art manuscripts require much preparatory work. The years that Lorna Price spent on *The Plan of St. Gall* would, if paid by the Press, have made that book look even more impossibly expensive than it was.

Try as we might to explain what was going on, we could not make so many changes, even over two years' time, without stirring up fear and resentment. Even before we got around to the Richmond warehouse, which was found to be operating with more positions than needed, the smolder had become a flame and the new employee union, hot to prove itself and attract more members, was after us. In the spring of 1971 the ever-helpful personnel office led us into a trap over the maternity leave of a woman in the business office, advising us to deny a particular kind of leave and, two weeks later, deciding that she should have it. The union blamed us, of course, and put out a flyer with the headline "MOTHERHOOD DENIED (Did the U.C. Press manag-

MOTHERHOOD DENIED!!

(Did the U.C. Press managers ever have mothers?)

The University of California Press management, formerly renowned for its liberalism, has turned the organization into a chamber of horrors. One of the most natural and necessary of biological functions has been deemed a liability by the managers of the UC Press.

On February 25, 1971, Betty Larry, a Black union member-- and 6 months pregnant--requested maternity leave from the Press business manager, Norman Koerner. She was told that Personnel would have to be consulted and he would reply to her in a few days. On March 8th, Betty again went to ask for her leave and was told then that she should direct her request, in writing, to the Assistant Director of the Press, Lloyd Lyman.

On March 19th, Betty, now 7 months pregnant and hemorrhag- ing in the hospital, was sent a letter from Lyman stating that she had been denied maternity leave. Management, holding true to form, offered Betty a token gesture. They were willing to give her a 6 months leave of absence so that she could continue her group medical insurance. However, at the end of the leave, there would be no guarantee of a job. Thus, if Betty were to accept this token, she would in effect be signing her separation papers.

The U.C. Press management is hereby publicly charged with sexism, mental cruelty (Betty had her baby 2 months premature), and harrassment of the union. We openly solicit community and campus support in helping Betty Larry get real maternity leave with a guarantee of reinstatement to her job.

JOIN THE UNION!

HELP PROTECT MOTHERHOOD!!

AFSCME 1695
UC Non-academic Employees
2483-A Hearst Avenue
Berkeley 94709   549-3440

labor donated
4/2/71

ers ever have mothers?).'' Below that the text began, "The University of California Press management, *formerly* renowned for its liberalism, has turned the organization into a chamber of horrors. One of the most natural and necessary of biological functions has been deemed a liability." I never learned who was author of that piece of prose.[8]

8. The episode is described in Minutes of the Board of Control, 31 March 1971.

The union produced a forty-four-page document, describing how the Press could save $160,000 without the lay-offs. Whether this has survived, I do not know, nor do I remember much of the contents, except that the chief saving would have come from using the Editorial Committee's fund for Press purposes, publishing fewer monographs, and paying the employees, whether they had work to do or not. I tried to explain to Dave Comstock that the money was not ours to use.

I don't recall how much Dave had to do with compiling the forty-four pages, but it was he who became the intellectual and spiritual leader of the dissidents, although, later, when the strike came in Richmond, he continued to work in the Berkeley office. (Berkeley, in a different county from Richmond and with a different labor council, was not struck.) About once a day Comstock sent in a memo asking whether we were ready to negotiate, and I would answer, saying no, but you are welcome to come in and talk. So talk we did, a number of times, and I think we both enjoyed the exchange of ideas, different as our viewpoints were. He was having a good time, I thought.

The group wanted to explain its position to the Editorial Committee, and I recommended to Ralph Rader, our northern chairman, that they be heard. Although the Committee had no jurisdiction in such matters, it always seemed to me that its members should be allowed—encouraged—to discuss anything about the Press that interested them. The more they knew and understood, the more strongly would they support us—as long as we were acting with sense and for the benefit of the Press. And so it turned out a number of times.

Four of the union group, led by Comstock, appeared at the May meeting and made their case at length but, to the best of my memory, without convincing anyone. Hugh Kenner, with his usual astuteness, remarked that the union thought of the Press as a collection of jobs and not as an organization with a purpose larger than any of us. Sometime during the meeting Dave Comstock said—with not quite a grin on his face—that the first of September that year might be the last of August.

It may be worth noting that Dave became a great friend to Susan and me. Not long after the union affair he or his wife Ardis inherited some money, and they moved to Grass Valley, where Dave built a house with his own hands, set up a free-lance book design and production shop, and did business with several university presses, including California. Susan and I have gone to Dave's art shows in Nevada City and own several of his water colors. He and Ardis have visited us on the desert where we live.

In June, when the warehouse and periodicals lay-offs were announced, the union (AFSCME 1695) called a strike and picketed the warehouse in Richmond. Since most people in the billing office there continued to work and shipments could be made from the New York warehouse, the effect was not great, and the union decided to shut down the University's other offices in Richmond, including the hospital supply center. At that point the University went to court for an injunction, and the strikers had to return to work.

All banal enough, perhaps, but during the two weeks of picketing the union paper published a cartoon by Vince Hickey, one of the strikers, that showed a scruffy fowl—U.C. Press Management—walking away from a clutch of eggs labeled Lay Offs, Racism, Speed Up, Sexism, and Unemployment. The legend underneath read: "A bird that lays such rotten eggs is long overdue for evolution." Union graphics, I thought, were superior to union prose.

Troubles, for better or worse, have a way of coming one on top of another and not one at a time. As the events above took place, and as all publishers struggled in a financial down-turn, the Press was bitten by a computer, and then came an attack on the Editorial Committee. We were not the first to acquire a computer for invoicing, but we might have waited longer, until the publishing software had been fully de-bugged. In those early days many firms, including publishing houses, were plagued by machines that worked only part of the time or that spewed out pounds of faulty paperwork. Some companies did not survive. In my mind I could see a tombstone with an inscription something like this: Here Lies the ——— Press, Murdered by a Com-

"A bird that lays such rotten eggs. . . ." Drawing by Vince Hickey.

puter. (A few years later I was wondering whether *The Plan of St. Gall,* with costs running out of control, might not turn into that kind of monument.)[9]

Our computer, an IBM 1130, was supposed to make invoicing faster and records better. What it did was to slow down the work and confuse the records. When the technicians sent out by IBM proved unable to correct the troubles, we were fortunate enough to find a young man whom I remember as John, who seemed to understand the infernal machine; he gradually got the programs in order, shipments went out on time once more, and we could begin to repair our reputation with booksellers.

We would have been lost, I think, without our assistant director, Lloyd Lyman, who hired a new business manager, found the other right people, took on the periodicals management himself, and in

9. A faulty computer system at Harvard University had much to do with the great deficits incurred by the press there at about the time I write of. The press survived, but the director did not.

general masterminded the renovation of our entire business operation. Lloyd had come from Oregon, as I had, but from the southern end of the state. He graduated from Reed College in Portland, took a masters degree in American history at Berkeley, then taught history at Cal Tech before coming back to Berkeley for an advanced library degree. Bored with study, he wandered into the Press, was taken on for miscellaneous tasks, and worked his way into the administration, where he managed most of the operating departments while doing editorial work on the side. After leaving California, he was chief editor at Louisiana State University Press and then director of the press at Texas A & M, personally chosen by the great Frank Wardlaw—a southern boy turned westerner choosing a real westerner to succeed himself.

But it was our small periodicals department that blew up in our faces. There were only a few journals, managed with the left hand while we concentrated on book publishing; some were inherited from the time of Sam Farquhar, who had paid for them with printing profits, while others were taken on to please faculty members at a time when we still had state money. Our journals manager, a very intelligent man, had worked well for several years but suddenly fell head over heels in love with the computer—as others have done since then—intrigued by all the complex things it could do when he might better have worked toward simplicity in the programs. The subscription records became entangled; there was trouble providing mailing tapes for new issues. And worse perhaps was an error of judgment that I should have caught sooner; unlike most journal publishers, we were providing copyediting for the academic editors and sometimes retyping manuscripts. The printing of new issues fell months behind. The academic editors held indignation meetings. Several of them signed a letter of protest to the Editorial Committee, which discussed the matter with us and reported back that repairs were being made. They were, but one critic preferred blood.

The Press was at fault, as we had told the Board of Control several weeks before; we had also pledged ourselves to clean up the mess by July 1971, a few months ahead. By that self-set deadline, Lloyd and his people managed to straighten out the records; meanwhile diagnosis of the copyediting trouble suggested a simple cure—surgery, editectomy. Giving the two copyeditors generous notice, we eliminated the work they had been doing, and asked the academic editors to prepare their own copy and send it directly to the production department. They did, and soon the issues were coming out on time. But it was not surprising that the two copyeditors were among the more vocal of our critics at the time of the strike described above.

So the problem was now solved—with pain and difficulty, but solved—and most of the academic editors accepted our expression of regret. But not the one. At that time his motives seemed obscure, and perhaps they were, but a re-reading of the documents is suggestive. In a memo to the Editorial Committee after the first attacks, I had recalled an appeal from the Davis campus a few years before: the concerned academic department had no money; the chancellor was short of funds; could I squeeze a few thousand dollars from the Press budget to acquire the journal and make our man editor? I did. And now, annoyed and unwary, I added to the memo a few words about biting the hand that . . .

Was this the unforgivable remark? We cannot be sure, but possibly so. In an earlier century the man might have defended his honor by challenging the Press to a duel, and I would have had no choice but to shoot him. In a nonvital spot, probably, and by shortly after dawn the whole affair would have been settled, bandage in place, honor preserved. In modern academia matters take longer.

At this distance and viewed with rational eyes, the affair of honor, if such it was, looks small, almost laughable. But the biter was not amused; he embarked on a vendetta, talking to those who would listen, sending memos and letters wherever they might do some good (harm). Since he could not get directly at the Press—an administrative department—he took aim at the nearest academic target, the Editorial Committee. In this he was aided by an accident: the chairman of an academic council reorganization committee happened to be resident of his campus. That officer was memoed, buttonholed, sold a bill of goods—a sale he seems later to have regretted. As well he might have: the one little piece of mischief making brought about dozens of meetings, reams of memos, the resignation of one Editorial Committee member, the appointment of a special investigating committee—and no changes at all, good or bad.

The Editorial Committee, said our friend, and after him the reorganization group, was too big, spent too much time on manuscripts and not enough on policy, accepted the bribe of new Press books from the director, and in some unexplained way failed to stand up to the director. Anyone, I thought, who could credit such passive behavior to a group of hard-nosed senior faculty members, might also believe that the earth is flat. To better ride herd on the director, it was proposed that the Committee be smaller, with shorter terms, that it take no free books, and keep its eyes fixed on policy. Nothing could have been sillier than books as bribes; the other proposals would have weakened the Committee vis-à-vis the director, something neither he nor they wanted. All in all, a sorry piece of academic thinking when the thinkers have lost their way. To the proposers the Committee's prime purpose was the narrow one of protecting the interests of faculty members. The Committee saw itself in a larger role: helping to build a first-rate publishing house.

It is heartening to record that the Editorial Committee stood up for itself, defended its purpose, its record, its practices, and succeeded in putting down the critics. One member, a biologist from Santa Barbara, Bill Purves, resigned in a letter to the council, describing the Editorial Committee as the finest university group he had ever served on, calling the attack unreasonable, and the whole "dismal" affair harmful to his scholarly work.

So the proposals were stopped, and the academic council appointed a special committee to study the Editorial Committee: Albert Hofstadter of Santa Cruz, Richard P. Longaker of UCLA, and as chairman, Mortimer P. Starr of Davis, a past chairman of the Editorial Committee. To me it seemed strange that the attack had come from Davis, where we had always had good relations—with the chancellor, Emil Mrak, and with others, many of them through Starr. It was he who had spoken for the campus in asking me to find funds for our critic's journal. Which was the more foolish mistake, finding the money or remembering it?

Although the study, the investigation, was of the Editorial Committee, we welcomed the ad hoc group to the Press, hid nothing from them, let them see the work, gave them all the documents they wanted, allowed them—in effect—to investigate the Press as well as the Committee. This kind of open strategy had always worked well in dealing with rational members of the faculty, even those who had doubts about us, and the three men of this group were all intelligently concerned with the larger good of faculty, Press, and University. After several months of work the Starr Committee turned in a balanced and sensible report, much of it concerned with the Press. Instead of proposals that might have weakened the Editorial Committee they made one to strengthen it by preserving the useful experience of former members. Thus they recommended a Press Council, made up of former and present members plus a few Press officers; this group would have had financial and general responsibilities. But after considering the report for a couple of years, the academic council took no action. Good advice and bad advice both came to naught.[10]

If there is glory in publishing of any kind, it comes in finding great books, great in content or in sales, and in producing beautiful volumes, even perhaps monuments like *The Plan of St. Gall*. But if we fix both eyes on high glory, it is all too easy to fall on our faces or into a pit. Despite the danger of something that might be called schizophthalmia, the publisher had better keep one eye on the ground while the other roams above. While we were happily courting historians and anthropologists, chasing off to London and Frankfurt and Mexico in pursuit of intellectual and literary riches, we had to take care of the house we lived in, repel the termites, patch leaks in the roof, keep the rain out, and chase several kinds of wolves from the door.

This we managed to do, more or less, sometimes well, sometimes

---

10. "Report of the Special Committee of the Academic Council on the Editorial Committee," 25 June 1972.

not so well, for a number of years after our little declaration of independence from the printing office. And then, about the turn of the decade from the sixties to the seventies, something caught up with us, growth perhaps, or market changes around us, and we found ourselves in a series of financial and managerial crises. That the University was suffering through the student wars at about the same time is only a coincidence; there was no connection. That it was a time of financial recession for all universities and their presses was an underlying condition.

I cannot say that all this was unexpected: the Board of Control minutes, beginning at the end of 1961, show that we had some idea of what was coming, or at least knew that something was coming; the Board did much to help us prepare for the crunch. In the last few pages I have tried to show how we dealt with these problems, overcoming some, sliding out from under others.

With luck then, and in about 1972, when I still had a few years to go, we suddenly burst into open water, the only clear sailing in all my years at Berkeley. The Press flourished, bringing out about 150 new books each year, and better ones than before. We made regular surpluses without the help of an operating subsidy, built up a balance sheet with assets worth many times the liabilities. All this came, in part and of course, from the work of our editors in many fields, from selling by Harlan Kessel and his people, but came also from winning the financial battles of the critical years.

In these long and sometimes bitter battles there were no true villains, although there were troublemakers enough, roadblocks, dead weights hung about the neck. Among the albatrosses may be counted, in no order of magnitude, the union, the personnel office, the computer, and the editor from Davis. These, together with our own mistakes, were handicap enough. The great Captain Maxwell need not be listed; his delinquency was minor and allowed us to laugh at ourselves. But if there were no villains, there were heroes, members of the Board of Control: Harry Wellman and Angus Taylor, our first two chairmen, both academic vice-presidents; Jim Bannerman and Loren Furtado, who believed that accounts should help rather than constrict management; and others, including the Editorial Committee members who sat on the Board, notably Mort Starr and Ralph Rader. Without them and their guidance for a decade, the Press might have been left in the fiscal confusion of the 1950s. With them we managed to clean up our act—not all but most of it—to the point where we could call ourselves a scholarly publishing house.[11]

11. The financial parts of this chapter are based on a longer, soberer, and more detailed account that I wrote in May 1987 and that may be found in the Press files and in the University archives: "Notes on the Financial History of the University of California Press 1893–1976."

21   Waiting for the God from the Machine

I t is best to write about the past. The present overwhelms us with details, many of little consequence; we cannot see it for what it is. The young Fabrice del Dongo (if I remember aright) wandered all day through the fighting at Waterloo and when evening came had to ask passers-by who had won the battle.[1] And the future is boring; it has never been lived, has no substance, is no more than a wraith, a shadow, the idea of a woman without the flesh (male point of view). But the past—ah, the past! It is real, it is true. It still lives because it once lived in us and made us what we are. To piece together its reality, to recover the *temps perdu,* is immensely difficult, requires more insight than research, but a measure of both. So I sometimes think that the historian—true historian and interpreter, not recorder of small facts—is the essential scholar. And that the lesser among us may follow in lesser ways. In my lesser way I have tried to realize a partial picture of a recent time in scholarly publishing.

The present is for the doer, the future for the reformer, one out of my reach, the other beyond my nature. But if a cat may look at the king, the skeptic may glance at things as they are, as he thinks they are, and try a few potshots at what may come after.

---

1. In that great novel by a man who used a German pseudonym, liked to think of himself as Italian, dedicated the book in English "To the happy few," but was none of those things—*La Chartreuse de Parme,* by Stendhal.

2120 Berkeley Way.

In 1944 when I walked into the old Press on Oxford Street, it was clear that I was coming into a printing plant. On the way to the second floor—where a kind of publishing went on—one could pause on the curving stairs and look into the shop, where skilled workers were setting and locking up metal type and tending the big flat-bed presses. When one opens the front door of the new Press on Berkeley Way, nearly fifty years later and four blocks to the east, a broad set of carpeted stairs leads to the second and third floors, where modern publishing offices are arranged around a central light well. Business offices are on the ground floor. Everything is publishing; there is no evidence of printing except for the hundreds of printed books that fill every office. Computers abound, especially in the production department where Tony Crouch and his people produce several hundred books, new and reprinted, in paperback and in cloth, each year. Although I had something to do with the great change from printing to publishing, the computers, except for the troublesome one in the billing office, have come after my time.

In the 1970s, when we could not get University housing and

bought a small building on Durant Avenue and began to set up our own building fund, we could not know what good use Jim Clark and his lieutenants would make of this beginning. Buying a kind of storage building near the northwest corner of the Berkeley campus, they have converted it into a modern publishing house—not so handsome on the outside as Farquhar's old Press on Oxford Street but far more attractive inside. Here are the main offices. The book stock is warehoused a few miles away in Richmond and also in New Jersey, where a fulfillment office has been set up jointly with Princeton University Press.

The selling network, as befits a large scholarly press and as noted a few pages back, extends around the world. Manuscript acquisition is almost equally widespread. Parallel editorial offices are maintained in Berkeley and in Los Angeles, under assistant directors Lynne Withey and Stan Holwitz. Neither office bears much resemblance to the offices of the old Press, described in my third chapter. And the Press, like the University, takes the whole world as its province, concerns itself with all major areas of scholarly research—as we had intended so long ago.

Some of the recent books have been named in earlier chapters, as I brought their topics (art history, book design, and others) approximately up to date. Some of the more important publishing fields of my time have also been described, but emphases change as research patterns do, some of them for intellectual reasons, others with fashions in social thinking. The most productive scholars of one generation may not be replaced by their equals; other stars arise in other quadrants. For a while in the 1980s much effort went into large pictorial books of semipopular nature; the emphasis has moved back to scholarly books, some of them also large and illustrated. The great sets of the past, the Donne and Dryden, the Larkin, the Pepys, have been followed by the *Papers of Martin Luther King*. The volumes of Mark Twain go on and on. As the one hundredth anniversary approaches, one hundred books are being chosen to be called Centennial Books—not an easy choice among so many.

And I, who embarked on expansion long ago in order to do things a small press could not do, have begun to wonder whether growth of this Press, and of all American presses together, has not gone far enough. Others must see what I see; Jim Clark and his staff are now holding the Press to about the present number of new books. In the current financial recession, which may not soon pass away, the Press is holding its own as well as others do.

When Chester Kerr conducted the first survey in 1948–49, thirty-five universities held membership in the Association of American University Presses. One of these was in Canada. There are now more than one hundred member presses, domestic and foreign. In the survey year, the thirty-five members published 727 books. In 1990 the number had risen to nearly 5,000. In the twenty years after 1970 the number doubled, from 2,504, and these figures do not include the books of Oxford and Cambridge, both of which issue many titles of American origin; their increase is even more striking—more disturbing, perhaps—although I am not sure what kinds of books the figures include. Cambridge went from 202 to 872; Oxford from 547 to 1,027.[2]

What are all these new books? Are there really nine or ten times as many research books than there were forty years ago? Some more of course as higher education has expanded, but surely not that many. A few may come from commercial firms as those publishers grow more timid about serious books. Many more, I think, are regional and local books, a kind that has proliferated with simpler manufacture and the growth of the paperback market. Scholarly or popular, they find a market among individuals and in public libraries and are thus not dependent on research library budgets. From where I sit we can almost see the University of Nevada Press, with its series about the Basque people, many of whom have settled in that state, and its books about the intermountain region of Nevada and eastern California. And Nevada is only one. This skeptic who once reasoned that Cali-

2. All figures except the first are from surveys conducted by the AAUP.

fornia should not be a regional press, has become an admiring customer for some of these books.

But the sales figures show that there are more scholarly (research)
books than the market can absorb. Still more appear to be coming.
And how can one speak against the Great God Growth, who will cure
all our ills, the economists say, if we can get Him to smile on us? A
list of 25 books will surely do better, or at least feel better, if increased
to 50. Or 50 to 100. But we might remember what happens to figures
when they are compounded a few times. And what if boom times do
not come again? The observer cannot help wondering whether the
urge to growth has not brought about the publication of more mediocre books, not bad but not excellent.

It is not surprising, then, that the average sale per book has gone
down sharply. On this I have no specific figures; university publishers,
although less secretive than commercial ones, are not eager to give
out the numbers. But we used to claim in the 1970s that we could sell
1,500 copies of any reasonably good scholarly book and that many
would do better; I am now told that the average is more like 700 to
800, and some sell fewer copies.

Along with our own over-production there is trouble in the university libraries, whose directors were complaining, long before the
current recession, about smaller book funds. Since annual budget increases were then averaging 8 or 9 percent, compounded, enough to
please most of us, skeptics suggested that staff salaries might be eating
up the book budget, and this may still be true. But a more voracious
eater may now be discerned; the increasing cost of serials, particularly
in the sciences, is taking more and more of the funds in large libraries.[3] Much also goes to satisfy the librarians' infatuation with elec-
tronics. We, the book publishers, can only hope that the electronic
monsters will some day swallow up a host of serials and release more
money for books. But if we are not rescued by this or some other

3. See "The Serials Crisis and the Response to It," a group of articles in *Scholarly
Publishing*, April 1992.

deus ex machina, and if the production curve continues up and the market curve down, what shall we do with all those books?

I have no talent for prophecy. And wonder whether anyone since ancient Delphi and ancient Judaea has been able to bring it off. The most celebrated political and economic prophet of modern times got virtually everything wrong, which, of course, did not prevent millions from believing him. Among those who like to play the historical game of What If (What if Hannibal had not hesitated at the gates of Rome, if indeed he did? What if Napoleon had not been ill on the day of Waterloo?) few trouble themselves to wonder what modern history would be like if Karl Marx had had the good sense to keep his thoughts to himself.[4] Perhaps not very different; big ideas often spring from several minds, although only one gets credit in popular thinking. We may note in passing that more accurate predicters, such as Marx's contemporary Tocqueville, have had little influence on political history.

So, in our smaller way, we may express skepticism about predictions on the future of the book or on its demise. In truth, none of us knows what will happen. As long ago as I can remember, technology lovers have been announcing the end of the codex book. First—I think—microfilm was going to replace it. Then microprint, or microfiche, with an entire book printed on one card, even on a catalogue card. Book lovers protested that no one would want to take a microfilm reader to bed.

No one did, I think, but microfilm proved useful in making available large collections of manuscript letters and the like. And when all American dissertations were put on film at University Microfilms in Ann Arbor and made available by Xerox printers, one copy at a time, there could be no further excuse for publishing dissertations, and university presses could ignore them, praise be, except for the very few. This kind of on-demand (OD) publishing proved useful for supplying journal articles, out-of-print books, copies of old classics; and some variation of it—disk replacing film, perhaps—may still have a

The skeptic looks on.

future. Microfilm, joined to Xerox printing, took over one kind of publishing but had little or no effect on a more central concern of publishers—new books, popular and scholarly.

Film may disappear before the book does. We now have several kinds of disks including CD-ROM, letters that look like a formula for gypsy magic but turn out to stand for nothing more esoteric than Compact Disk-Read Only Memory. On a small disk, like those used for music recording, can be put a huge amount of data, which can then be called up and displayed on a computer screen. And since

4. If the nose of Cleopatra had been a little shorter, the whole face of the world would have been changed.—Pascal.

nearly everyone now owns a computer, why bother with the printing press? Unless you want to read in bed, that is. And even that might be managed with a screen on the wall, while your companion wears a mask.

The enormous utility of these disks is at once apparent. All kinds of reference works—encyclopedias, dictionaries, indexes, compilations of many kinds—can be stored in a small space and searched at computer speed. And since the computer, although incapable of thought, is as fast as twenty thousand clerks, we may as well put it to work for us. Already the great Oxford English Dictionary (second edition, twenty volumes) is available on disk, along with other works I know not of. The death of the book is imminent, it seems.

Or is it? I do not predict. A reference book, used for quick access to facts, is one thing; a book to be read is another. Only a lover of gadgets would want to read an entire book on a screen—but then our descendents may all be hooked on computers, as we have been hooked on the gasoline engine and the crudities of TV news. Here perhaps I can cite myself as a small test case for the older generation. Because the retina of my one good eye has deteriorated, I can no longer read a book directly but can read only on the screen of a closed-circuit TV monitor, which provides the enlargement needed. This works reasonably well and I—considering the alternative—prize my reading machine. But were there a choice? An ordinary book is much faster to read, more convenient, more pleasant, more everything desirable, immeasurably superior for straight reading. The inventors of the codex, a couple of thousand years ago, knew what they were doing. But I covet a set of dictionaries on disk.

It remains to be seen whether one of these disks or some other electronic device will appeal to people for pleasure, as opposed to factual, reading, or for contemplation of an author's reasoning rather than the search for data. Perhaps there is a difference of kind between book and information—true book, that is, and not data between book covers. As an old lover of Glenmorangie, Glenlivet, and other Glens, I see virtue in Colin Day's remark that "information is the mash that is fermented . . . the essential and distinctive nature of the spirit comes from . . . distillation. The barley is brought in truck loads, the whisky is distilled drip by drip."[5]

It may be that I am thrown off by the buzz-word "information," assuming—unjustly, do you think?—that some of those who use it fail to see the difference between one thing and another, things that look alike but are not alike. My old School of Librarianship in Berkeley is soon to be renamed School of Information Studies. Can its leaders see, more clearly than do the rest of us, where they are going? If the intellectual content—not great but of value—is poured out of the curriculum, is it possible that the school may be dead before the book is? The use of computers, when the period of invention is over, may not call for study in a university. In the seventeenth century Samuel Pepys studied shorthand at Cambridge University.

The orientation packet from an important company serving libraries and scholars speaks ecstatically of a "world of information"— faster and faster access to larger and larger quantities of data—but with no intimation that more and more data may not be good for us. The computer can deal with almost infinite numbers, grains of sand on the beach, one at a time but with great speed. The human mind at its best can do something rather different—can leap from one point to another, passing up the details in between, in an intuitive recognition of values and relationships, called by Pascal the *esprit de finesse*. But if that mind is overloaded with trivia, it may be forced into its lesser and duller mode, the adding and weighing of details.

How does it happen that Alexis de Tocqueville, sitting in his manor house in Normandy 150 years ago, reflecting on a single visit to the United States and deriving intellectual stimulus from sending and receiving handwritten letters—how is it that he managed to see American democracy more clearly than almost anyone since then? A more subtle mind, you may say, and that could be true, but is it possible that there was advantage in dealing with fewer (and better?) pieces of information?

The present-day scholar or thinker must find his way through vast

5. In *Scholarly Publishing*, October 1991, pp. 35–36.

volumes of data, typed, printed, processed, stored in archives. So the computer, as Voltaire said of God, had to be invented. If it can be used to relieve the human mind of detail, it will be a great boon. But if it becomes the excuse for compiling and recording more and more undigested pieces of data, where will that lead us, even with the fastest of sorting by word or topic? To the best of my knowledge, no one has come up with a computer program that will separate the significant from the trivial, the kernels from the straw, unless a human mind has already made the choices. Judgment is the province of the mind. But if it is assaulted by too much trivia, too much "information," then it will be more difficult for the mind to work.

So we may think about ways to use a formidable tool without letting it use us. Several years ago I offered my Second Law of Progress: the better the technology, the less efficient the human use of it.[6] Anyone who has dealt with construction workers or has observed public projects will know what was meant. I cited the Central Pacific and Union Pacific railroads of the 1860s, which with pick and shovel constructed two thousand miles of track over mountains and deserts in five years, while the BART system in San Francisco one hundred years later built seventy-five miles in thirteen years. Let us hope that we shall not have to revise the law to read: the more "sophisticated" the technology, the more foolish the human use of it.

We shall have to wait and see. Meantime we may ask whether computers and disks (or whatever comes after disks) can help with the problem of too many scholarly books—too many for the market. Regional books are no problem; they have a market of their own. The best scholarly books, the wide-ranging and well-written ones, even those of real distinction on narrower topics, these too will find buyers enough. And whether they gain a little or lose a little, the publisher will know that they justify the human effort put into them as well as their monetary cost.

Most important in defining them, perhaps, is the quality of the author's mind, for we know that the right author can make any topic

6. In *Scholarly Publishing*, October 1975. There was no first law.

significant while the merely methodical can make anything dull. The latter, often enough, do not know the difference, and not everyone is willing to tell them. The problem, then, is the quantity of adequate but not excellent manuscripts, mostly on small or not very significant topics but also the mid-level treatment of larger matters. And these will always exist for, without prophetic sight and a licensing system, we cannot have the greater without allowing the lesser to be written. Many of these lesser are honest enough, competent enough, useful to some degree but not useful enough to find much of a market. We need not scorn them. Nor, perhaps, publish them. Several years ago I suggested to the board of the National Enquiry into Scholarly Communication that it consider for mid-level manuscripts a national system of on-demand publishing similar to that used for dissertations and out-of-print books. Publishing, we called it, but in truth it amounted to recording, indexing, and retrieving—a kind of library service that would preserve research results without cranking up the great publishing mechanism.

My fellow members of the board, knowing that scholars would not be happy with second-level treatment, with no handsome volumes for their shelves, did not go along. Now older and possibly wiser, I see that such a system—this or another—will never arise out of rational planning. Need—the lack of any other course—and available technology may bring it about. Until then and while we wait for the god to spring from the machine, tie up the loose ends of the plot, and tell us what will be best for everyone—until then we remain on the stage and may think about ways to help ourselves.

Since we cannot know what is to come, perhaps we shall be well advised to make a wager like that of Pascal—not that God exists, as he proposed, but in our smaller way, that scholarly presses as we know them will continue to exist. If we lose the wager, if the electronic devices devour all scholarly publishing and make university presses redundant, we can then lean back, try to avoid teleological thoughts, and remember what we did for an earlier generation. If we win, and the machines relieve us of the lesser works while leaving us the greater ones, we can murmur our thanks as we contemplate smaller but better lists of books.

In the meantime and sustained by a provisional faith, we may take a look at our present lists and ask whether we might steal a march on the future by lopping off the bottom tenth or other fraction—each press defining its own bottom. For lop them off we can if we are willing to drop responsibility for the lesser manuscripts and leave them to the eventual care of another system and another agency. To those who will then call us elitist, we can answer that we hope so. Universities and university presses do not deserve to exist if they do not serve an elite of the mind.

If we should embark on this course and find ourselves making more strenuous choices, we have ready at hand some of the fine, big criteria already displayed here: significance, breadth, style, quality of the author's mind. But these big words, "defaced by ages of careless usage,"[7] are not always helpful. A few little tricks can sometimes be of use. Long ago, with the temerity of one who would square the circle, I proposed a simplistic little formula for selection: a book should be good or it should sell. If it is good enough, if it promises high renown or lasting importance, one can forgive a poor sale if the loss is not too grievous. If on the other hand it will have a strong continuing market, helping to support other books, one need not demand outstanding quality as long as the book is intellectually respectable.[8]

It can be added that the good and the salable are often the same. At California many years ago, manuscripts for our old monograph series of book-length studies in the humanities and social sciences were selected by the academic editors on the single criterion of scholarly quality, without regard to sales. The results, the titles published, were less than great. When we discontinued these series and chose

7. Conrad, in his preface to *The Nigger of the Narcissus*. In a different context, of course.
8. "The Service Agency and the Publishing House," *Scholarly Publishing*, January 1976, p. 123.

326 Waiting for the God from the Machine

manuscripts for scholarship *and* salability, the list at once became more distinguished. The best list of books, we were forced to believe, comes from the use of a kind of double standard: intellectual quality plus market appeal.

This is of course no argument for popular books. If we try to make ourselves into something we are not, trade publishers, we shall soon be second-rate and expendable. But at our own specialty we can do better than others can, and we need only get the best possible scholarly books. When I was very young in this business, Datus Smith of Princeton taught me that the best book was the safest—not the biggest seller but the one least likely to bomb. And the best scholarly list will always, I think, be composed mostly of what we call short discount books—a term that refers not to intellectual importance but to the method of marketing.

Formulas and practical games are manageable, and it might be well if we stuck to them. But from time to time, and in spite of our wariness, we come up against things less manageable, called moral issues, and we cannot always sidestep them. Or always see them plain. The best we can do, perhaps, is to be aware of their complexity and not expect too much of ourselves as we try to get along in a chaotic world. The wisest journalist I know of, José Ortega y Gasset, once wrote that human life is forever shipwreck—not drowning but shipwreck. And that the awareness of shipwreck as the truth of life constitutes salvation.[9]

Philosophically or morally, the commercial publisher is in a more secure position than we are. He (or she) is free to pursue his own ends, to save the world, if that appeals, or merely to make money. These two projects are proper to him, but the university press is in a more ambiguous position in regard to both of them. It exists to publish learned works; when it uses commercial methods and when it

9. This paragraph and two or three others are based on my "The Ambiguous University Press," *Scholarly Publishing*, October 1976. Ortega's words are paraphrased from *The Dehumanization of Art and Other Writings on Art and Culture* (1956), 126.

seeks books that will sell, it is walking close to the moral edge. And it must walk close. If it finds too few salable books, it can die of deficits. If it finds too many, it may lose its soul, its character. And if it lets itself be used for an alien purpose—worthy or unworthy—it can lose its soul in another way. So it must live constantly with the danger that the means may corrupt the end—an old-fashioned danger, no longer of concern to many liberal intellectuals, but the corruption takes place with or without their concern. Those who wish to avoid it may find it useful to *look* at what is going on, to *see*, and—as I have said elsewhere—not spend too much time thinking.

A young editor once said, defending his project, "This book will help make the world a better place." How could one deny such missionary zeal? How explain that we are not missionaries? And could we really expect him to *see* what lay in front of him? Anyone can recognize propaganda when the cause is a "bad" one. But when the cause is perceived as good, it takes sharper eyes to see the danger, although the same danger is there. No matter how noble the cause—noble at the moment and to some of us—using the press to promote a cause is using it for a purpose alien to itself.

Saving the world may safely be left to those, including private publishers, who are morally free to indulge in politics. It is in any event a large and unlikely project for our small secular minds. The skeptic will prefer to save Mono Lake,[10] a task not too great for human powers and not subject to the moral and practical doubts that haunt the saving of large and worthy parts of the world—the middle class, the Republican Party, labor unions, minorities, the poor—perhaps even the undeserving poor, like Eliza Doolittle's father in Shaw's *Pygmalion* (*My Fair Lady*).

The Achilles heel of the secular unbeliever is that he must doubt his own doubts. The book mentioned above was part of a larger project being pushed by an eager foundation, which offered money to the

---

10. A lake east of the Sierra Nevada, threatened by the Los Angeles Department of Water and Power, which has already made a sandbox out of Owens Lake, where steamships ran in the nineteenth century.

willing publisher. Although not dazzled by their money, I could see virtue in some of the books, thought I might be drawing too fine a line, and wondered whether it was not proper enough to be bought for a cause deemed by others to be good—thus the virtuous whore. Letting the project go forward, I found myself in a more dubious moral position than that of the editor. I knew better and he did not.

The university has—used to have, perhaps—its own nonpolitical ends. We may shy away from big statements about Truth with a capital T, but the role of a true university is to foster honest research (and teaching), as free as possible from political intent; and a press, if it wishes to keep its university character, will look in the same direction. Not an easy thing to do these days, when well-meaning people would convert the university into a force for change, a social and political propaganda machine. Some will say that I am asking a press to be more true to the university than the university is to itself, and perhaps that is so. A press is smaller and less resilient than a university and less able to withstand an amount of corruption of purpose without suffering character change. Lost purpose as well as bad means may corrupt the end, which is honest scholarship, with as little politics as humanly possible.

The line between polemic and legitimate point of view can be hard to discern. Where does the attempt to find new (or old) truth merge into the promotion of some cause? They tell us that objectivity is impossible, and of course that is so in the sense that perfection is not human. But the scorning of objectivity as an ideal can lead to the loss of honesty, which *is* possible. Difficult, of course, and approachable only when we see it—and not some political good—as of first importance.

Since skeptics are not allowed to preach, let us try a kind of parable. On a tedious railway journey the aunt of three children tries to keep them quiet with stories about good boys and girls. Of course she fails, and a stranger in the coach takes over with his own story about a little girl who was very, very good—horribly good, he says, holding his audience. She was awarded three medals for three kinds of goodness and wore them pinned to the front of her dress. Because of her goodness she was also allowed to play in the Prince's park, where all went well enough until along came a big bad hungry wolf. By happy fortune the little girl managed to hide where the wolf could not find her but—alas—when she trembled the three medals for goodness clinked against each other. The wolf pricked up his ears, ran to her hiding place, dragged her out, and ate her completely, all but her shoes and the three medals for goodness.

"The most beautiful story I ever heard," said one of the children. And so, except for the Gospels, it probably was.[11]

Doing good is only one of the sins that lie in wait for scholarly publishers. Other sins and mere mistakes are strewn through the pages of this book and might be compiled into a sizable catalogue. And although a skeptic does not preach, he may confess that he has committed them all, made all the bull moves, as the gangster Dutch Schultz called them,[12] and survived. Surviving, he sometimes recalls the story of a mountain climber and his guide, who were traversing a steep and icy slope that fell off for thousands of feet to a glacier below. The guide said: "If you slip here, you will be sliding down that slope for the rest of your life." In our precarious business, I like to think that it is possible to slip and recover.

And it is sometimes possible to live with grave moral issues even without understanding them. There was once a monastery in Provence—not far perhaps from the mountain mentioned above—that had fallen into poverty and was in danger of dissolution. In this extremity it was remembered that one of the brothers knew the formula for an unusual cordial and was also skilled in making it. He was set to work, the cordial found a market, the monastery prospered. But, as so often with new-found fortune, there was a catch—like any good cook, the monk had to sip his concoction from time to time and, sipping, became drunk, sang bawdy songs, danced lascivious dances.

11. See "The Story-Teller," in *Beasts and Super-Beasts,* by H. H. Munro (Saki).
12. On his death bed he is supposed to have advised his followers, "Don't make no bull moves." I am reminded also of Satchel Paige, the great old-time baseball pitcher (in the Negro leagues) and philosopher, who left us many fine precepts, including, "Don't look back; something may be gaining on you."

In the morning, sober, he feared for his immortal soul and told the others he could not go on with the work.

For this dilemma, which threatened either his soul or the welfare of the monastery, a typically French solution was found. The brother went on making the cordial, and all the while he sang and danced, the assembled monks in another room knelt and prayed for his soul. The prayers were deemed equal to the sin, counteracting it, and all was right with the world.[13]

13. From a story in *Lettres de mon moulin* (1868), by Alphonse Daudet. Retold here from memory.

22 Earthquakes and Endings

Anyone can *write* a book, said the sales manager. Anyone can *start* a book, I would say, but not everyone can finish one.

In his finest work the great author named in the very first sentence of this volume floated his two protagonists, white boy and black slave, down the long, wide river through adventures revealing, grotesque, and funny. After a thousand miles and more the journey came to an end, but the book did not. The book, in its book nature, could not just stop but hung there, needing an ending that would give the reader some sense of finality.

Since the book was a comedy, the author could not take the easy way out, as a Renaissance dramatist might, by killing off the main characters, with minor ones left to blow trumpets. Or like another novelist of his own century, who sent his three protagonists, ship, master, and whale, down to a watery grave, thus demonstrating beyond all doubt that the business was finished.

He may have thought about the deus ex machina, but there was no Olympus in the sky above the antebellum South, no Apollo or other god to swing down from a crane, impose a kind of order, and tell the audience to go home. In a similar spirit and with the help of a clever boy, Tom Sawyer, who liked to play god, the author fabricated a kind of happy ending. There was too much of it, perhaps, and it did not fit the spirit of what went before, but no one minded much except a few sober-sided critics, who would have had him confront the social situation. And ruin the novel.

A small book, like a great one, must have some kind of ending, natural or contrived. The events set forth in the preceding pages have come to a kind of milestone, end of one hundred years, half of which I observed. In our fascination with round figures, we may imagine that the turn of one century has come around to meet the turn of another, and so made a kind of entity or unity. An artificial one, of course, but the only one we have. In reality, learned publishing will go on without regard to milestones, and in ways that will almost surely elude my speculations.

In the desert where I live the earthquakes have rattled the house all summer long. Near the back gate or under the fig tree, a snake sometimes rattles. Not often, but we know the sound and keep our eyes open. And are reminded that we live with uncertainty.

AF September 1992

ADDENDUM I

God, Swahili, Bandicoots, and Euphoria

Hugh Kenner

G od's hand—so captioned—emerged from clouds to rest on the smug bald head with the pince-nez: a rite for the effortless delegation of power. Baldhead, "Director," portly in banker's stripes, rests his right hand negligently on a blanker head, labelled "Editorial Committee," from whose owner, hand to head, power next descends to a slighter, more harried entity: "Sponsoring Editor." Following the gesture of his hand in turn, we find ourselves among the infra-structure of Copy-editing, Production, Sales, the small and busy beings. Some wag whose suspicious facility with a Speedball would connect him either with Design or with Advertising prepared this large cartoon to help orient newcomers.

I suppose it should have helped, though in the years—was it six? seven?—that I served on an Editorial Committee (of the University of California Press) the lines of delegation were never clear at all. There were always people who wanted them made clear, but they weren't on the Committee (more about them later). The chart's details were misleading. The Director, for one thing, wasn't bland and portly but a hirsute and brooding man who eventually grew a beard. And we weren't neatly located on some stream of energy between him and the Sponsoring Editors.

The one sure thing about our function was that we controlled

Reprinted with the author's changes from *Scholarly Publishing* (Toronto), July 1974.

The Imprint, a phrase one of our chairmen always pronounced in capital letters, made graphic by a downward punch with an invisible Great Seal. No printed thing, save after formal Committee action, could have "University of California Press" on its title page. Formal Committee action meant a presentation, a pow-wow, a vote, and an entry in the minutes. Some books for which we authorized The Imprint have not appeared and possibly never will, the Director having taken the responsibility of deciding that they were too expensive, too unsaleable, or umbilically linked with an author just too impossible. To go ahead and actually produce a book, taking due account of the vectors between idealism and bankruptcy, was a managerial decision, so the Committee had no formal obligation to think about costs. This freedom made its deliberations not less but more responsible. It's being nagged all the time by thoughts of costs that can drive committees into bouts of defiant idealism.

Manuscripts get before the Committee like this. All the impossible ones are bounced (politely) by the professional staff. The possibles go out for readings. Each survivor then becomes the personal project of a Sponsoring Editor, who next persuades a Committee member to "present" it when it's docketed. "Presenting" it means reading its dossier—readers' reports, sometimes author's responses, sometimes too half a ream of peripheral correspondence, plus as much as you need to of the manuscript itself, which is frequently all of it. At the meeting, when your manuscript's turn comes up, you speak a piece which culminates in a motion, to publish or not to.

The fifteen or twenty people to whom you are speaking have in front of them a Xeroxed wad they have supposedly studied already: what you have waded through in a streamlined version, with at the very least the readers' reports *in toto*. It's chiefly in drawing also on the ms. itself that your information is more extensive than theirs. They ask questions. What about the acerbities of Reader x, over which you so negligently glided? You answer that Reader x is a compulsive sniper, requiring routine 40 percent devaluation. Do you really think anybody wants this book? That's a tougher one; after a few experiences you learn to pose it to yourself in deciding which way your motion is going to go. There's no worse danger than forgetting that readers, not writers, are the proper beneficiaries of a publishing operation, despite all those colleagues who think that your job is to get their work published.

But what readers? How many? Two or three times some meritorious treatise came up whose potential readership consisted, worldwide, of perhaps six specialists. Our decision each time was to commend it but not publish it, and get word to the author that he should circulate six Xeroxes. What about a few hundred buyers at most for a text that bristles with diacritics and tables? Publish, yes, but stipulate camera-ready copy for photo-offset. And a big long book on Rattlesnakes, with hundreds of illustrations, some in colour, and 1,533 text pages? How many herpetologists are there in the world? Are we really running a charity for their benefit? Somehow that one got published, 2 vols. boxed, $50, and underscored the folly of fine-tuning such speculations by turning into a surprise best-seller, the *Zeitgeist* having apparently decreed that Klauber's definitive word on Rattlesnakes should be *de rigueur* on post-Christmas coffee tables. (It's a fascinating book. Do *you* know how to catch a rattler with a piece of string? See p. 1036.)

A great reward of Committee service was lore gleaned from books one wouldn't otherwise have read. In theory manuscripts went to Committee members already expert in the subject field, but so broad and continuous is the spectrum of submissions that Omniscience itself couldn't select that knowledgeable a Committee, not even from California's nine-campus faculty. So Sponsoring Editors grow expert at spotting unlikely zones of responsiveness in committee members. For years all our Film mss. were presented by a man whose certified competence, French Literature, was rarely called on, and everything pertaining to Music by a biologist. Another biologist was our Swahili expert. If you want random wide-ranging expertise you seem to strengthen your chances by stacking the deck with biologists. Things were never so lively as in the days when by some miscalculation there were five of them on the Committee at once.

Nearly every member's presence on the Committee might be

traced to a miscalculation somewhere, rooted in a hopeless snarl of age-old misunderstandings. Members get appointed by a statewide Committee on Committees, which receives nominations from campus Committees on Committees, and observes just one formal rule which pertains to the balance of representation among California's numerous campuses. Beyond that, the more *ad hoc* rules these bodies make for themselves the wilder their decisions become. Local committees have all sorts of notions, including the idea that the real charge of a Committee member is to fight like hell on behalf of the local authors, or the idea that since he will be concerned with books he ought to be bookishly and stuffily eminent. The statewide Committee on Committees suffers from the periodic delusion that the Editorial Committee's office is to assert Faculty Control over hirelings whose daily ambition is to build empires. They also have sporadic illusions about representing Subject Areas, and these criteria, the latter only slightly less irrelevant than the former to the Committee's real way of functioning, were in frequent conflict in my time. The days of the five biologists (how did that happen?) gave way to the bleak year when the Committee was purged, out of suspicion that it was getting on all too well with the Director and the Sponsoring Editors. (Some influential man's book had been turned down.) That simply meant that we had to break in a quorum of bewildered neophytes, while for months a handful of survivors of the purge did nearly everything. No member was ever really effective till perhaps his second year, a feel for principles and procedures being impossible to receive by inoculation. One man I remember (a biologist in fact) said nothing whatever during his entire first year of attending meetings. The second year he was suddenly our most eloquent member, and the year after that a co-chairman (we had two, North and South). Then the statewide appointing body dumped him.

There is no rationale at all for any of this, and yet the Press flourishes. Moreover no University Committee (in a university worm-eaten with them) has such *esprit de corps*. It's a charmed committee, the only committee assignment a rational person ever welcomed, even though it meant monthly statewide travel, a nuisance of feeder airlines and rent-a-cars and hassles with the Accounting Office. It wasn't what it might easily have become, a routine of voting on manuscripts and let's-get-out-of-here; it was the nearest thing at California to what we kept saying was the Idea of a University: the free and ebullient exchange of ideas. I didn't see that happen anywhere else except sometimes by accident for about five minutes, but it happened regularly, off and on all day, in the Press committee rooms. Rather than miss a meeting, one man would routinely interrupt research trips and zoom in from half-way around the world. The lure, and the force that got so much homework so conscientiously done (Sponsoring Editors having among other bad habits the habit of mailing 900-page typescripts just days before a scheduled meeting) was simply a shared zeal for producing good books. No other committee anywhere in the system helps produce anything. There were no factions, no pockets of mistrust, because everyone very quickly sensed that their charge was unique: that they weren't meeting to *prevent* something: empire-building, the autocracy of deans, over-facile promotions. No, we met to facilitate something, the enhancement of the Press's list: hence our committee's spontaneity, its receptive patience, its massive, nearly majestic dedication to the belief that a bureaucracy-ridden University might lend its name to something done triumphantly right.

No grass-roots efforts to explain to us that Directors are by hypothesis megalomaniac and require restraining ever persuaded any of the fifty or sixty members I worked with over the years. Newcomers, old university committee hands, often experience sensations of free fall, and one or another of them every year would try to get a Policy formulated about something. How can you make decisions without a Policy? Well, you can, but you can't explain how. What you can do is outline case histories, incidents when a policy would have been a fearful encumbrance. Faced by unanimous lack of enthusiasm, the policy-hungry newcomer would subside. In a few months he would be free-falling like a veteran.

Or if he was lucky, as I was, some incident at his very first meeting would woo him into perpetual enchantment. At my first meeting one manuscript that came up seemed from the dossier to have as little going for it as a monograph on topologists' left feet. It was a fiercely detailed account of the taxonomy and habits of the Tasmanian Bandicoot, concerning which I'll save space by asking you to look it up in the encyclopaedia if you're hazy. The member presenting this item had contemplated the photographs attached, and simply fallen in love with the furry creatures. He set out to sell us not on the monograph but on a higher theme: the Bandicoot. He passed around photos. He rhapsodized on their sharp little eyes. He sketched impassioned sagas of their ways with one another in the night. After five minutes he had us panting to emigrate to Tasmania. After five more, his trajectory terminated, he turned around twice out of sheer undissipated rapture, and sat down. In the silence that followed, we voted to publish the monograph. I never heard how it did, except that it wasn't a bestseller, not like *The Teachings of Don Juan* (another of our books) nor like *Rattlesnakes*. But the members of the Editorial Committee who filed out for lunch that day were life-long Bandicoot-lovers to a man.

ADDENDUM II

Publishing
The Plan of
St. Gall

James H. Clark

F ollowing is a letter that deserves to stand as a landmark—
perhaps only a minor one, but a landmark—in the history
of the sometimes-troubled relations between scholarly authors and
the publishers of scholarship. The director of the University of California Press, August Frugé, had just put the authors of *The Plan of
St. Gall* on notice in January 1975 that his press was halting production
of their book. The senior author, Walter Horn, felt abused. The letter
followed.

President Charles J. Hitch   January 1975
University of California

Dear President Hitch:
For your information I am sending to you a copy of a letter addressed
to the Director of the University Press, Mr. August Frugé. This letter prepared by me details a situation which I believe to have been
caused by an unreasonable administrative act involving a scholarly publishing project. The contents of my letter are self-explanatory. I consider Mr. Frugé's action to be an affront to me as author of this work
and as General Editor of the series California Studies in the History of
Art in which it appears. The project entitled *The Plan of St. Gall, A
Study of the Architecture, Economy and Life in a Paradigmatic Carolingian*

First printed in *Scholarly Publishing* (Toronto), January 1982. Reprinted separately
by the University of California Press in 1983.

Monastery is co-authored by architect Ernest Born in San Francisco. It has broad cultural implications, is of interest to an international audience and, I believe, a credit to the University of California.

Sincerely yours,

Walter Horn

Professor Emeritus of the History of Art

General Editor, California Studies in the History of Art

cc: Vice President Angus Taylor, Chancellor Albert H. Bowker, Vice Chancellor Ira M. Heyman, Assistant Chancellor Errol W. Mauchlan, Provost and Dean Roderic B. Park, Dean Anne Kilmer, Professor Chalmers A. Johnson, Chm. Editorial Committee, Professor Leopold Ettlinger, Co-Chm., Dept. of Art and History of Art, Director August Frugé, U.C. Press, Associate Director Philip Lilienthal, U.C. Press, Members of the National Committee Advisory to the General Editor of the California Studies in the History of Art: Professors H. W. Janson and Donald Posner, New York University, and John R. Martin, Princeton University, Architect Ernest Born, Editor Lorna Price

It is hard to remember when our press was not publishing *The Plan of St. Gall.* Now considered a classic in medieval scholarship, the book is a magnificently detailed study of a Carolingian monastery plan that was preserved in the Convent of St. Gall, Switzerland, for more than 1,100 years. In Horn's words, "The plan gathers as in a lens an image of the whole Carolingian life." The authors began thinking about the work in the early 1960s, producing a 1,000-page manuscript with some preliminary art work in 1967. It was accepted by the Editorial Committee of the Press in the same year. In January 1980, after thirteen years, *The Plan of St. Gall* was finally published.

It is truly a massive work, at least twice the size the authors originally anticipated and the Press planned for. The three volumes weigh twenty-two pounds and contain over 1,000 illustrations, many in color and most works of art conceived and rendered specifically for the book by Horn's co-author, Ernest Born. The composition, printing, artwork, paper, bookbinding, binding cloth, and endpapers all have a quality, integrity, and excellence normally considered impossible in publishing today. That the subject commanded such magnificent treatment cannot be denied. Rarely are the content and form of a work in such harmony. Such a book could be published only by a scholarly press.

But behind the story of the book and its publisher, revealed in selected correspondence, is the story of a conflict between author and publisher. It is not the full publishing story but it indicates the special character of a major publishing enterprise. If one reads the correspondence literally, money would seem to have been the central issue, but this was not so. Authority, control, and responsibility were at the heart of the conflict.

In publishing, as in any joint venture, each party has a role to perform and a domain of responsibility. The author creates the manuscript, prepares it in an acceptable form for publication, and bears final responsibility for the content of the work. The publisher selects a manuscript, conceives and executes the design, arranges for and oversees the printing and binding, and then promotes and sells the finished book. It goes without saying that without the author there is no need of a publisher.

Most books are published with these lines of responsibility honored by both parties. Certain factors unique to *The Plan of St. Gall,* however, encouraged the blurring of the traditional roles of author and publisher. The authors brought with them substantial funding— ultimately more than $100,000—and naturally felt that they should participate in making decisions relating to the use of these funds. They also became deeply involved in the book's design, which was exceptionally complex, ambitious, and important to the whole conception of the work. Ernest Born selected the typeface and even redesigned one of its characters. He chose the paper that the book was to be printed on and the cloth for the cover. He planned and executed the illustrations. He determined the layout of every page. He even hand-pasted hundreds of tiny stars that, photographed and reproduced, became the pattern of the endpapers. He did or supervised everything that related to the appearance and physical makeup of the volumes. Because of Born's great talent, it would have been a disservice to the book to have him do less. But the consequences of his involvement at times reduced the publisher's role to that of bill-payer.

The three principals themselves—Walter Horn, Ernest Born, and August Frugé—intensified the drama of this shift in traditional roles. Each possesses a powerful intellect, a dedication approaching religious zeal, and the experience of a full and eminent career. None of them is uncertain about his convictions or wanting in will power. Walter Horn is a distinguished art historian and scholar. He has the gift of seeing behind particular events the grand schemes that may span centuries. He invests himself completely in his work. Ernest Born has taught and practiced architecture for sixty years. He is a dedicated artist able to render an abstract concept of beauty and perfection into the real and tangible. August Frugé, a gifted publisher, had been director of the University of California Press for twenty-five years at the time of his retirement five years ago. He knows and has written extensively about what is at the heart of publishing. With such forces at work, all matters associated with the publication of the book, including disagreements, were elevated above the ordinary.

Thus the issues of responsibility and control dominate the correspondence. Money, which is mentioned often, serves as its metaphor. The letters tell of these and other matters in rich detail.

The opening of this article marked the midpoint of the story—now to its beginning.

FRUGÉ to HORN   October 1963

Dear Walter:
This note is to acknowledge your phone call about the St. Gall book. You asked whether we want to publish it or whether you should give it to a Swiss firm, and I assured you that we do want to publish it here and that we should be able to finance it with the help of a subsidy from the account controlled by the Editorial Committee. I feel *very strongly* that we do not want to miss out on a first rate work by the editor of our California Studies in the History of Art.

I hope this letter will give you some assurance of our good intentions.

For a manuscript to be accepted for publication at California, it must receive the endorsement of two authorities on the subject. One of the readers who evaluated the manuscript wrote:

The main objective in this tremendous effort on the part of Walter Horn has been to extract all possible information *from this most important of documents* for the history of monastic building in the early Middle Ages.

It will I fear be a considerable undertaking to issue the book complete with all the plans and illustrations, which are necessary not so much for an understanding of the text as to demonstrate their full significance for the scholar. I should like however to express my hope and to advise that it should appear with as full a documentation as possible, in view of the fact that it will constitute for all time a standard work on this essential document for the history of Carolingian art. It is a work of sufficient importance to be considered fundamental for a comprehensive knowledge of the history of Western architecture. I also consider it of especial significance as being the epitome of the life-work of a scholar.

With unqualified support, the manuscript went to the Editorial Committee of the Press. Seventeen faculty members representing the campuses of the University of California must give final approval for a manuscript to be accepted for publication. *The Plan of St. Gall* was enthusiastically granted the imprint.

FRUGÉ to HORN   September 1967

Dear Walter:

It is a pleasure to tell you that the Editorial Committee approved your big manuscript on *The Plan of St. Gall*. The reports were highly favorable, as you know, and there was little left for us to do but applaud.

There remains one worry: the finances of the project. Even with the Kress money and with a small amount that I was able to get from the Committee, we are going to be hard pressed to make ends meet.

I don't like to be so cautious before committing myself to a royalty, but we are buying a pig in a poke, especially when we are dealing with Ernest, who is excellent on quality but not overconcerned about other people's money.

The period from 1968 to 1971 was one of quiet and work on the manuscript by the authors. Then matters started to move and new lines of responsibility began to emerge.

Dear Ernest:

It is a little embarrassing that I cannot give the Kress Foundation some sort of schedule for the appearance of our magnum opus, *The Plan of St. Gall.*

It is not easy to push Walter, as you must know. If you can give us a schedule for your own part of the work, I think I can manage to get behind Walter and Lorna Price to see that they move rapidly this fall. Can you let me know what is possible for you?

I am thinking that this book may be the finest thing that the Press has done.

From 1971 to 1973 Born was hard at work on the design and illustrations.

Dear Walter:

I am just a little bit concerned about Ernest Born's recent memo on the growth of the St. Gall book. There is no point in saying more than that now or in stirring you up, but we are going to have to make a definite settlement on the size and cost of the book.

I know that Ernest wants to make a great work of art, a sort of monument [the first time the word monument was used, but not the last!], but we may not be able to pay for something of the kind. We simply have to keep within our estimates of some time ago—either that or look for another source of funding.

This letter is merely an advance warning that we shall have to get together a couple of weeks from now and come to some firm agreements.

Then in the summer of 1973 it became clear that profound changes were occurring in the manuscript. The original estimate, in 1970, had envisaged 700 pages of text and 561 pages of illustrations. By August 1973, these numbers had grown to 1,100 and 800 respectively.

Dear Walter:

I continue to think about how we can finance the additional cost of *The Plan of St. Gall*—$21,334 over the previous estimates, most of it caused by the increased number of illustrations.

As I tried to explain when last we talked, I do not have an extra $21,334 that I can reach for and place on this book. And I cannot go back to the Editorial Committee, which has already given me enough money to subsidize about 12 books by other members of the faculty and which is, in any event, short of funds this year. I am acutely embarrassed by the high cost of this one project.

You know, I am sure, that I like the idea of putting out one super handsome book—a kind of monument. But I do not have the right to spend the University's money on a monument to you or to the Press. In one way or another, it is my obligation to do what I can to bring the expenditure on the book within the resources that we have.

MEMO

FRUGÉ to PRODUCTION MANAGER OF PRESS   October 1973

You will—
1 Not allow any additions to the book as presently planned.
2 Not approve any miscellaneous expense items, whether from Born or from anyone else.
3 Not spend any money on reproducing the 80 pages from the actual plan of St. Gall and not commit us in any way to go ahead with this part of the book. This is part of volume 3, I think.
4 Indeed, you had better call a halt on all expenses until we know what the final book is to include.
5 And please keep me fully informed.

HORN to FRUGÉ   October 1973

Dear August:
You have written in your letter of October 8 what I have heard you state more than once in informal conversation: that with the St. Gall books Ernest and I are out to set a "monument"—to ourselves, to you, and to the Press. You must allow us to correct this impression because it is erroneous. Neither Ernest nor I is interested in a monument. We are involved passionately, body and soul, because the subject, the Plan of St. Gall, is not only one of the most fascinating creations of the human mind, but has proved at every level of investigation to be a cultural gold mine.

The St. Gall work is not one, but three books. They are not going to form a "monument," but rather will stand as a comprehensive, thoroughly researched, well and succinctly written treatise concerning one of the greatest humanistic statements of the Western mind. Because of Ernest's taste and genius, this treatise is going to be laid out with consummate skill, beautifully printed, superbly illustrated. It is going to be well composed all the way through: in scholarly argument, in supporting historical documentation, and it will be not "monumental" but "good"—as good as we can make it, and the best we can do, because, believing what we do, we have no other choice.

You ask me whether such an extensive treatment of the explanatory titles of the Plan is really necessary. My answer to that is: no! Nor is it necessary for this—or indeed any—book to be written, nor is it necessary that there be a University Press to publish such books, nor—as Governor Reagan puts it—that there be libraries to purchase them, when knowledge has been so successfully synthesized in the Encyclopaedia Britannica. The fault is mine. I have obviously not succeeded in conveying to you the reasons why a separate and comprehensive treatment of the explanatory inscriptions of the Plan is a matter of importance.

Horn ended the letter with a request that August Frugé secure more funds from the Editorial Committee and a promise to seek additional financing himself. At this point it was clear that matters would probably go public. Correspondence began to take on the character of documentation.

Born to Horn   December 1973

Dear Walter:

When you showed me August Frugé's letter of 8 October concerning the St. Gall book, I was surprised, and more.

At that time you and I decided to carry on with equanimity. What else was there to do? I reviewed the status of the work with you, and it was clear that retreat would solve nothing.

The last two months, October and November, have been full of work. By toil, rather than brooding, I cool off best.

My feeling is that if August had had a full comprehension of what has gone into our collaboration, over such a long period of time, and of the circumstances that gave rise to this effort, he would never have expressed himself as he did. It is my impression that his letter was written during a wave of pressures that sometimes clutch an administrator in a grip beyond endurance.

The Plan of St. Gall is not something that either you or I sought out as an instrument for self-advancement. [There follow eight pages on the work that led us to *The Plan of St. Gall.*]

What I have outlined may help to suggest that the Plan of St. Gall is part of something much bigger than the book. It is part of a long-range scheme of situations and events in the University life stream that will be a worthy incident in the history of the Press, consonant with the University symbol, a book, over which shines a star, below which one may read *Fiat lux*.

If August detects a monumental quality in the design and typography, I am not displeased, for the union of functional, practical, and pleasing typography together with some sense of the monumental is not easy to achieve, and is too seldom seen in books these days.

I would be derelict, in a review of this kind, if I did not tell you what an angel Lorna Price has been. We are thrice blessed to have her for our editor. How she stands us, I do not know.

FRUGÉ to HORN   December 1974

Dear Walter:

The tentative revised figures on your big book are rather worse than I expected. In the year since my letter of 8 October 1973 the cost of printing, paper, and binding appears to have gone up by about $22,000. This is an addition to the $21,000, which I mentioned in the earlier letter and which had largely to do with the new material, text and illustrations, that you and Ernest wish to add to the book.

I simply cannot steer the Press into what appears to be a large financial disaster. Nor can I leave this project as a sort of time bomb to be defused or exploded by my successor. Consequently, I am calling a halt to our participation in the project until it is refinanced, either with outside money or by reduction to the 1970 plans or perhaps in both ways. This is formal notice, then, that the Press will not continue with the project under present circumstances. We shall, of course, be happy to take it up again if you can bring it back down to a feasible size and find outside funds. And of course any new agreement will have to depend on the date when all the material is ready for the printer.

You know, of course, that I have tremendous admiration for your work and for that of Ernest Born, and I hope that it can see the light of day, either here or elsewhere, in a form that will be pleasing to you.

HORN to FRUGÉ   January 1975

Dear August:

In your handling of the St. Gall book you have appeared inactive and timid. You are still unaware of its research values, of the project's cultural qualities and implications, although opportunities to survey the work have long been available. You suffer from a ludicrous misconception that Ernest and I are hell-bent to set ourselves "a monument," a feeling you have expressed more than once. You have at this stage not even taken the trouble to look at the available page-proofs. You appear to be totally unaware of the fact that the co-operation of a man who happens to be an architect of unusual stature, and one of the world's greatest architectural draftsmen, with the more traditional kind of scholarship that I represent, is an entirely unique situation. You have, apparently, no understanding of what is involved in a co-authorship of this kind, nor do you seem to realize how different *The Plan of St. Gall* is from the usual "run of the Press" publications.

It took me twenty years to write the book. By the time it is available on the market it will have taken Ernest ten years to guide it through design, illustration and production.

When all of this is done we will have produced one of the finest books ever to have been published anywhere in the world, not a monument raised in self-glorification, as you so erroneously like to think, just a god-damned good book, the best we can do; a book that will be illustrated with hundreds of drawings of superb quality and immaculate precision; a book that will be alive for some time to come; a book that will excite people, visually and textually; a book that, I hope, will raise a welter of controversy; a book that tells the story of the architecture, economy, and life in a community of three hundred to four hundred men, who have chosen to render themselves to the service of God, under the guidance of a man who is responsible for their physical and spiritual welfare and has to account to God for his success and failure; a man, who in order to free his monks for the "Work of God" has to have the managerial ability to control a vast web of manorial estates, some encompassing as many as 40,000 non-religious men and women. It is a book that tells the story of the first great Western effort of urban planning, a masterpiece of planning, produced in the ninth century, by some of the greatest intellectuals of all times . . . a book that tells the

story of the scholarly and visual conversions of a simple line drawing of
the ninth century into full three-dimensional reality, portrayed in drawings so accurate and precise that this entire monastery could, today, be
built with the aid of these drawings; a book that tells the story of the
medical services of that community, its educational facilities, its agricultural facilities, horticulture, viticulture, animal husbandry, cooperage,
and half a dozen other crafts; the story of harnessing water for sanitary
purposes and the running of such technological machinery as mills and
mortars, to grind and crush grain for the making of bread and the brew-
ing of beer.

August . . . you do not know what you have in your basket! Your
trouble is that when you took over the demanding task of running the
Press, life was plush. You did not think that you would have to do such
menial chores as raising money, and not having practiced that craft,
now that inflation ruffles your hair, you get scared and angry and in
this mood, even reject the help that is proffered.

Ernest and I are fully aware that as authors we are rough customers
for a Press Director. But we have something very unusual and very exciting to offer. We have announced our willingness to help raise the
needed $40,000. To do this successfully requires the full weight of
your office behind our efforts. We may need support from the Chancellor's Office, and perhaps even some friendly advice from the President's Office. This is not the time to slam the door, send the workers
home, and shut the plant. This is the time to get together. The going
is not as rough as you make it, but it requires concerted effort by all
of us.

FRUGÉ to ANGUS TAYLOR   February 1975

(Vice President of the
University of California)

Dear Angus:
I am grateful for the offer to help in my little duel, as you call it, with
Walter Horn. I may need your help before we are through.

We are jockeying for positions, as you will see. He is trying to get
me off balance and I am trying to retain what leverage I have. Let us
see how he reacts to the enclosed letter, which repeats—in a quieter
way—what I have said before.

FRUGÉ to HORN   January 1975

Dear Walter:

Thank you for your long letter.

In discussing the problem before us, let us see whether we can focus our attention on the matters at issue, putting to one side other matters that are not critical and those on which we are agreed. *Item:* Much of your letter is devoted eloquently to telling me how long your work has been, how culturally important it is, how great a draftsman Ernest is, how hard he has worked, and the like. All these things I gladly accept; I now stipulate them in the hope they need not be mentioned again and that we can turn to questions less easily resolved. *Item:* You keep coming back to my jest about a monument to you and Ernest. I had not dreamed that so lighthearted a thrust could strike so deep. In any event, I have no objection to a monument provided it not also become a tombstone for the Press. *Item:* When you charge that I am not willing to help raise money, you are setting up and striking down a straw man. Of course I shall help to the extent I can. I have already requested and obtained the largest grant ever made by the Editorial Committee of the Academic Senate.

Let us try to be clear also about the antecedents of our financial plight. You accept responsibility for the enlargement of text and for added illustrations, but you ask to be excused from responsibility for inflation. In general terms, no one could argue with that. But I keep remembering that the manuscript was approved by the Editorial Committee in 1967, when we were told it would be ready to go after one more editorial pass. We made a fresh start in 1970, agreeing on the number of text pages and illustrations; the cost was estimated; through your efforts and mine, jointly, we found adequate financing for the book. Had we gone ahead from there, all would have been well. But when I now look at my calendar it says 1975. And you tell me now that drawings and captions will not be completed for another year and a half. I even wonder about that promise, remembering the others in our file. While you are not responsible for inflation qua inflation, you and Ernest do have responsibility—or so it seems to me—for holding up the project for several years while inflation was steadily undermining its financial support. That responsibility also—using the word in a pure and non-pejorative sense—you ought to accept.

It would be a psychological and tactical mistake, I expect, to go on with the work while hoping to solve the financial problems at a later time. In any event, I must protect the Press as best I can, and my present obligation, as I see it, is to make sure that the entire project is adequately financed before we spend more money.

We have now—I hope—cleared the table of extraneous matters. Perhaps also we may have an end to recriminations, in one direction or the other, and attend to the problem that lies before us. If there is a solution—and there may not be—we can try to find it.

There is another possible direction for you to take. Although your suggestion of sharing costs and revenues with a commercial firm does not seem likely to me—who is going to buy into a losing venture?— you might try getting another publisher to take over the entire project, buying our investment at cost and without an overhead charge. Or you and Ernest might want to publish the book yourselves, investing your own funds and any money you can obtain from donors, and hoping to recoup later from sales.

I think that I have now batted the ball back into your court, offering 1/ a way to continue that project as you want it but not at our expense; and alternatively, 2/ to step out of your way so that you may find another publisher or constitute yourselves as one.

The matter did become public. Various university officials helped to mediate. In the end both parties secured additional funding. Frugé went back to the Editorial Committee for an additional subsidy. Horn and Born obtained support from foundations and friends of art, and even made contributions themselves to help finance the work.

If the correspondence is read too quickly, August Frugé may seem just to be the keeper of the purse or the brake on what he perceived as excesses. He was both, and more. He was a full partner in the enterprise. He did pull back when necessary, but he pressed forward as well, committing scarce resources that could limit the Press's subsequent publishing programs. He supported the project from the original decision to publish to his final decision to allow Born the printer of his choice. His actions and judgments were a reflection of a lifetime of publishing experience, which gave him a genuine understanding of his dual responsibility to the author and book at hand and to the publishing enterprise he directed. It is the maintenance of that delicate balance between the demands of a dedicated, talented, and forceful author and the survival of the publishing house that tests the publisher and defines his worth.

FRUGÉ to BORN   January 1977

Dear Ernest:

A note to thank you—and Esther—for the very fine lunch yesterday.

It is exciting to find that we are at last approaching the time when we can think of producing the first volume. I will be retired before it is actually out, but I will always retain an interest. In spite of our little difficulties, which were inherent in our differing responsibilities, I am proud to have worked with you and Walter on a remarkable project.

With this note August retired. Three years later the volumes were published.

In just two years the book sold out its first printing and was honored with more than a dozen awards—including the Carey Thomas Award, the most important honor within U.S. publishing. The reviews have been superb for both the book and its publisher.

Was the project a financial disaster for the Press? A simple balance sheet would indicate not:

2,000 sets at $250 net	$500,000 gross income
actual manufacturing costs	$359,749
subsidies	$152,000
overhead *	$281,000
NET INCOME	$ 11,251

*The overhead figure is a way of accounting for all the expenses that are not directly charged to the production of the book, such as administrative salaries, sales and promotion costs, and shipping, warehouse, and order processing expenses.

But a closer look confirms August Frugé's concerns about a financial shortfall. Advertising costs ran $30,000 over budget. In production for well over ten years, the book was the most labor-intensive project the University of California Press has ever published. The production manager spent almost three full years on the book, and two directors, several editors, and various staff worked countless hours on the project over the years it was being produced. It is clear that even with the large subsidy the book will never break even. The final accounting will surely show that even August Frugé's highest estimate was less than half what the book actually cost to publish.

Publishing such a work placed tremendous demands on the Press, which is just now, two years after publication, returning to normal. But what is a university press for if not to take these kinds of risks, make these investments, and publish books that make a difference? If there are lessons to be learned from these letters and the publishing of *The Plan of St. Gall,* they are that great people produce great books and that in publishing, as in other enterprises, the institution must survive or what it does will not. *The Plan of St. Gall* has now been recognized as a monumental work of scholarship representing the best a scholar and a publisher can achieve. It also stands as a monument to three exceptional men who care deeply about ideas, publishing, and excellence.

October 1981

Index

Compositor:	G&S Typesetters, Inc.
Text:	10.5/15 Galliard
Display:	Galliard
Printer:	Edwards Brothers, Inc.
Binder:	Edwards Brothers, Inc.